BUSINESS
LETTER WRITING
MADE SIMPLE

BUSINESS LETTER WRITING MADE SIMPLE

REVISED EDITION

Edited by

IRVING ROSENTHAL, MS.

Associate Professor, The City College of N.Y.

AND

HARRY W. RUDMAN, Ph.D.

Professor, The City College of N.Y.

MADE SIMPLE BOOKS

DOUBLEDAY & COMPANY, INC., GARDEN CITY, NEW YORK

ABOUT THIS BOOK

In a business civilization such as ours, almost everyone is in some way involved with business correspondence, and inevitably meets with numerous occasions when he or she is called upon to write business letters. And when that occurs, as it must, there is often a feeling of frustration and bewilderment, a sense of unpreparedness. This book has been prepared to provide reliable and authoritative guidance in all matters relating to business letter writing.

Following a thorough consideration of the problems of "approach" to business correspondence and complete explanations and descriptions of letter-structure and appearance, there are extensive treatments of the major kinds of business letters: the sales letter; direct-mail sales letters; credit and collection letters; employment letters; complaint and adjustment letters; post cards and telegrams; and, in the section on "Miscellaneous Letters," other kinds of business correspondence. Every aspect of business letter writing is explored in detail and illustrated with numerous model examples—models from which the reader may gather valuable and helpful ideas and suggestions for his own letters.

The Appendixes are another unique feature of the book. Here you will find—simply explained and outlined so that it may be rapidly digested—explanations and illustrations of the rules of spelling; scientifically prepared lists of words most frequently misspelled; the rules of punctuation, with illuminating illustrations; the correct forms of abbreviation; carefully prepared lists of words often confused or wrongly used, according to their frequency; lists of words and expressions to avoid in the interest of better writing, followed in each instance with suggestions for improvement. The final Appendix is the most complete available Glossary of terms used in business and formal correspondence.

Throughout the book the editors have been especially careful to reflect everywhere the most modern, up-to-date forms, usages, customs, practices, and norms. In the best sense of the term, this is *modern* business letter writing.

This book is intended for use as an office and home manual in business letter writing not only for men and women in business, but for everyone who will ever have occasion to write a business letter of any kind in our business society.

—Irving Rosenthal
—Harry W. Rudman

ACKNOWLEDGMENTS

The editors wish to acknowledge their warm appreciation to the following firms and executives who have so generously responded to their requests for some of the illustrative material used in this book:

American Hotel Association, New York, N.Y.
The American Magazine, New York, N.Y.
The Atlantic Monthly Magazine, Boston, Mass.
Buescher Band Instrument Co., Elkhart, Ind.
The Dartnell Corporation, Chicago, Ill.
Elkhart Band Instrument Co., Elkhart, Ind.
Essley Shirt Company, Inc., New York, N.Y.
Greater Little Rock Chamber of Commerce, Little Rock, Ark.
Life Magazine, New York, N.Y.
Look Magazine, Des Moines, Iowa
Newsweek Magazine, New York, N.Y.
Tide Magazine, New York, N.Y.
Time Magazine, New York, N.Y.

TABLE OF CONTENTS

CHAPTER ONE

CHAPTER TWO

CHAPTER THREE

CHAPTER FOUR

CHAPTER FIVE

CHAPTER SIX

CHAPTER SEVEN

CHAPTER EIGHT

CHAPTER NINE

CHAPTER TEN

BUSINESS
LETTER WRITING
MADE SIMPLE

BUSINESS LETTER WRITING TODAY AND YESTERDAY

If you compare business letters written a generation ago with business letters written today, you will be startled by the difference. Some words once in common use in business correspondence, like **ultimo,** meaning "last month," or **instant,** meaning "this month," may puzzle you, for they have disappeared from the vocabulary of business. What will strike you most, perhaps, will be the formality of the business letters of the past as contrasted with the more easygoing business letters of our day.

Fashions change and there may be a return, in the future, to formal ways. But the present trend favors informality. If you want to be in tune with the times, you will avoid the boiled shirt-front in your business correspondence.

But changes are rarely complete and final, and old forms and habits linger. Echoes of the past may sound in your mind while dictating, and stilted expressions may slip in. Therefore it may be helpful, now and then, to glance at Appendix F where you will find a list of obsolete and over-formal expressions that you should avoid in your letters.

These lists also include stale, needlessly stiff, and indirect expressions of our own time. Such phrases reflect uncertainty or merely fatigue. If you are on guard against their occurrence in your letters, you will be able to strengthen weak points.

PERSONALITY

Let us now turn to the current informal trend in business letter writing. This informality is really part of the general tendency toward the expression of personality in all our activities, including business. Today impersonality is avoided, even in the most impersonal of business relationships.

Thus, big public-service corporations like gas, electric, and telephone companies, which were formerly satisfied with sending the monthly bill, now seek to "personalize" all their business operations. They pay substantial fees to public relations agencies to improve their methods of personalizing these transactions.

You will observe this trend even in seemingly unimportant details in the second-class mail you receive. Instead of the firm name in the return address, companies which do mass mailings often use the name of an individual in their organization. In that way they add a personal touch to the outside of the envelope. Some firms print only the return address on the envelope without even mentioning the name of the firm.

In current business correspondence, therefore, the aim is not to be reserved and impersonal but to communicate personality. In that respect business letters increasingly resemble personal letters. Business letters, too, seek to give the impression of one person talking to another.

THE OBJECTIVE

How, then, do business letters differ from personal letters?

There are two main differences. One is in

17

what we may call the "restricted objective" of the business letter; the other is what we may term "its restricted attitude." We shall first take up the restricted objective.

Personal letters are unlimited in their aims. They may express any emotion; they may drift from one thing to another; they may have no object at all other than a chat by mail.

A business letter, on the other hand, has a very definite objective. In almost every instance its purpose is to induce the reader of the letter to take some action desired by the writer. This action may be to buy the writer's goods; to extend credit to him for purchases he wishes to make; to effect payment of an overdue bill or, on the contrary, to avoid legal action on a bill he has left unpaid; to obtain a new job; to get satisfaction for his claim for damages, or to refuse a claim upon him in such a way as not to lose business, etc. In brief, he writes the letter to influence the reader to do something he wants, and the contents of the letter are the reasons he presents to accomplish that result.

We turn now to the second major difference between business and personal letter writing.

THE "YOU" ATTITUDE

Since the restricted objective of a business letter is almost always to induce the reader to some action desired by the writer, its chief means will be persuasion. A number of components enter into effective persuasion. Here we will take up what is generally acknowledged to be the primary component. It is something which people who provide professional counsel in business letter writing call the "you" attitude.

In personal letters both the "I" attitude and the "you" attitude occur; generally, the "I" attitude predominates. In personal letters the writer usually counts on the reader's interest in him, in what he, the writer, thinks and feels.

He will, of course, if he is not either inconsiderate or foolish, take some trouble to show reciprocal interest in the reader's thoughts and feelings. But on the whole, it is the writer's thoughts and feelings that will be paramount. His letter, then, will be written from the "I" attitude.

The situation is entirely different in the business letter. There the writer, seeking to induce the reader to take a certain action, must consider the reader's thoughts and feelings. He must somehow manage to put himself in the reader's place in order to anticipate his reactions. Only in that way can he gain the insights that will enable him to persuade the reader that it will be to his advantage to act in the way the writer desires.

Therefore the writer cannot risk the "I" attitude. He must adopt the "you" attitude, the attitude that will enable him to identify himself with the reader. He must write the letter so that you, the reader, will feel that **your** point of view is being considered, **your** interests are being served.

NO CONFLICT

The foregoing analysis may appear to contradict what we have said about business letters being an expression of personality. Actually there is no contradiction. For just as the objective of business letters is restricted, as is the attitude from which they should be written, so too is the expression of personality in them restricted.

As a businessman you must give the impression of being an understanding and fair person and an efficient performer. That is the side of your personality to be expressed in your business letters. All the better if you can do so with some display of individuality or even temperament. Unless your letters leave an impression of fair dealing and efficient performance, you are not likely to get very far with your readers. The "you" attitude in a business letter is necessary not only to persuade the reader but also to win his confidence in the writer's fairness and effectiveness.

In short, write with brevity, courtesy, tact. Make your meaning clear—in simple, everyday English. Visualize the person to whom you are writing, plan your letter carefully, and make it accomplish what you would like to achieve if you had him in front of you.

CONCISENESS

Since business letters have a specific and restricted objective, the writer cannot afford to be wordy. He cannot risk being indirect or indulging any irrelevant interests, his own or the recipient's. He should be concise and to the point.

There are additional reasons for directness and brevity. Business mail is much heavier than personal mail; and it is often read under unfavorable conditions, amidst telephone calls, summonses to conferences, and other interruptions. To assure attention a business letter should not look discouragingly long or complicated. It should be direct, readable, and logical so that its message is quickly communicated and easily retained.

Like other rules, however, the rules of directness and conciseness have their exceptions. A conspicuous exception is mail-order sales letters.

Unlike most other business correspondence, a mail-order sales letter (unless it is a follow-up) has no previously established connection to count on. It must establish a bond with the recipient before it can proceed to "sell" him.

This aim is usually accomplished by means of some **attention-catching** opening to induce the recipient to examine the letter and then, by the stratagem of some interest-sustaining matter, to hold his interest. Both the **attention-catching** opening and the **interest-sustaining** copy may be only remotely connected with the sales message. In that sense the rules of directness and conciseness are often deliberately violated in mail-order sales letters. But once attention is caught and interest is held, the rules begin to apply. The sales message itself, to be effective, must be direct and concise.

We shall amplify this topic in the section on mail-order sales letters. There are exceptions to be noted in other types of business correspondence as well. These, too, will be discussed in the sections devoted to them.

TYPES OF BUSINESS LETTERS

In business letter writing, as in other fields, no one list of types can exhaust all the possibilities. However, the main categories of business correspondence, to be treated in separate sections, comprise the following:

Sales letters
Direct-Mail Sales letters
Credit and Collection letters
Employment letters
Complaint and Adjustment letters
Miscellaneous letters
Post Cards and Telegrams

APPEARANCE AND PRECISION

Before discussing classifications section by section, we must deal with the very important prerequisites—appearance and accuracy.

We have seen that business letters have been approaching personal letters in the tendency to informality. It is not likely, however, that this trend will ever reach the degree of informality of personal correspondence—just as the business suit, which has departed so far from the striped trousers and frock coat of men's former business wear, will never reach the ease of lounge dress at home.

You would not think of appearing unshaven and in crumpled clothes in your office. Similarly, in your letters you want to have a crisp and tidy appearance. And you want no errors. Inexactness cannot be tolerated because whatever suggests sloppiness, ignorance, or inefficiency forfeits the most important thing in business—confidence in your ability to deliver a sound product or render an efficient service.

In business your letter must suggest, by its very appearance, that you are competent, alert, neat, accurate—in every respect first-rate in your field. Obviously no letter will give that impression if it is on inferior paper, poorly spaced, typed from a dirty or faded ribbon, full of erasures and glaring errors, or confused and illogical in its structure.

We shall therefore begin with rules and suggestions governing the appearance and construction of the letter.

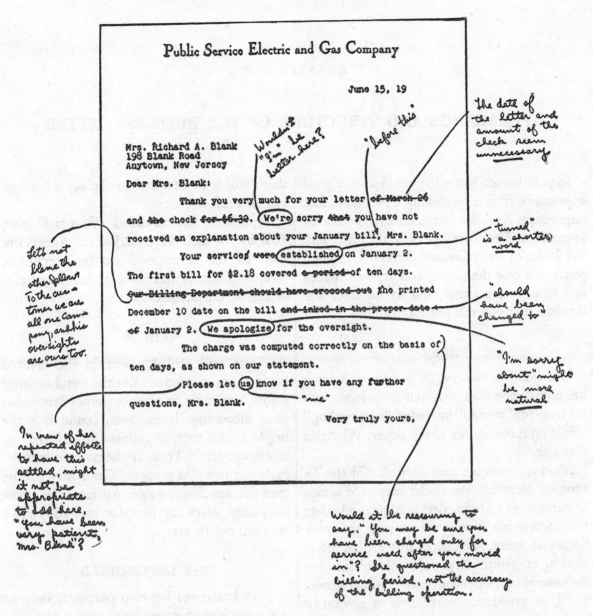

Fig. 1. If studied carefully, this revised letter can provide essential instruction in the strategies of business letter writing. Pay close attention to each revision, as in each case an important point is illustrated.

In general, it may be pointed out here, the letter's author has sought consistently to achieve specific qualities which make for excellence not only in business letter writing, but in all writing. The qualities are: simplicity, clarity, economy, succinctness, directness, natural informality; and the avoidance of ambiguity and unnecessary words. Notice that he seeks to establish a warm *personal* relationship with the client, while at the same time maintaining personal dignity and the dignity and unity of the firm.

CHAPTER TWO

APPEARANCE AND STRUCTURE OF THE BUSINESS LETTER

In your letters, just as in your clothes, a good appearance is vital to making a favorable first impression. And the first is usually the lasting impression. Therefore it pays to take pains with the looks of your business letters. Use good paper; see that the typing is neat, well spaced and free from erasures; and let no error slip through that you can possibly catch.

PAPER

Use good stationery. A secretary, sorting her employer's mail, may put your letter into the heap for "second" instead of "first reading" if it is on recognizably cheap paper. Why run that risk?

Showy, expensive stationery should also be avoided. Certainly the reader may take notice of parchment textures, deckle edges, and other ostentation; but it may not be with the reactions you desire. Such paper may arouse suspicion or contempt. A paper stock suitable for diplomatic correspondence, ceremonial invitations, or graduation certificates is obviously out of place in business correspondence.

Moreover, the most expensive paper is not always the best for correspondence. It may take ink poorly and prevent even and legible typing.

SIZES

Use standard 8½ by 11 inch sheets for longer letters and half sheets, 5½ by 8½ inches, for shorter letters. A brief message on a half sheet will look better than the same message lost on a full-size sheet.

Sometimes the so-called "Baronial" size, 10½ by 7¼ inches, is used. But this is generally reserved for correspondence by executives, with their names and titles engraved and embossed on the letterheads.

COLOR

White will probably remain the favored color of business letters. But the trend to other colors, especially in sales correspondence, has been increasing. It has been found that the bright colors, such as yellow and red, are "attention getters." These are being used increasingly for just that purpose. Color may also be used for associative value. An air travel company may select sky blue for its stationery; a vacation resort, green.

THE LETTERHEAD

Your letterhead has two purposes. Because it is your identification, you want it to be attractive and impressive. And because it supplies the reader with essential information about your company—name, address, telephone number, etc., you want it to be clear and readable.

Fussy lettering and fancy symbols, mistakenly intended to impress the reader, unfortunately produce a different effect. Like pretentiously expensive stationery they may

THE LETTER PICTURE

AVOID THIS

> 1 Oakly Avenue
> Elmont, New York
>
> June 24, 19
>
> Box C123
> Times
>   New York, N.Y.
>
> Dear Sir:
>   For the past six years I have been fortunate
> enough to work at an occupation I really enjoy -- sales
> promotion. At college I prepared for the work I knew I
> would devote my life to. Since then, I have helped, both
> as a salesman and as a sales executive, to develop succ-
> essful techniques of marketing plastics in the United States
> and in South America. I believe that I am now ready
> to assume the responsibilities of complete sales promotional
> management.
>   I have enclosed a personal data sheet outlining my qual-
> ifications for the position you offer. If my qual-
> ifications interest you, I should be grateful if you would
> allow me to come in and talk with you.
>
>   Very truly yours,
>   *Warren Finzer*
>   Warren Finzer

> 1 Oakly Avenue
> Elmont, New York
> June 24, 19
>
> Box C123
> Times
> New York, N. Y.
>
> Dear Sir:
>
>   For the past six years I have been fortunate enough
> to work at an occupation I really enjoy -- sales promotion.
> At college I prepared for the work I knew I would devote
> my life to. Since then, I have helped, both as a salesman
> and as a sales executive, to develop successful techniques
> of marketing plastics in the United States and in South
> America. I believe that I am now ready to assume the
> responsibilities of complete sales promotional management.
>
>   I have enclosed a personal data sheet outlining my
> qualifications for the position you offer. If my qualifi-
> cations interest you, I should be grateful if you would
> allow me to come in and talk with you.
>
>   Very truly yours,
>   *Warren Finzer*
>   Warren Finzer

DO THIS

Fig. 2. In the example of the letter to "avoid" there are many glaring violations of good form. The typist reveals very bad compositional sense: the margins are erratic and inadequate; the crowding of the letter into the upper half of the page distorts the proportions; the left hand margin is slovenly; the indented and modified block forms are randomly combined, etc.

Notice that the model letter, on the other hand, is well composed and in every way pleasing to the eye.

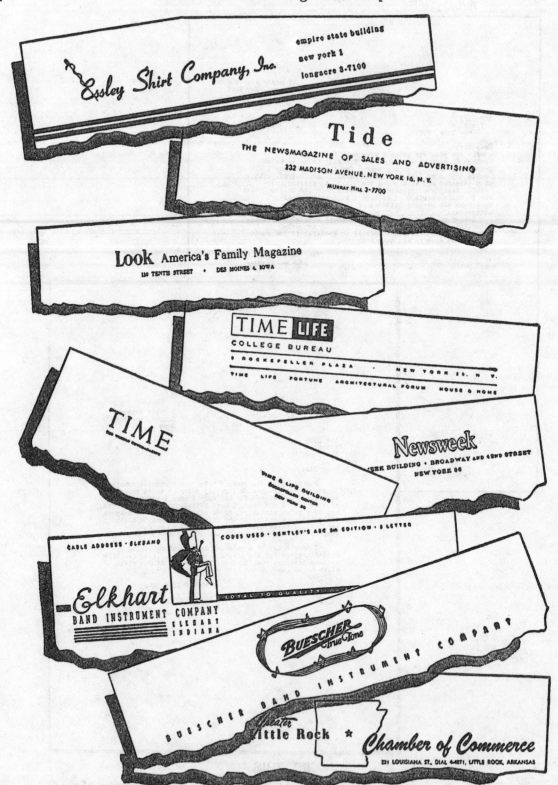

Fig. 3. Letterheads

evoke annoyance and ill will instead. In any case, if they serve to make a letterhead hard to read at first glance, they may be considered unsatisfactory.

Below are some letterheads showing attractive lettering and symbols that are impressive and in good taste without sacrifice of clarity.

BOTTOM AND SIDE-MARGIN MESSAGES

Business stationery sometimes carries printed matter at the foot of the sheet or down the side-margins. The foot-line (it is seldom longer than a line) is usually the motto or slogan of the firm or a special sales message. Such messages may also be printed on the side margins, usually the left-hand margin. Most marginal matter, however, consists of lists of officers, sponsors, or branches of the organization.

ADDITIONAL SHEETS

Whenever a letter is longer than one page, the extra sheets should be of the same paper stock but without the letterhead imprint. A continuation line carrying the name of the addressee (the person to whom the letter is addressed), the page number, and the date should be typed at the top of each additional page. See that a minimum of three lines of text, besides the complimentary close and the signature, appear on the final page of the letter. For the sake of appearance it will be worth retyping the preceding page, if necessary, to make that possible.

FRAMING

Good typography requires proper placement of type on the page so that it sits in its margins like a well-framed picture. Since type-writing is a form of typography, accordingly it follows the same rules. The typewriting on a letter should be so arranged that, within its margins, in the spacing of dateline, salutation, and closing lines, and in its paragraphing, it resembles a well-composed and well-framed picture.

To achieve this pleasing effect the typist does not have to be an artist. She need only follow her own orderly habits of care in her margins (which should be larger in a brief letter), in her paragraph spacing, and in her indentations.

INDENTATIONS

When letters were hand-written, paragraph indentations were necessary for visual clarity. The universal use of the typewriter has tended to make indentations encumbrances instead of conveniences. Many business letters, today, dispense with them. It is becoming general practice to use line space separations instead. This devise speeds up stenographic work and improves the appearance as well. But whichever practice is used, it should be employed uniformly throughout the letter.

Nevertheless, the change from indentations to line spaces for paragraph in dictations and other purposes has not been complete. Today four forms are in use: The "full block" form; a kind of transitional form called "modified block"; the old "full indentation" form; and a type used for special effects, called "hanging indentation."

THE "FULL BLOCK" FORM

The "full block" form is gaining in usage because of its simplicity. In the full block form everything under the letterhead—dateline, inside address, salutation, body of the letter, complimentary close and signature—is aligned along the left-hand margin.

THE "MODIFIED BLOCK" FORM

The "modified block" form is the style in widest use. Here certain parts of the letter, such

ADDITIONAL SHEETS

Mr. John Jones -- page 2 -- January 14, 19

therefore feel that we cannot accept the return of the

merchandise at this late date. We like to cooperate

with all our accounts....

Fig. 4. It was necessary, because of its length, to continue this letter on an additional sheet. The additional sheet is headed by the addressee's name, the page number, and the date. There is the requisite minimum of three lines of text, in addition to complimentary close and signature.

THE "FULL BLOCK" FORM

February 28, 19

Mr. John Jones
1492 Columbus Avenue
Louisville 3, Kentucky

Dear Mr. Jones:

I was very pleased to receive your prompt response to my

and I look forward to seeing you on your next trip to the city.

Sincerely yours,

George Sabrin

Fig. 5. In the "full block" form all the letter's contents are aligned on the left hand margin.

THE "MODIFIED BLOCK" FORM

```
                                          February 28, 19


    Mr. John Jones
    1492 Columbus Avenue
    Louisville 3, Kentucky

    Dear Mr. Jones:

    I was very pleased to receive your prompt response to
```

```
    and I look forward to seeing you on your next trip to
    the city.

                                 Sincerely yours,


                                 George Sabrin
```

Fig. 6. All the letter's contents, with the exception of the date, the complimentary close, the signature, are aligned on the left hand margin. This is still the most widely employed form.

FULL INDENTATION

```
                                      19 Elm Street
                                      Oswego, New York
                                      April 5, 19


    Mr. Gilbert Kahn
      67 Wren Road
      Miami, Florida

    My dear Mr. Kahn:

              In undertaking the assignment you gave me
    when I was in your office last Thursday, I made it clear
```

```
    nevertheless intend to do the best job I can.

                                 Sincerely yours,


                                 Lucille Graham
```

Fig. 7. This form is all but obsolete, and there seems little doubt that in time it will cease entirely to be used.

as the date line, the complimentary close, and the signature, are aligned to the right to help balance the rest of the letter, which has a left-hand alignment.

Some companies use the full block form for short letters (where it makes a better appearance) and the modified block form for longer letters.

FULL INDENTATION

As mentioned before, the fully indented letter is a survival of the period when letters were hand-written. The typewriter has rendered this form obsolete. Today only a small proportion of business correspondence is typed in the full indentation form.

In the full indentation form not only paragraphs are indented but also the separate lines in the inside address and other sequences of lines in salutations and complimentary closings.

HANGING INDENTATION

"Hanging indentation" is seldom seen in business correspondence other than sales-promotion letters. There, it is used to focus attention or attain a repetitive, "hammering-home" effect.

PUNCTUATION AND ABBREVIATIONS

Along with the dropping of indentations there has been a tendency to do without unessential punctuation and to avoid abbreviations, especially in the inside address where these would necessitate punctuation. This economy is for improvement of appearance—lines without terminal punctuation marks look less fussy—and for speed and convenience. The typist, freed of the bother of punctuating and figuring out abbreviations, can turn out more letters a day.

A stark, attractive simplicity, characteristic of the full block form of business letter, is increasingly to be noticed in the modified block letter as well. Periods are being omitted from the end of the dateline and after ordinal numbers such as 43rd and 44th; and commas, from the ends of the inside address lines. It is now also allowable to omit the colon from the salutation and the comma from the complimentary close. Most letters, however, still retain these marks of punctuation.

Abbreviations of cities and states are being avoided. Such abbreviations as Mr. or initials for first names are being retained and are followed by periods.

The new, unpunctuated form, where all punctuation is omitted, is called "open punctuation." The practice of using some punctuation is termed "mixed punctuation." The old form is called "closed punctuation." See the examples below:

Open Punctuation	*Closed Punctuation*
Mr. Ferdinand L. Shorey	Mr. Ferdinand L. Shorey,
12 West 44 Street	12 West 44 Street,
New York, N. Y. 10036	New York, N. Y. 10036.
Dear Mr. Shorey	Dear Mr. Shorey:
Yours sincerely	Yours sincerely,

Mixed Punctuation

Mr. Ferdinand L. Shorey
12 West 44 Street
New York, N. Y. 10036
Dear Mr. Shorey:

Yours sincerely,

Even in the past the use in the salutation of the semicolon or the colon and dash was incorrect. Such practices today are grossly illiterate. Do not use **Dear Mr. Shorey;** or **Dear Mr. Shorey:—**

ELEMENTS OF THE LETTER

Business letters should have at least the following elements: the letterhead, dateline, in-

HANGING INDENTATION

Dear Sir:

If you've been reading COSMOS for years, I hope you'll for-
give me for sending you a letter you don't need --

-- But you'll understand why I jumped at the chance
to write a special letter to a list (on which your
name appears) of successful executives who have been
appointed to even more responsible posts.

For readers of COSMOS know that the busier a man is the more
rewarding COSMOS can be. And if you haven't yet discovered
the added advantage of reading COSMOS for every week's
news, then I hope you'll look into it now.

It's a quick, reliable short-cut to information you'll use a
dozen times a day. A readable, reliable report on the
....

Fig. 8. It is to be noted that this form is not appropriate for normal
business correspondence, but is widely used in the sales letter for the
apparent reason that it readily strikes the eye, arrests attention.

Newsweek
152 West 42nd Street, New York 36, New York

NEW YORK
N.Y.

POSTAGE
PAID

RESERVED SEATS

USE ENCLOSED AIR MAIL REPLY

Fig. 9. Window Envelope

side address, salutation, body, complimentary close, two signatures (the name of the company typed out and the written signature of the writer), and the dictator's and typist's initials, the former, usually in capitals and the latter in small letters. In addition, depending upon the operating procedure of the writer's company, there may be a file number, an order number, or a subject line for the purpose of future reference; an "attention" line where the letter is directed to a particular person or department; notice of an enclosure; and a postscript.

THE DATELINE

Usually the dateline is typed at the right. In full block letters it may be typed flush with the left margin. Sometimes it is centered under the letterhead.

The customary sequence is month, day and year: as April 5, 1954. Some logical persons have been advocating a usage, now standard in Great Britain and in our armed forces, of a progressive time-interval sequence—the shortest interval, the day, first, followed by the month, and then the year: as 5 April 1954. Although not common, this form is acceptable.

THE INSIDE ADDRESS

Inside addresses are included in business letters for several practical purposes. The inside address serves as a ready identification since envelopes are usually thrown away; it helps in filing correspondence; and it can be used with window envelopes. It is also useful to the post office when checking misdirected letters or letters with no return address on the envelope.

The inside address usually consists of three lines: the name of the person or the firm, the street address, and the line carrying city, state, and zip code. In foreign mail a fourth line carries the name of the country. If the ad-

dressee is associated with a company, its name may appear under his as the second line.

Examples: Mr. Thomas Smith
24 West 98 Street
New York, N. Y. 10025

Mr. Alan May
16 Charing Cross
London, N.W. (Zone No.)
England

Mr. Thomas Smith
West Side Riding Academy
24 West 98 Street
New York, N. Y. 10025

THE SALUTATION

Present-day usage for the normal salutation is the word **Dear** and the title and name of the addressee: as **Dear Mr. Doe** or **Dear Mr. Roe.** In personal friendships between businessmen it is permissible for them to use first names or nicknames in salutations: as **Dear John** or **Dear Hank.** In formal address the expression, **My dear Mr. Doe,** is often used.

Sales letters addressed to regular patrons may use terms like **Dear Customer, Dear Madam, Dear Subscriber,** etc. In mass mailings any general terms such as **Dear Sir, Dear Madam, Dear Friend, Dear Fellow Citizen, Dear Reader** or any other salutation considered appropriate may be used—or none at all.

Whenever open punctuation is used, the colon may be omitted after the salutation. But, as we have mentioned before, it is more customary to retain it. The colon-dash and the semicolon, however, are never correct.

There are special forms of address for persons of high rank in government, the armed forces, the church, and the professions. These will be found in Appendix D.

BODY

The body of the letter is, of course, its most important part. In appearance it should be clearly typed, neatly spaced, and uniform in typographical construction.

Long paragraphs should be avoided. The paragraphs should not be so short, however, as to give any impression of talking down to the addressee. But in sales letters short paragraphs are almost always the rule, in order to sustain interest.

Underlining to indicate italics or to give emphasis is being displaced by capitalizing. Capitals are regarded as more readable, more emphatic, and more pleasing in appearance. Moreover, capitalizing makes for easier and more rapid typing. Titles of books and names of periodicals, however, should continue to be underlined or placed in quotation marks.

The contents of the body will be dealt with at greater length in the separate sections discussing the different types of business letters. Here we may generalize as follows:

The opening paragraph should be short and, unless there is a compelling negative reason, it should immediately introduce the subject of the letter or connect it with a previous development in the correspondence. The middle paragraphs should do the main job of the letter—expand on the subject in such a way as to persuade the addressee to act upon it in the manner you desire. Let it convince him that it will be proper for or advantageous to him to conclude the purchase or the agreement, or to make the postponement, the payment, or the adjustment you are seeking.

The closing paragraph should summarize your message and make clear the action you desire. Avoid wavering words like **hoping, wishing, trusting,** etc. Be positive. Say something like "We feel certain that you will agree that this is the most satisfactory solution." Avoid dangling participial endings, such as "Hoping we hear from you."

THE COMPLIMENTARY CLOSE

Just as you open your letter with a word of friendly greeting, so you close it with a cordial expression—what is called the complimentary close. Some people propose dispensing with both, and recommend plunging into the letter without salutation and closing abruptly with the signature. But the convention is so firmly entrenched as to render it unlikely that this suggested procedure will take hold.

The customary forms are "Yours truly," "Yours sincerely," or "Yours very truly" where the relationship is formal. The terms "Yours sincerely," "Sincerely yours," "Faithfully yours," and "Cordially yours" express rising degrees of intimacy. "Respectfully yours" has gone out of fashion and is now generally restricted to correspondence with dignitaries or official superiors in formal situations.

THE SIGNATURE

It is considered a discourtesy not to sign a letter personally. If this becomes an impossibility and a rubber stamp has to be used, it should be inked and imprinted in such a way as to resemble the true signature as closely as possible. If the writer's secretary signs for him, she should put her initials under the signature to make that fact clear.

New attitudes regarding the position of women do not seem to have penetrated into business correspondence, at least as regards their marital status. That has to be indicated in the signature. A married woman who wishes to use her maiden name in business should add her married name (Mrs. ———— ————) in parentheses. A widow retains her married name unless she takes legal steps to resume her maiden name. A divorcee retains her former husband's surname but may not use his initials or his first name.

Where the company name is included in the signature, it is typed one or two lines below the complimentary close. Four spaces should be left for the writer's signature, and his name and company position should follow:

Yours sincerely,

Thomas Smith

THE JOHN JONES COMPANY

Sales Manager

To make sure that the signature is not misread, the name is often typed above or below it.

Yours sincerely,

THE JOHN JONES COMPANY

Thomas Smith

Thomas Smith
Sales Manager

SPECIAL PARTS OF THE BUSINESS LETTER: FILE NUMBERS

In addition to the standard parts of the letter special requirements may call for additional lines or items. On traffic or mail order correspondence file or other reference numbers may appear, usually at the left of the dateline or under it.

ATTENTION LINE

When a letter is addressed to an individual in a firm but is not intended for him exclusively, or if it is intended to be routed to a certain department, a line is added to that effect. Letters are often addressed to the **attention** of an individual instead of to him directly so that, if he should be away, the letter will not be held up but will be acted upon by the person temporarily taking his place.

The attention line is usually put between the inside address and the salutation, and may be placed either at the left, as in the example below, or in the center of the line.

The John Jones Company
710 West 10 Street
New York, N. Y. 10011

Attention Mr. Thomas Smith, Sales Manager

Gentlemen:

Note that where the attention line is used, the salutation is **Gentlemen,** not **Dear Mr. Smith.**

ENCLOSURE LINE

The enclosure line in the letter is not for the addressee, who will be informed about the enclosure in the text of the letter. It is for the mailing clerk or the stenographer herself as a reminder to include the enclosure in the mailing. It should therefore be in an inconspicuous position. It is usually typed under the stenographer's initials, as an abbreviation: Encl.

POSTSCRIPTS

Postscripts in business letters differ from those in personal letters, which are afterthoughts set down after the letters have been finished. In business correspondence, postscripts have a definite, planned function. They may emphasize a point made elsewhere in the letter, or they may make a special offer. They are more customary in sales letters than in other business correspondence, and are designed to draw special attention. Examples will be found in the section on sales letters.

ENVELOPES

As much care should be observed with the envelope as with the letter itself. It is the first part of the letter to be seen, and, as we have already observed, the first impression is important. It should, of course, be of the same paper

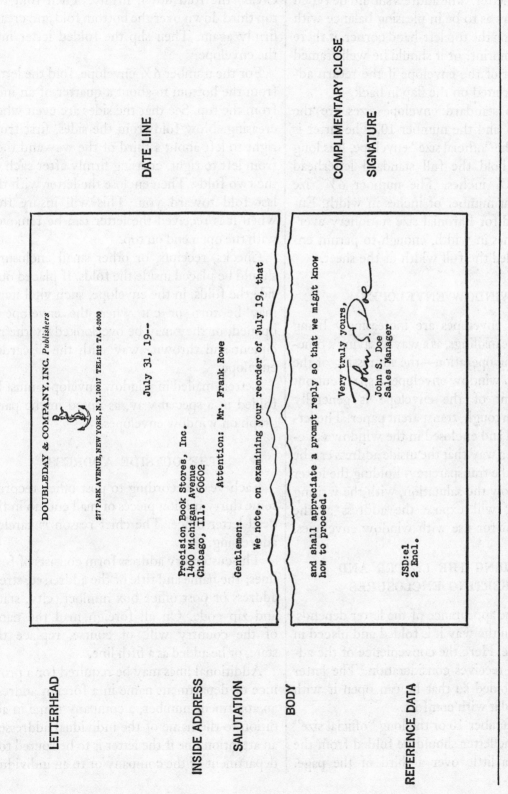

LETTERHEAD

DATE LINE

INSIDE ADDRESS

SALUTATION

BODY

COMPLIMENTARY CLOSE

SIGNATURE

REFERENCE DATA

DOUBLEDAY & COMPANY, INC. *Publishers*

277 PARK AVENUE, NEW YORK, N.Y. 10017   TEL.: 212 TA 6-2000

July 31, 19--

Precision Book Stores, Inc.
1400 Michigan Avenue
Chicago, Ill. 60602

Attention: Mr. Frank Rowe

Gentlemen:

We note, on examining your reorder of July 19, that

and shall appreciate a prompt reply so that we might know
how to proceed.

Very truly yours,

John S. Doe

John S. Doe
Sales Manager

JSD:el
2 Encl.

Fig. 10. This model letter includes in standard form *all* the elements normally employed in the business letter.

stock as the letter. The address should be typed in such a way as to be in pleasing balance with the imprint on the top left-hand corner, if there is such an imprint; or it should be well framed on the front of the envelope if the return address is imprinted on the flap in back.

The two standard envelope sizes are the number 6¾ and the number 10. The latter is also called the "official size" envelope. It is long enough to hold the full standard letterhead width of 8½ inches. The number 6¾ size averages that number of inches in width. Envelopes used for Baronial size stationery average 7½ inches in width, enough to permit enclosure folded the full width of the sheet.

WINDOW ENVELOPES

Window envelopes are increasingly being used, in large mailings, as a way of saving a time-taking typing operation—the addressing of the envelope. In window envelopes a space cut out of the front of the envelope is generally covered by a tough, transparent paper. The letter is folded and enclosed in the window envelope in such a way that the inside address can be seen under the transparency. Folding the letter directly below the salutation, with the writing facing you, will expose the address at the proper point for use with window envelopes.

FOLDING THE LETTER AND INSERTING ENCLOSURES

Part of the appearance of the letter depends, of course, on the way it is folded and placed in the envelope. Here the convenience of the addressee also receives consideration. The letter should be folded so that he can open it with ease and read it with comfort.

For the number 10 or the long "official size" envelope, the letter should be folded from the bottom to a little over a third of the page.

Crease the fold down firmly. Then fold the top third down over the bottom fold and crease firmly again. Then slip the folded letter into the envelope.

For the number 6¾ envelope, fold the letter from the bottom to about a quarter of an inch from the top. See that the sides are even when creasing. Now fold from the sides, first from right to left about a third of the way and then from left to right, creasing firmly after each of the two folds. Then enclose the letter with the last fold toward you. This will insure that when it is received the letter can be removed with the open end on top.

Checks, receipts, or other small enclosures should be placed inside the folds. If placed outside the folds, in the envelope, such vital items may be torn or cut when the envelope is opened; or they may be overlooked by the recipient and thrown away with the discarded envelope.

Letters mailed in window envelopes must be folded in a special way, as noted in the paragraph on window envelopes.

THE OUTSIDE ADDRESS

Each year, according to post office records, some thirty million pieces of mail end up in the dead letter office. The chief reason is careless addressing.

The customary address form consists of four lines: the name and title of the addressee, street address or post office box number, city, state, and zip code. On all foreign mail the name of the country will, of course, replace the state, or be added as a fifth line.

Additional lines may be required for a province or department name in a foreign address, an apartment number, a company name in addition to the name of the individual addressee, an attention line if the letter is to be routed to a department of the company or to an individual

FOLDING THE LETTER

a. 8½ X 11" LETTER IN SMALL COMMERCIAL ENVELOPE

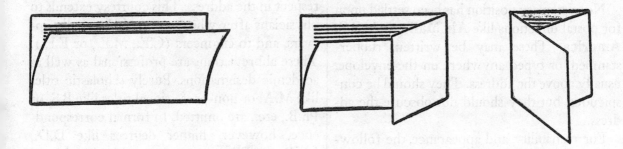

b. 8½ X 11" LETTER IN LONG COMMERCIAL ENVELOPE

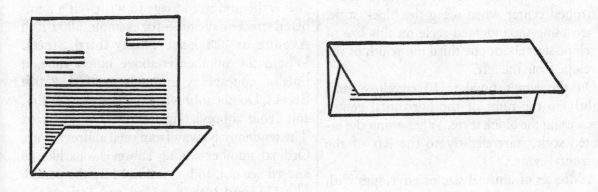

c. THE FOUR PAGE LEAFLET

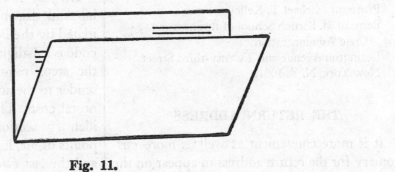

Fig. 11.

in a department, or the specification, **Personal** or **Confidential,** where the letter is intended for private reading by the addressee.

Except where they are part of the address, such additional lines are typed in the lower left-hand corners of the envelopes.

No customary position has been settled upon for postal directions like **Air Mail** or **c/o S.S. America.** These may be written, rubber-stamped, or typed anywhere on the envelope, usually above the address. They should be conspicuous, but they should not obscure the address.

For readability and appearance the following positions have been found most satisfactory. In all cases start the address slightly below the vertical center of the envelope. On a number 6¾ envelope start slightly to the left of the horizontal center when using the block style. When using the indented style on this size of envelope start about one third the width of the envelope from the left.

On the larger number 10 envelope start slightly to the right of the horizontal center when using the block style. When using the indented style, start slightly to the left of the horizontal center.

Addresses of unusual size or envelopes with the return address on the flap in back may call for variations of these positions.

Professor Michael T. Kellogg
Bernard M. Baruch School of Business and
   Civic Administration
Lexington Avenue and Twenty-third Street
New York, N. Y. 10010

THE RETURN ADDRESS

It is more convenient as well as more customary for the return address to appear on the front of the envelope than on the back flap. In any case make sure it appears somewhere on the envelope. This practice will be an additional precaution against the letter's ending up in the dead letter office.

TITLES OF RESPECT

It is customary to include certain titles of respect in the address. This courtesy extends to physicians after whose name M.D. usually appears, and to engineers (C.E., M.E., or E.E.). These abbreviations are professional as well as academic designations. Purely scholastic titles like M.A. or non-professional titles like B.S. or Ph.B., etc., are omitted. In formal correspondence, however, higher degrees like D.D., LL.D., Ph.D., etc., may be used in the address.

NUMBERS AND ABBREVIATIONS AND THEIR PUNCTUATION

It is the preferred usage to write out a numbered street or avenue—for example, **500 Fifth Avenue** or **223 East Thirty-third Street.** Where the number is above ninety-nine, it usually appears as a number: **2204 220th Street.** Do not abbreviate the name of the city, and avoid abbreviating the name of the state. The tendency is away from such abbreviations. Ordinal number-ending abbreviations like **th** and **rd** are not, today, followed by the period. Use 33rd and 34th, not 33rd. and 34th.

ZIP CODES

On July 1, 1963, a new system of mail sorting and distribution called zip code was initiated by the Post Office Department. The zip code is a 5-digit number designed to cut down the steps required to move mail from the sender to the addressee, thereby holding down postal costs. The first three digits of the code identify sectional centers, which are main points of air, highway, and rail transportation, and the last two digits identify the post office or delivery station. In cities that previously had local postal zones, the first three digits of the zip code identify the city and the last two digits (which are generally the same as the former zone number) designate the branch post office or substation.

The first numeral of the zip code, 0 to 9, identifies one of ten national service areas. The second and third digits indicate the service area subdivision and the post office, and the last two digits identify the station from which the mail is delivered.

While the use of zip codes is optional but strongly recommended for first-class mail, it is *mandatory* for second-class and third-class bulk mailers, who must also presort and bundle their mail in accordance with detailed instructions that appear in the *Postal Manual*. Large-volume mailers should familiarize themselves with the regulations regarding zip codes by consulting the *Postal Manual* or their local post office, since failure to conform to the zip coding requirements can result in refusal of the post office to handle improperly zip-coded mail at the lower bulk rates.

Placement. The zip code should appear on the last line of both the address and return address following the city and state. There should be not less than two nor more than six spaces between the last letter of the state and

the zip code, and no characters of any kind should follow the zip code:

```
Mr. Harold Jones
3025 Theresa Street
Arlington, Va.    22207
```

SOME FINAL REMARKS

Some individualistic correspondents omit the salutation and the complimentary close. They may be anticipating future usage but they are violating present conventions. The practice will attract attention, certainly if that is what is desired. But the accompanying responses may not be desirable.

It is advisable that you personally look over all the letters sent from your office. If that cannot be done by you, make sure that some other responsible person examines them carefully.

It is also advisable, periodically, to make a critical reappraisal of the appearance of your letters. Perhaps you should change your style of correspondence. Even if you find nothing that, in your opinion, needs improving, it will be a pleasant reassurance to ascertain that such is really the case.

CHAPTER THREE

THE SALES LETTER

The concern of all business is to sell goods or services. Consequently all business letters are, directly or indirectly, sales letters.

Your best collection letter, for example, is one that does more than induce a delinquent customer to pay up. It is the one that leaves him convinced, after the payment, that he has been dealing with a fair and considerate house with which he is glad to continue doing business.

Sales letters, as such, are distinguished from other business letters by the fact that their sales objective is not indirect but direct and, more or less, immediate. The qualifying phrase, "more or less," is used because some varieties of sales letters are not intended to make an immediate sale but rather to lead **gradually** to sales. And others are intended to pave the way for sales by other means.

Certain sales letters, for example, may be written to help a salesman make the sale. Others may be written to bring customers for your products to one of your dealers.

The most common and largest variety of sales letter is used in direct mail selling. Devices employed in that type of sales letter are presented in a later section; here we shall deal with the more general aspects of sales letters, and take up types of sales correspondence that are part of regular business operations.

YOUR SATISFIED CUSTOMERS

No selling job is ever over. The alert businessman keeps analyzing his accounts. Can A's volume be increased? B's orders show a slight decline over last year's; does that mean a decline in his business? Or is he sampling the wares of a competitor? Whatever his conclusion, the alert businessman sends off the appropriate letter.

IN AN EFFORT TO INCREASE SALES

Dear Mr. Martin:

I have been very pleased to note the steady increase in the frequency and size of your orders since we started doing business together. It is gratifying to know that our product is being well received in your area and that you are making money with it.

My reason for writing is twofold—to thank you for your patronage and to offer our cooperation in any way that will build your sales of our product even further. Under separate cover I am sending you some advertising aids that can be used in window and counter displays; mats for newspaper ads; and suggested spot announcements for your local radio station. Frank Moss, our representative in your territory, will drop in on you next Thursday to help you set up these displays and to offer his assistance in every way. If there is anything special you may need, don't hesitate to get in touch with me.

I look forward to the continuance of our pleasant and, I hope, mutually profitable relationship. With all good wishes, I am,

Sincerely yours,

Robert Johns

IN AN EFFORT TO RETAIN
GOOD WILL

Dear Mr. Burke:

Somewhere or other we read: "There are many good excuses for losing an order—but no excuse whatever for losing good will!"

That's why we're writing you—not to ask why you preferred to place your recent order with somebody else, but to make sure it wasn't because of something which has lost us your good will as well.

If it was the latter, we'd be most grateful if you'd write us about it.

But regardless, we sincerely hope your new equipment gives you the kind of performance you expect of it—and that you won't hesitate to make use of our nationwide service facilities should the need arise.

Next time, perhaps, it will be our good fortune to take care of your requirements.

Sincerely,

William H. Wolcott

The alert businessman never feels smug about his satisfied customers. He does not leave the initiative to them, content merely to take orders. He bears in mind those two business adages: "It costs less to keep a customer than to get one," and "Your customer is your competitor's prospect."

If he starts a new line, if he makes an improvement in one of his staples, if he has a plan for reducing the price to a customer by quantity shipping of combined orders, the alert businessman lets his satisfied customer know about it. He does not wait for the word to get around; he sees to it that it gets around. Keeping the satisfied customers posted is a good way of keeping them satisfied.

Dear Larry:

I hope this finds you well and your business booming. I think I have something that you ought to be able to go to town on.

I've just picked up a special lot of piece goods off-price that I'm going to cut tomorrow in Style 637, with which you have done so well. I plan to bring out the number at two dollars less than you have been paying, and I know it will fit in well with your January sale.

I can get a limited number of garments out of the lot, so I'd like to know how many you can use before I offer it to anyone else. We'll be able to ship within ten days.

All good wishes.

Sincerely yours,

Phil Nelson

Dear Mr. Forman:

When you were in the city several weeks ago, you mentioned the difficulties you were having in getting fast deliveries of merchandise shipped to you by us and by other manufacturers. I think I've come across something that can help you.

I have just had a conversation with Jack Bell of Vanguard Trucking, 247 Terhune Place, Jersey City, N.J., who runs a fleet of trucks through your territory. He told me that if you can work out an arrangement with a few other merchants near you to consolidate shipments, he will be glad to set aside one of his trucks to serve your group. If the amount of freight warrants it, he can provide daily overnight deliveries, and is confident he can cut your present transportation costs by forty per cent. I think it's worth looking into, and I suggest you get in touch with Mr. Bell for more particulars.

Sincerely yours,

Robert Glass

FREQUENT COMMUNICATION

Keep the contacts with your customers unbroken and, so far as you can, make the contacts personal. Some firms regard communication with their customers, once a month, a minimum requirement for good customer relations. They do not limit the correspondence to invoices and routine acknowledgments of orders and payments. To the routine mail they add interesting enclosures. And they take advantage of every suitable occasion to extend the contact. They avoid formalities and try to set up a personal relationship. For signatures they do not use only the firm name but rather the name of an officer of the firm, the head of a department, or a salesman.

Some concerns go about unobtrusively getting personal items about their customers and keep the data current. Birthdays are remembered. If a buyer gets married or has an addition to the family, the event is observed.

Many service firms such as laundries and cleaning establishments find it profitable to send their customers and prospective customers blotters bearing calendars and reminders of seasonal cleaning needs.

Department stores keep in touch with their charge-customers by sending them advance notices of sales, seasonal announcements, and letters about special services. Whatever your business is, there are sure to be occasions for getting in touch with your customers other than through routine notices and acknowledgments.

YOUR EX-CUSTOMERS

Some customers die and some go bankrupt. Others move too far away or get into some other situation that makes further business with them unprofitable. So a certain calculable amount of lost business must be anticipated.

But there are other lost customers who must not be given up without prolonged and persistent effort. These are the customers who have been won away by your competitors or have been driven away by the rudeness or inefficiency of someone in your organization.

Where the customer has been lost to a competitor, your letter starts a job of reselling. Write about new lines or about improvements. Make some attractive offer.

Where the customer has been lost through rudeness or inefficiency, ask him for the whole story. Express regret in a dignified and manly way. Offer an adjustment, if it is called for, or some special inducement to bring him back into the fold.

The alert businessman keeps a regular check on his customers' buying. When one has stopped or tapered off, he does everything he can to find out why.

The point is, of course, to regain the business as soon as possible. But an important, additional reason is to discover whether the lost business signifies some weakness in the organization.

SPECIAL CUSTOMERS

In every business there are customers who rate or demand special attention. Some should get it merely because the large volume of their business calls for every possible special and even personal consideration. Special and personal letters, if feasible, will be in order.

Others may have special needs. For example, dealers located in hot, moist regions may require special packaging or other measures to keep the wares they receive in good condition. Letters dealing with such special needs are in order.

Others may be merely fussy or eccentric. These may be hard to do business with and require special sales correspondence. If you decide that the volume of their business justifies it, carry on that additional correspondence with good grace.

LETTERS TO HELP YOUR SALESMEN

The salesman may be assisted, through letters, in two general ways. One type of letter prepares the ground for him—introduces him, mentions the new line he will demonstrate, some special offer he will explain in detail, etc.

Such help to a salesman may be needed for several reasons. One is the lingering effect of the fictional presentation of the salesman as an

Dear Mr. Watson:

I have just heard with chagrin from a mutual friend of
ours that you feel you haven't been getting the same attention here that you received when we were a smaller firm. I
was wondering why I hadn't seen you in our showroom lately.

I am very sorry if anyone in our organization has been
remiss or negligent in taking care of you the way you deserve
to be looked after as an old and loyal customer through the
years. I offer my personal apology, and I hope you will give
us another chance.

I shall appreciate your coming in to see me personally
the next opportunity you have to drop in on us, and I shall
see to it that you are taken care of to your complete satisfaction. We have had a very pleasant relationship for a number of years, and I would feel hurt -- more for personal than
business reasons -- if through some fault of ours that relationship was marred in any way.

                                        Sincerely yours,

                                        David Redmond

Fig. 12. This letter is written in what is obviously a difficult and delicate
situation, requiring graciousness, tact, diplomacy. Ruffled feelings must be
smoothed, and a disgruntled customer won back. The kind of letter to be
written must be appropriate to the sort of relationship which exists between
the involved parties, and the special requirements of the particular case.

Dear Miss Filene:

    Thank you for your order of January 13. I have issued
instructions to our shipping department to fill it exactly
the way you wrote it -- without a single substitution in
size or color. I have also told them to get in touch with
you before shipping, if for any reason they can't fill the
order as written.

    I am sure you will have no more trouble with our ship-
ments, and I shall appreciate your getting in touch with me
personally if we can be of service in any way.

                                  Very truly yours,

                                  Ben Sloan

Fig. 13. This letter serves the valuable purpose of assuring the customer that her order is receiving the very special and personal attention of a responsible person—who is not content merely to place the order, but who has taken pains to arrange for its smooth execution.

Dear Mr. Sanborn:

As you know, John Williams, who traveled your territory for us, is no longer with us. We have been fortunate in adding a new man, George Alexander, who I am sure will be able to look after you the way John did.

During the training period George spent with us here, he impressed me as a sincere, conscientious, straight-shooting fellow. He just came out of the service, but he has had considerable experience in our industry, so he is familiar with your needs and with our operation.

George will call on you during the week of February 14 with our new line, which looks stronger than ever. We've added a few novelty numbers that I am sure you can do well with, and I look forward to an even bigger volume with you in the future than we have enjoyed in the past. With all good wishes and regards, I am,

Sincerely yours,

Sid Frank

Fig. 14. This letter introduces to the customer a new salesman, who is in the sometimes uncomfortable position of replacing a man whose service to the customer has been entirely satisfactory. The dual purpose is thereby served of at once reassuring the customer that he need in no way fear a deterioration of service, and assuring the new salesman of the firm's solid support in his new venture.

Dear Mr. Graves:

    Thank you for your reorder of our Style 986. I am going
to look after it personally and have it sent out right away.

    When I visited you last month on my round through your
territory, I knew the strength of this number and I am happy
my recommendation worked out well for you. We've just added
two more styles that I have equal confidence in; one account
where we tried them out sold them out in three days. I am
enclosing pictures of them, and if you'd like me to send you
some, just let me know and I shall be glad to see that you
get a prompt delivery.

    I expect to leave for my next trip in about three weeks
and look forward to seeing you around the first of the month.
In the meantime, if there is anything I can do for you here,
please don't hesitate to write.

                        Sincerely yours,

                        Clarence Kell

Fig. 15. This letter serves several purposes, chiefly that of sustaining and strengthening salesman-customer relations in the period between visits. At the same time that it assures the customer of the salesman's personal attention to his needs, it also exploits the opportunity provided by the letter to advance suggestions for new sales.

intrusive, high-pressure man with his toes wedged in the door sill, launched on a non-stop spiel. Even dealers who have good relations with salesmen and have found them helpful may think of those they know as exceptions and look for the obnoxious type in a new man. A letter can help the new man by presenting him in a friendly light, stressing the useful service he is to perform—the demonstration he will make or the plan he will explain, etc.

In such letters, however, take care not to tell the customer too much. Remember that the purpose is to introduce the salesman, not to substitute for his call. The letter should stimulate the customer's curiosity and leave it to the salesman to satisfy it. Similar letters can serve to bring customers to your show rooms, to exhibition booths, to dealers handling your products or services.

Letters sent between sales calls can strengthen the salesman-customer relationship. The seasonal nature of certain kinds of merchandise or the fact that salesmen will make only a few trips a year in the ordinary course, gives rise to considerable correspondence about reorders, substitutions, cancellations, returns, complaints, and the acknowledgments and adjustments these call for. As much of this correspondence as is practical should go out under the salesman's signature.

In addition it is frequently advisable to send out, also under the salesman's signature, letters advising the customer of new developments, new lines, new policies, etc. Even in business the strongest bonds are personal, and a good salesman-customer relationship means a good relationship with the customer for the firm.

TESTIMONIALS

When enough time has elapsed for a new account to have tested your products and your business procedures, it is a good plan to write to the customer and ask whether he is satisfied and whether he has any suggestions or comments to make. This kind of inquiry should be the first step in the continuous keeping-your-customer-sold campaign that was mentioned earlier.

Such letters may evoke testimonials that will prove valuable in your promotion. And the letters will probably have the additional value of providing a running check on your business methods by revealing from time to time the need for changes.

Build up a testimonial file from the favorable letters your inquiries bring you. You can draw upon such a file when approaching prospects in the same area or in the same general line as the writers of the testimonials. The signer of the testimonial can say more for you than almost anything you can say for yourself.

Dear Mr. Seaman:

It is now eight months since we first started doing business together, and I note with satisfaction that the volume each month has been increasing nicely. At first, we were skeptical about the possibility of developing sales in your territory, because our product has been sold mainly in colder sections of the country. Your experience, therefore, has been gratifying.

My purpose in writing is to find out whether you have any thoughts about how we can increase our volume to mutual advantage even further. As you can see, we're trying to work with you the best way we know how, and we'd appreciate hearing from you with any comments you may wish to make about our service and product. We like to receive brickbats as well as pats on the back. We can correct our faults—to the advantage of all concerned—only when they're pointed out.

Sincerely yours,

John Thomas

THE INQUIRY LETTER

Answers to inquiries are a major part of business correspondence, and can be the most important type of sales letter. Those that are part of a direct-mail sales campaign will be dealt with in the next section. Here we touch upon the type of inquiry that originates in other ways.

Someone in the market for your sort of goods or services has looked up your firm in a trade directory; or has had it recommended to him by one of your customers with whom he is acquainted; or has heard of you in some other way. He writes to you for information. His inquiry to you may be the only one he is making. But the chances are that he is simultaneously asking for similar information from your competitors.

It is wise to assume that that is the case, and that your answer must stand the test of competition. Do your best to make your reply a sales letter that wins the inquirer's business.

Promptness is of the first importance. Your prospect will be quite as much sold by evidence of your alertness and efficiency as by what you may say.

Directness is also important. Give specific answers to the questions. If the questions are vague, don't follow that bad example; be specific about what you have to sell and thus you will probably answer effectively the questions your prospect has not been able to express.

Being specific does not mean being detailed. Leave the details to the catalogue or the other enclosures you send. A good sales letter is organized to have a certain impact. It cannot have that impact if it interrupts itself to go into minutiae.

ENCLOSURES

Your postage outlay pays for an ounce per unit of reading matter. That ounce gives you leeway for several sheets besides your letter which—barring necessary exceptions—will usually be less than a page in length. Business-

men have found it profitable to take advantage of the full permissible weight by adding enclosures that reinforce the sales punch.

The enclosures can be particularly useful in supplying details which, if put into the body of the letter, might blunt its impact. If the prospect had to pause, while reading the letter, to take in details of measurement, construction, delivery schedules, etc., his interest would be too diffused for him to react as you would like him to.

Your letter should do two things. It should put the prospect into the buying mood and whet his interest so that he will want to look up the details. These can be furnished in an effective enclosure.

However, avoid a clutter of accompanying "literature." Some mailers believe in the more-the-better principle. But experience has shown that beyond a certain point **more** can become **too much.** Then, no matter how colorful and clever the enclosures are, they begin to clash with one another. They distract attention from the letter. They even become a nuisance to the recipient—and the letter may lose its effectiveness.

Moreover, the enclosures should not overshadow the letter. The letter itself should be attractive to look at, but above all its copy should be so carefully, sensibly, and effectively prepared that it produces the results desired.

It is generally advisable, when dealing with a small enclosure, to fold it into the letter so that it comes out along with the letter when the envelope is opened.

Dear Mr. Merton:

I am going to make this letter brief. I feel the enclosed brochure speaks for itself. But I am writing merely to let you know that the sales potential of the lamp described has been tested carefully in thirty selected stores similar to yours. Every one of them has come back with quick reorders. So we know WE HAVE SOMETHING YOU CAN DO WELL WITH.

We developed this item with a view to shooting for volume. We've brought it out at the lowest price possible, and we have complete confidence in its sales potential.

We all get a steady stream of mail across our desks, but I hope you will take a few minutes to study the brochure carefully, and to try out a sample order of the lamp. We'll let the selling talk for itself.

Sincerely yours,

Ivan Hubbell

FORM LETTERS

Whatever the special function of the sales letter you write, make it personal if possible. If the volume of the correspondence makes this impractical, use forms and methods that will make it appear like a personal letter.

There are two main kinds of form letters— **complete** and **paragraph.** The complete form, even when it is individually typed and signed, is prepared in advance to cover certain standard needs.

Usually **complete form letters** are multigraphed or mimeographed, depending on the purpose they serve. Multigraphing is useful in letters where spaces can be provided to fill in dates, individual salutations, addresses, etc. In virtually all cases, the name of an individual, even in rubber stamp or stencil reproductions, is preferable in the signature to simply the name of the firm.

Complete form letters are usually identified by some combination of letters or initials under which they can be filed. Thus there may be a series of form letters with which catalogues are to be enclosed. These are keyed with the letter C and their numbers in the series. Then the secretary can be instructed to send out Form Letter C-4.

The greater flexibility of the **paragraph** **form letter** makes it possible to meet a larger number of calculable special situations. Such a letter is assembled from designated prepared passages kept on file in a "paragraph book." Some firms have several paragraph books with hundreds of paragraphs in each.

For illustration let us take a paragraph book containing ninety passages. Of these, one to ten may be devoted to letter openings; eleven to forty may consist of second paragraphs; forty-one to seventy may consist of third paragraphs; and the remaining twenty entries may be closings. Thus a typist may be instructed to use 7: 24: 51: 82, and will construct the letter from the corresponding paragraphs in the paragraph book.

STRUCTURE OF THE SALES LETTER

In **sales letters** the same general principles of structure apply as in all business letters. But greater latitude is allowed in sales letters, just as greater latitude is allowed in the sales approach in general. You can be more unconventional and use more color and typographic tricks; and you will be pardoned a certain amount of puffing. Of course, if any one of these is carried to excess, it will prove self-defeating.

The salutation: One of the liberties that may be taken is with the salutation. In mass-mailings, where fill-in salutations and inside addresses are impossible, anonymous salutations such as **Dear Friend, Dear Sir,** or **Dear Madame** may be used; or, if the list is a selected one permitting such specifications, **Dear Doctor, Dear Business Executive, Dear Fellow-Angler,** etc.

In some cases the salutation may be dispensed with and a flattering introductory phrase substituted for it, such as "To a Forward-Looking and Ambitious Young Businessman" or "To a

Young Lady Who Keeps in Step with the Times." Or just a catchy headline like "Play Ball!" may be employed. However, these devices should be shunned in ordinary correspondence, and might be resorted to only where the multitude of identical letters is so great that individual salutations are impractical.

The opening: The opening is more crucial in a sales letter than in any other business correspondence. It is the sender's bid for attention; if it fails, the whole effort is wasted.

Some firms go to considerable trouble and expense in striving for attention-getting openings. In a conspicuous position on the letter they may have—stapled, glued on, or affixed in some other way—a small metal, cloth, or plastic object that pictorially symbolizes the opening line.

For example, one firm used a cord lasso, fastened to an upper corner of a letter so that the rope end touched the first line, to give animation to this opening: "Yes, we want to rope you in—and you'll be glad of it. . . ." Similarly a small aluminum bat glued to another letter helped to fix attention on this opening: "This is the season to go to bat for . . ."

Devices like these must be used with care for they are novelties that may appeal to some readers and by their "cuteness" irritate others. You may not be able to afford such expensive attention-getters; but still less can you afford a dull or lifeless opening. You can always attract attention with an imaginative thought and vivid words.

The question opening: One sure method is to put your opening in the form of a question. In that way you can take advantage of a quirk of human nature. We always react to a question as a challenge, and it is a rare person who does not feel the compulsion to make some response.

Of course the question should be provocative and relevant personally to the prospect, and should bring in the article or service being promoted.

This question opening was used by a home development company: "Are you over thirty, married, and a churchgoer?" Since the mailing list had been selected to concentrate on mature, married, churchgoing people, the reader was bound to answer "yes" and was thereby put in a receptive frame of mind to the rest of the proposition.

The striking statement: Another good type of opening is the **striking statement.** A good example is the one used, some twenty-five years ago, by the New York *Daily News* when it introduced itself and tabloid journalism to the metropolis. To its advertising prospects it sent a letter advising them to "Tell it to the Sweeneys" (through its pages) because "the Vanderbilts don't care." This was followed, of course, with interesting material on the advantages of the mass market and its lower sales resistance.

Another example of the striking statement as an opening was the following, used in a letter to advertisers by a large woman's magazine: "Yes, men still carry on most of the nation's business—but their wives do still more of the buying!"

A **proverb,** too, can provide a good opening, especially when it is given an arresting new twist: "The early bird catches the worm—but was it wise for the worm to be early?"

Body of the letter: Having gained attention by your opening, you must next sustain interest while making sales points in the body of the letter.

The anecdote: Some writers have recourse to a story or anecdote for this purpose. An organization arranging outdoor exercise and entertainment for businessmen used this anecdote in a sales letter to its prospects:

"A vigorous man in his nineties was asked

the secret of his longevity. 'Wal," he replied, 'when my wife and I got married we agreed to do something to spare our nerves. If I was the grumpy one she'd go into the other room and take up her knittin'. And if she started to pick on me I'd put on my hat and go out for a walk. . . . So you see I been outdoors most of my life.'

"Being outdoors, that tried and true recipe for a long life and a healthy one, can be made easy for you by joining the ———— Outdoors Club. (And equally easy for your wife as well, who won't be so inclined to pick on you if you include her.) Drive out in your own car or one of the Club's limousines will pick you up outside your office and bring you to the club grounds. Then you can swim, golf, swing a racket, walk or do anything else you like in clear sunlight and unpolluted country air."

Enclosures gave further details.

Facts and figures: Other writers rely on facts and figures. They support tempting descriptions of the article or service they are marketing with data giving the results of laboratory tests, consumption statistics, testimonials, guarantees, and other inducements.

Incidentally, experienced sales-letter writers advise that the core of the sales message should appear about two-fifths of the way down the letter.

The closing: In earlier business correspondence, in the days when businessmen dressed in frock coats and striped trousers like diplomats, it was considered proper to close sales letters with polite wishes like "hoping" or "trusting we shall hear from you." Such expressions tend to linger on. Usually they are left in mid-air as dangling participles. If you find them in your correspondence, pull out the blue pencil!

Sales letters now end with forceful suggestions for immediate action. They ask for the order; and they enforce it with all sorts of in-

ducements, bargain offers, samples, free examination privileges, and a wide variety of other appeals.

Here is an example of the appeal of **exclusiveness:**

"There are many more than three thousand discriminating readers who will want this book, but only three thousand copies were printed. As this letter is being mailed, the day's orders reduce the number still available to 422. Better make sure of getting **your** free-examination copy by filling out and mailing the enclosed card **today.**"

The "You" Attitude again: Among the numerous factors that contribute to effective correspondence, the "you" attitude, referred to earlier, is paramount. The seller takes care not to show his anxiety to make a sale. What he stresses is the buyer's interests. The buyer will get a bargain; he will be guaranteed against dissatisfaction by the privilege of returning the merchandise; payment will be made easy for him by special terms, etc. In sales letters as much as in any other form of business correspondence be sure to consider the reader at all times.

The postscript: In that same frock-coat-and-striped-pants business era alluded to above, the postscript was frowned upon. It was considered unkempt—allowable, perhaps, in private correspondence but distinctly incorrect in well-dressed business correspondence.

Today, however, few sales letters are without postscripts. As a typographical device, the postscript has won general adoption because of the special services it can perform. It can remove from the body of the letter, whose unity it might impair, some special matter which should be brought to the reader's attention. Or it can give a needed emphasis to something as no other method can.

"P.S. Special discount terms can be arranged" stands out in a postscript, yet does not interfere with other persuasions as it might if set in the body of the letter. And if you have already mentioned your booth at a convention, a postscript reminder can do a lot to draw visits there: for example, "P.S. We're looking forward to seeing you at booth 16. Ask for Mr. Elkin."

"LETTERS YOU DON'T HAVE TO WRITE"

A recent speech by Maxwell C. Ross, a well known sales promotion expert, listed **sixteen** ways letters can be used to create good will— and, eventually, sales. "There's just one prerequisite," he said; "the person using them has to be a nice guy, courteous, friendly, and, above all, sincere."

Each is simply a friendly, personal letter that you send on some occasion when nobody would have thought very much about it if you hadn't sent the letter at all. They don't *have* to be written, but they create a tremendously favorable impression because they *are* written.

1. *You can use a letter to follow up a salesman's call.* You don't need to, for it isn't expected, but you'll be surprised at the reception it gets. You could start something like this: "John Smith told me today of the pleasant visit he had with you about your insurance program. I know that John will do a fine job for you." Then finish off in your own words.

2. *You can use letters to make appointments.* You say, "It's about time for me to sit down with you, Jim, and go over your insurance in the light of the new tax changes. I want to do this when you have the time for it, but it should be soon. I suggest that we get together late Friday afternoon. How would 4 o'clock be?" You don't need to say much more, but you'll be surprised at the nice reception you get.

3. *Whenever a customer or client has been promoted or changed jobs*, it's a nice gesture to send a letter like this—"Congratulations on your appointment to District Sales Manager. This is fine news, and I know you'll do a great job. If I can ever be of any help to you, please let me know."

4. *When a customer is ill*, there's no more appreciated time to get mail. All you need to say is—"I'm certainly sorry to hear that you are laid up for an operation. I hope it won't be many days before you're back at your desk." Add to that a book, or the loan of one, a magazine, or a box of candy, and the good will you build is far above the effort you take in doing it.

5. *When there is a death in the family*. If it's tactfully done a short message of sympathy can mean much.

6. *When a daughter or son gets married*, or *a new baby arrives*. These letters make no tangible effort to sell; they're simply good-will builders—the kind that some day will bring something nice to you because you went out of your way to do something nice for somebody else.

7. *When people buy a home*, write to them. Your letter doesn't need to be long or fancy. Perhaps: "I hope you are enjoying your new home, and that you have recovered from the trials of moving." If you have something to sell, go ahead and mention it. Tell these folks you'd appreciate a chance to call when things are squared away. In some cases, an inexpensive gift like a small rosebush or a young tree creates far more good will than the cost.

8. *When a customer has a birthday*. Quite a few successful salesmen make a practice of keeping birthday lists and sending cards or letters. A personal letter is best, but if you use a card, write something in longhand on it.

9. *When people move to your town* a letter of welcome is an excellent source of new business. They don't know where to go for dry cleaning, laundry, milk—what service station to trade with, where to do their banking, or the nicer places to eat. So you write: "Welcome to Omaha. We know you'll like it here. If there is any way we can help you get settled, please let us know."

10. *When people move from your town*, it may seem a futile gesture to seem sorry—but the intangible good will you create may come back to you in unsuspected ways. And sometimes people *do* return. So you write: "I am sorry you are moving away from Lincoln. We will miss you as a customer, but should you ever return we'll be waiting to serve you again."

11. *When you read about a customer in the newspaper*, send him a letter. Clip the article, send it to

him, and say: "I don't know whether your children keep a scrapbook of the nice things that happen to you, but just in case they do, here's an extra copy I clipped for you to give them." And if congratulations are deserved, give them!

12. *When a customer is elected to some office,* or honored in any other way, perhaps you would say: "I've heard some nice things about the work you've done for the Chamber of Commerce, so I was not surprised to see that you have been elected vice president for the coming year."

13. *When someone has done you a favor* he will appreciate a note from you. "Those two extra tickets got me off a rough spot. I hope I can repay the favor soon."

14. *When some product or service pleases you,* take time to write about it. "Quite often people write to you only with their complaints, but I wanted you to know how pleased I am with our new floor furnace, and with the courteous and efficient way your men installed it."

15. *When a serviceman comes home write to him* or to his parents if he lives at home. That's a small way to show your appreciation of all he has done for you and his country. Never again in his life will he so much *want* to be welcomed back; or want to feel that all he went through was not in vain.

16. *You can use letters to thank new and old customers for their orders.* Perhaps you do, but many don't. In Des Moines, a filling station operator sends a post card to new customers. All the card says is, "It was nice of you to stop at our station. I hope you'll come back often." That's all it needs to say.

Talent scout, G. L. Fultz, St. Louis' best dressed credit man, and staunch enemy of Whiskers and Goozle, says of the following assembled hogwash: "I know you will want to read this letter, for it's a dandy."

"Thank you very kindly (who was kind?) for your letter of November 12th, just received. I am sorry that our bookkeeping department (mass production) erroneiously (new spelling) billed you for storage on the car that we handled for you. I am attaching corrected bill for which (?) I am sure you will find in order. Thanking you very kindly, we remain, very truly yours."

CHAPTER FOUR

DIRECT-MAIL SALES LETTERS

What has been said in the previous section on sales letters in general applies, of course, to that concentrated type of sales correspondence, the mail-order sales campaign. We shall deal here with the special features and problems of such campaigns.

BIG BUSINESS

Though its peak may have been passed, mail-order merchandising remains one of America's biggest businesses. But realistic merchandisers bear in mind the following developments.

Our farm population, which once comprised the biggest mail-order market, has declined, in fifty years, from more than half to less than a fifth of our national total. At the same time, the automobile has made it possible for farmers to drive to town to do their shopping. So considerable is this trend that big mail-order houses have followed their straying rural customers to the towns by opening retail outlets there. At the same time, metropolitan department stores, following their straying customers to the suburbs with well equipped branch-stores, have also picked up many farmer shoppers.

Mail-order merchandisers, therefore, have had to show alertness and ingenuity to meet this challenge. That they are meeting it successfully is demonstrated by the continuing enormous volume of mail-order business.

The giants like Sears, Ward, Spiegel, and Alden continue to send out millions of catalogues every year. In the book industry mail order promotion has become one of the major merchandising methods. *The Literary Marketplace*, the directory for the book trades, lists some seventy book clubs! Correspondence and self-improvement courses continue to educate millions of customers by mail. Almost countless small firms sell specialty items like homespun textiles, hand-whittled toys, home-baked cookies, and even scalp massages. Increasingly, a good deal of banking, insurance, and other services, formerly conducted in person, are now carried on by mail. And the sale of such services is increasingly done by direct mail. Department stores and many other types of business supplement their regular sales with the business brought in by their mail-order departments.

Most mail-order campaigns are linked with advertising campaigns in publications, over radio and television hookups, on matchbook covers, and by other means. In many cases the advertising is done to produce the lists of prospects used in the mail-order campaign proper.

ADVANTAGES OF DIRECT MAIL

The chief advantages of direct-mail selling are, first, that it is selective as regards audience and market. The direct-mailer has generally built up classified lists of proved prospects. If not, or if he wishes to enlarge his lists, he can obtain the lists he wants from list brokers. When he sends out a mailing he knows, if that is necessary, the age, sex, trade, income level, etc., of the persons whom he addresses. And he can pick the territory, the time, and so on. In a well-organized campaign the part of the town and the day when the letter is delivered can be determined in advance.

Another advantage of direct mail is its flexibility. Through careful testing techniques every element in the campaign, from the price range to the color of the ink used, can be tested beforehand to assure the best return.

Still another advantage is economy. On a large variety of goods and services mailing and other costs are well under dealers' discounts and salesmen's commissions and expenses.

WHAT YOU SHOULD KNOW

You may be a clever copywriter but you will fail in your assignment if you start without certain essential information.

Know what you are selling. Study the article or the service that you are selling. Know it thoroughly before you write about it. The better you know it the better able you will be to choose your selling points, to write with conviction about them.

Suppose you are selling a table. Learn what wood it is made of, how it is finished, what style it is in. From your knowledge of it decide whether to stress appearance, durability, or price.

Know the market. What is the income level that is to be appealed to? How does the current economic situation affect your potential customers' buying habits? Will it be wise to propose time payments?

Know the prospect. Study the lists you use. Age, sex, locality, etc. all influence buying habits and trends.

APPEALS

In a certain book publishing house there were two schools of thought regarding the appeal to be used in promoting fiction. One school held that people bought novels for the story; the other held that it was literary values that drew people to the purchase of hard-cover books, that if they wanted merely story they turned to the magazines.

To settle the argument it was decided to send out two test mailings on the same novel. One emphasized story; the other emphasized literary values. But that experiment did not settle the argument. The two mailings brought almost identical returns.

Analysis of the two campaigns led to a number of conclusions. Each campaign was well prepared. In each the appeal used was made so attractive that it had a good sales effect. And it became clear that the audience wanted both story and literary quality.

Without realizing it, when they were writing the letters, the copywriters had taken this into account. In the letter stressing story, the copy implied that the novel also had literary quality; and the copy stressing literary quality implied that this enhanced a good story. From then on that publisher's promotion materials, whatever was actually stressed, featured several appeals.

You will find that most good sales letters use more than one appeal. The bargain appeal may be enhanced by stressing quality, and vice versa. And usually other inducements are added to break down sales resistance. It is good policy to offer a variety of inducements.

THE MAJOR APPEALS

A distinguished psychologist, Professor Starch, has listed the following, in the order of relative influence, as motives to which the sales-letter writer can appeal:

Appetite — hunger	Taste
Love of offspring	Personal appearance
Health	Safety
Sex attraction	Cleanliness
Parental affection	Rest — sleep
Ambition	Home comfort
Pleasure	Economy
Bodily comfort	Curiosity
Possession	Efficiency
Approval of others	Competition
Gregariousness	Cooperation
Respect for Deity	

Another list takes the following order:

> To make or save money
> To acquire beautiful possessions
> To gratify curiosity
> To satisfy appetite
> To protect loved ones
> To guard one's reputation
> To attract the opposite sex
> To be individual or "different"
> To "keep up with the Joneses"
> To avoid trouble or effort
> To seize opportunity
> To be popular
> To preserve one's health
> To be comfortable
> To be in style
> To enjoy life
> To be wholesome and clean

Other lists have been compiled. The owner of a big newspaper chain put popular reading interest in the following order: "Money, crime and sex." An advertising agency estimated sales appeals in this order: "Bargain, ambition, sex," —which seems to summarize all the appeals.

In selecting the appeal for your campaign two things should be borne in mind. First, as the book publisher's tests indicated, it is wise to exploit more than one appeal. Second, the nature of appeals varies according to age, sex, education, income level, and occupation.

"Sex attraction" will rank ahead of all others for most young men and women but will fall behind "bodily comfort" in appeals to the elderly. In buying a car safety of operation will outweigh all other considerations for a mother with small children; with a college boy, speed and appearance will count most.

CONCENTRATE THE APPEAL

Try to concentrate the mail appeal in a single phrase or sentence. If you do this you can use it as an opening sentence and re-use it, possibly with an interesting variation, in the body of the letter or in the postscript.

And make it direct. Two catchlines were proposed for a certain campaign. One was "161 New Ways to Win a Man's Heart." The other was "A New Recipe for Home Happiness." The first pulled four times as many inquiries as the second. Why? Mainly because terms like "recipe" and "home happiness," as used, are not as direct as "ways" and "a man's heart." And also because the appeal to curiosity, in the use of the number 161, was added to the other appeals, illustrating again the value of the multiple appeal.

Here are some examples of concentrated yet multiple appeals:

Exploiting the desire for security, an insurance company implied the possibility of attaining comfort and material happiness as well, and worked on the reader's curiosity in their semi-question catchline, "How we retired with three hundred a month."

Concentrating on prestige and success values, Oldsmobile added appeal to the spirit of adventure in the line "Four hundred thousand Oldsmobile owners who drive the Hydramatic way are blazing the trails tomorrow's motorists will follow."

The following opening was intended to appeal to curiosity and to vanity: "You are expensive but we think you're worth it."

INDUCEMENTS

Additional appeals in mail-order campaigns usually take the form of supplementary inducements. In some cases the appeal is a snobbish one. The merchandiser dwells on the small number of purchasers to whom the offer is limited. The inducement is in belonging to an elite. But in most campaigns the chief extra inducement is savings, or something free. The word **Free** in heavy type on an order form will pull many more inquiries than the same form without it, even if what is offered is nothing more than a catalogue.

Book clubs have had much experience in selling by mail. They find that "book dividends" —a gift book on joining, special rebates, "free" examination or combinations of such inducements—are strong sales inducers.

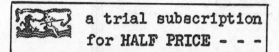

Fig. 16. In prominent type, and placed conspicuously at the head of the sheet, this offers in the form of a brief digest, assimilable at a glance, the contents of the sales letter which follows it.

Turkey is a very popular dish, but a turkey farm that sold its birds by mail found that giving away a stag-handled carving knife with each purchase nearly doubled its sales.

Fig. 17. Appended to a sales letter soliciting subscriptions, this original, eye-catching "special reduction" inducement is in the form of a series of "railroad tickets," only one of which is shown here. Notice that in addition to the attractive offer, a certain pressure for swift action is applied, as the offer holds for limited time only.

Mail order-shirt-sellers, copying mail order-jewelry sellers, boosted their business when they offered free embroidered monograms.

Food packers have found it worthwhile to give away quite costly books of recipes. Similarly furniture manufacturers have profitably given away books on home-decorating. One could fill a book with similar examples.

The giveaway, indeed, is the standard way to build up lists of mail order prospects. The offers of catalogues, booklets, free samples, bargains, gifts, entries into prize contests, etc. stimulate interest and produce inquiries that lead to sales.

Here a question enters, which the direct-mail merchandiser must answer according to the character of his product or service and according to the character of the prospect. Should the offer be completely free, or should a small charge be made to cover postage and handling expenses? If the offer is completely free, the number of inquiries will be much larger. On the other hand, if a small charge is asked, this serves as a screening process, eliminating the "deadheads" who write in for everything free. The result is a more selective list of prospects who are definitely interested in the product. Which is best for your campaign can be learned by testing. Testing procedures will be dealt with further along in this chapter.

THE ORDER FORM

The mail order campaign may be carried on exclusively through letters; it may be opened by an advertising campaign to draw inquiries; or it may be part of a larger selling campaign in which the mailings are coordinated with various forms of advertising. In any case, the order form, whether it is an advertising coupon, a separate mailing enclosure, or part of the letter or of another enclosure, is too important to be treated as a mere detail. The effects of force-

Fig. 18. This bases its appeal not only on the very substantial reduction offered, or on the attractiveness of the "invitation," but also on the extreme convenience of the method. The potential subscriber merely signs and mails, as the back of the coupon is a self-addressed, prepaid business reply card. He need send no money, and will be billed later, upon receipt of the magazine.

Fig. 19. Again the "half price" magazine offer, necessitating swift action on the part of the potential subscriber, and requiring of him only that he sign and mail.

ful copy can be weakened by an inconspicuous, unattractive, or unclear order form.

Care should be taken, if the order form is part of other printed matter, to set it off by some means or a combination of means. This emphasis is usually made by using broken or dotted lines that visibly separate the order form from the other matter.

Although some sticklers for typographical unity avoid it, most mail order men stress the separation by the use of distinctive, often bold-face type. Wherever practical, they go further and use blocks or accents of color and illustrations, such as pointing fingers or cutting scissors, to emphasize the separation.

Essentials of the order form include the firm's name, address and postal zone, and key number to identify the source of the form. If it is an advertisement coupon, it may be identified with the initials of the magazine and the number of the month—for example, WD 8 for *Woman's Day*, August issue.

If it is an order form enclosed in a mailing, the key may be an initial standing for a department of the firm and a number placing the letter in the position it occupied in a sales series. Thus P 2 may stand for Plastics Department and the followup letter in the current series. Or the key may be used to identify a rented list. Thus, assuming that a list has been rented from a concern named Harris, H 2 would stand for the followup letter in the campaign on the Harris list.

A concise description of the merchandise or service being offered should follow. If there is space for it, this can be made supplementary selling copy. Good copywriters can inject persuasion into the barest "Please send me . . ." phrase.

If the order form is to consummate a sale, the specifications should then be clearly stated —conditions under which a refund is guaranteed; time limit for the return of merchandise; method of remittance (cash, check, money order, C.O.D., on approval, installments, etc.); postage and handling costs, and whether borne by the purchaser or the seller; and other relevant information, such as added costs in Canada or abroad, etc.

If a booklet or sample is offered but, in order to screen the prospects, postage and handling costs are asked for, this should be clearly indicated.

Where choices of items, methods of payment or shipment are offered, boxes or spaces should be shown conspicuously so that the prospect may conveniently check off his choice.

In the lines for the prospect's signature and address, most order forms carry a notation in small type, underneath, "Please print plainly." If the prospect's signature is desired to make the filled-out form a valid contract, the small type underneath the lines should say, "Please write plainly."

In advertising, Post Office regulations restrict the size of the coupons to half the advertising page. In letters, however, you are free to make the order form as large and elaborate as you like. As in other fields, however, the simple approach is usually the best approach.

TYPES OF DIRECT MAIL LITERATURE

We shall deal here with the variety of pieces used in direct-mail campaigns.

The sales letter. Its characteristics have already been discussed. Here it should be noted that sales letters that are part of a series are often carefully varied in shapes and colors.

The post card. This may be of white or light-colored stock and may be printed on both sides. To meet postal regulations it must fit within the maximum ($4\frac{1}{4}'' \times 6''$) and the minimum ($3'' \times 4\frac{1}{4}''$) sizes. In other dimensions, first-class cards require more postage.

U.S. Government post cards, purchasable singly or in 40-card sheets, may be used. This allows a printer to "gang-run" them, imprinting the sales message on many cards at once, at savings in time and labor. The post office will redeem unmailed or spoiled cards provided the indicia (the official post office markings) are intact and the cards are tied in bunches of twenty-five all facing the same way to facilitate inspection.

The leaflet. A single sheet printed on both sides, in one or more colors, on white or colored stock.

The circular. A printed piece that may be folded, simply or in elaborate "accordion" style.

Broadside. A mailing piece unusual in shape, size, or manner of folding; and, usually, with conspicuously varied display types.

Self-mailer. This makes envelopes unnecessary. It is a folded sheet of rather tough paper. One side has a space to insert the addressee's name and address. It may also be a circular, broadside or booklet with the back cover used as the address side. The folds can be held together with gummed seal, a staple, or with the postage stamp. The printed message frequently permits detaching part of the piece by the recipient, who can fill it out and mail it back to the sender.

Brochure, catalogue book. These may be handled as more elaborate types of circulars.

INSERTS

Mailings usually consist of a number of inserted pieces. (Not, of course, self-mailers which have detachable parts for that purpose.) The following, in various combinations, may be included as inserts in mailings:

A piece carrying an order form; a business-reply envelope or card (self-addressed and postage prepaid) or an unstamped envelope; a piece carrying testimonial copy, usually a montage reproducing original letterheads and signatures); a guarantee that the goods or services offered will be satisfactory (usually printed in the form of a bond or other legal document); a gift coupon; a swatch of material or other sample; an advertisement designed to sell some other item; a blotter, etc.

Order-Form Inserts. As a mailing insert the order form may be a business-reply card; a self-addressed, government post card; a self-addressed, private mailing card; or a card to be inserted in a business-reply envelope.

As a business-reply card, the order form is frequently a self-mailer with perforations to facilitate detaching by the recipient. It should be on paper strong enough to stand double handling.

Because of its larger size, the inserted order form can have greater variety and elaboration in text and arrangement than advertising coupons in publications where space saving is all important. Illustrations and colors may be used; provision may be allowed for the sale of other items; etc.

The order form used as an enclosure may be used as a selling piece in itself or as part of another enclosure.

TYPES OF ENVELOPES

Two standard size envelopes are generally used in mailing. One measures $4\frac{1}{2}'' \times 9\frac{1}{2}''$, the other $3\frac{5}{8}'' \times 6\frac{1}{2}''$; the return envelopes enclosed in these measure, respectively, $3\frac{7}{8}'' \times 8\frac{7}{8}''$, and $3\frac{1}{2}'' \times 6''$.

To permit third-class mailing the top or one of the sides is left unsealed. Other envelopes have clasp closures.

If a carton or a mailing tube is used, sealing is permitted provided the wrapping plainly displays the statement that the item may be opened for postal inspection. The weight must be under 16 ounces. At 16 ounces or over,

Postage
Will Be Paid
by
TIME Inc.

No
Postage Stamp
Necessary
If Mailed in the
United States

BUSINESS REPLY CARD

FIRST CLASS PERMIT NO. 22, SEC. 34.9, P. L. & R. CHICAGO, ILL.

3¢—POSTAGE WILL BE PAID BY—

TIME

540 NORTH MICHIGAN AVENUE
CHICAGO 11, ILLINOIS

Fig. 20. A prepaid, self-addressed business reply card.

memo to:

OUR SUBSCRIBERS

This letter probably underscores some of
the reasons you had for choosing NEWSWEEK yourself!
It reached you because to invite new readers,
we use privately owned lists which
are not available for checking against our
subscriber files. Nevertheless, I hope you found
it of interest, and that if you know someone who would
appreciate joining you as a NEWSWEEK reader,
you will pass this invitation along.

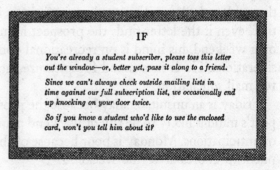

IF

You're already a student subscriber, please toss this letter
out the window—or, better yet, pass it along to a friend.

Since we can't always check outside mailing lists in
time against our full subscription list, we occasionally end
up knocking on your door twice.

So if you know a student who'd like to use the enclosed
card, won't you tell him about it?

Fig. 21. Inserts requesting readers to invite friends' participation in subscription offer.

the piece falls in the category of fourth-class matter.

A double-duty type of envelope is much used in mail order as an enclosure. It may not carry postage-paid indicia. Space is provided on it for the return address, advertising copy, and an order form. It is so cut that when the flaps are folded over and sealed it becomes an envelope that can contain the remittance for the purchase of the advertised article. The post office regards it as first-class mail.

A triple-duty type combines all the above together with an outgoing envelope. The top flap bears the prospect's name and address. When this kind is pulled up, the sales message is uncovered. The inside top flap carries the order form. The material below the flap has a gummed edge by means of which it can be made up into a return envelope in which the filled-out order form can be inserted.

WHEN TO MAIL

Many mailings are so arranged that they reach prospects on Tuesdays, Wednesdays or Thursdays.

The reason for this strategy is that weekend days, and the days neighboring on the weekend, have been found to yield fewer sales than the midweek days. The explanation given is that, even if the letter finds the prospect home on a weekend, his mind is on recreational considerations. He is in a mood for pleasure, not for mail solicitation.

Friday is an unsuitable day because the prospect's mind is likely to be full of weekend plans or anticipations. Monday is poor because of the piled-up chores after the weekend.

For similar reasons direct-mail merchandisers avoid holidays and widely customary vacation periods.

Other factors must also be taken into account for their possible effect on the pulling power of the offer. The character and circumstances of the prospect may have a bearing on the mailing time as also may the weather, changes in trends, sensational news, etc.

Thus it will be wasted effort to direct mail to farmers during planting or harvesting. If what you are offering is a luxury item, war threats should postpone the mailings; jittery people are not good prospects.

On the other hand, if you have been considering mailings regarding a non-fattening food specialty, take advantage of the current dieting trend. For this type of product the warm, figure-conscious months are good months, though they are bad for mail-order selling in general.

In the experience of mail-order concerns the months of the year are rated as follows:

JAN., FEB.
SEPT.–OCT. } BEST SEASONS
MAY–JUNE—LOW LEVEL

Some firms, however, mail in bad months either because they have some seasonal product, or because they believe that they will make up, in lack of competition, for the general buying apathy.

BASIC EQUIPMENT FOR A MAIL-ORDER DEPARTMENT

In the past, mail-order departments of most business concerns were set up to carry out all the mailing operations. Today little besides the planning and copywriting are done there.

New electronic and other machinery have vastly simplified cutting, folding, wrapping, labelling, billing, recording, filing, addressing and stamping processes. But this machinery is very costly. Only the very largest concerns can afford it. Specialized mailing concerns, which have installed such equipment, now service direct mailers at less cost than was possible with the older equipment. Consequently, even some

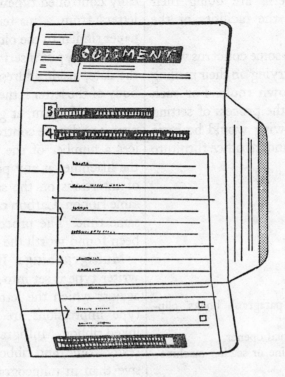

Fig. 22. Two forms of the double-duty envelope, one already folded, and one which requires folding—both combine the functions of order blank, request form, credit form, collection letter, business reply envelope, etc. A variation of this, allowing for the out-going envelope, is the "triple-duty" envelope.

sizable mail-order concerns are doing their mailings today through the facilities of the large mailing houses.

Nevertheless, there are some concerns which have good reasons for carrying on their mailing operations under their own roofs. For such concerns, if they are in the process of setting themselves up, the following would be basic equipment, aside from standard office furniture and stationery supplies:

Typewriter
Adding machine
Postal scale
Rubber stamps
Mailing labels
Stapler
Postal guide
Looseleaf binders for paragraph books, clippings, etc.
Mail slicer or electric mail opener
Postage metering machine or sealing machine
Multigraph
Mimeograph

REPRODUCTION PROCESSES

In mass mailings, which rule out individually typewritten letters, the processes described below are most common. Except where other effects are sought, the aim is usually to simulate the individually typed letter as closely as possible.

Letter-press printing: Ordinary printing. Advantages are clear, crisp impression. Disadvantages—expense, except in very large runs, and mechanical look.

Offset printing: Less expensive than letterpress for small runs, especially if art work is used. The plate from which impressions are made is rubber or some other material permitting softer and richer tones than ordinary print.

Hooven Process: Next to individual typing the Hooven process is the best method for use in the sales letter proper. A battery of electri-

cally controlled typewriters turn out identical letters from a master record on perforated paper similar to the old-fashioned player-piano roll. The typist inserts the letterhead, types in the date, inside address and salutation, and the body of the letter is then typed out by the automatic mechanism, at great speed. The mechanism is under the control of the typist who services a number of the machines. She can stop the machines at any point to permit typing in of insertions on the same keys and from the same ribbon. Carbon copies can be made at the same time. The process is expensive, but has been found worth the cost on special mailings.

Multigraphing: In multigraphing, typewriter type is set into a slotted, flexible drum, against which the letterheads are rolled. The type impressions are made through a large inked ribbon. Multigraphing takes more "make ready" time, and ribbon inking is more expensive than in mimeographing (see below) but it is neater and resembles actual typing more closely.

Multilith: An improvement on multigraphing. The process resembles offset printing. The multilith machine is actually a small offset press. It becomes more economical than multigraph for large runs.

Mimeograph: Least expensive of reproducing processes. Reproduction is from a stencil, a tissue longer than a standard letterhead, coated with cellulose. "Cutting" the stencil involves the same process as typing. The keys cut their impressions out of the cellulose, leaving a blank space which is later filled with ink from an inked roller and impressed on paper. In addition to type matter, drawings and hand-lettering can similarly be "cut" out of the stencil with a "stylus," an instrument resembling a pencil with a metal tip.

From the cut stencil hundreds of copies can be rolled off. The machine, which is easy to operate, is comparatively inexpensive. The cost of materials, stencils, ink, etc., is also comparatively low.

Mimeographing, however, has the disadvantage of never looking quite clean. It is very hard to keep from spotting the paper and smudging the lines. Careful work, however, can produce a presentable job, and with a signature cut by a stylus, has been found useful in large mailings where expense is a consideration.

Nahmco Process: A refinement upon multigraphing. An added operation at, of course, added cost gives a uniformly even type impression, improving the appearance of the letter.

Varityper: An accessory process. The varityper is an electrically operated typewriter with interchangeable sets of keys, which permits the use of varieties of type. It is capable of "justifying," that is, evening out the lines of type as in typesetting machines. Its advantages are that it provides variety in type, a crisp finish, and neat appearance. It can also be used to prepare "originals" from which letter-press or offset plates can be made.

SOURCES OF LISTS

Crucial in any mail-order campaign is the list of prospects. Usually a firm's customers make up its basic list, and other lists are used to expand it.

The sources of names for other lists are responses to advertising in publications, over the radio, on match-book covers and other media calling for orders or inquiries; various public lists such as are supplied by public agencies and utilities; and purchases or rental of lists of other concerns.

Lists available to the public include telephone books, trade directories such as Thomas' Register, financial-rating books, college catalogues, national, county and city directories, and bureau records such as incorporation lists, voting registers, license and permit records, etc.

Some city directories show residences arranged according to street numbers. These are useful in campaigns that include house-to-house circularization. They may be copied at the local library, the county clerk's office, or the local Board of Elections.

Numbers of valuable lists are obtainable from the Superintendent of Documents, Government Printing Office at Washington. In any new large mailing it might pay to send for an index of these lists, to see whether there are any that might furnish prospects.

Another means of developing lists is to run contests. The names of the entrants will constitute a list of prospects whose interest in your product has been stimulated by participation in the contest.

Questionnaire cards or bargain or gift offers inserted into merchandise are good sources of lists. Some book publishers enclose business-reply cards asking intriguing questions on literary matters. Those who answer not only furnish their names as prospects but define their tastes, thereby facilitating accurate classification of the lists. Food packers and manufacturers of household goods offer bargains on enclosures or on detachable parts of the packaging.

Where the article offered has a touch of rarity or special interest, a request to the customer for the names of like-minded friends generally brings names of good prospects. A mail-order distributor of craft objects—textiles, pottery, basketwork, etc.—built up substantial and profitable lists by this means.

Where the articles offered are related but not competitive, list-exchanging is frequent. For example, art galleries will exchange names with musical groups or rare-book dealers, women's specialty shops with fashionable restaurants, etc.

PURCHASE OR RENTAL OF LISTS

In addition to exchanging lists, as mentioned above, lists can be purchased or rented. The purchased lists constitute, of course, an outright addition to your list. The rented list, in addition to the business it brings, will add good general prospects to your list.

Lists may be purchased or rented from various types of organizations—civic, labor, fraternal, religious, educational, sports, etc.— from magazines and book clubs, and from other business concerns.

These transactions can be carried out directly or through list brokers. The brokers, for a twenty per cent commission, arrange the rental of names. Many brokers also handle the entire mailing procedure—sorting the names, stenciling, inserting, sealing and delivering the letters to the post office for a certain fee. They do so either because their brokerage business has developed as a sideline to their mailing business or because they have connections with organizations or agencies willing to make lists available.

If the list is purchased, a set of stencils or other records is delivered to the buyer. If the list is rented, the renter delivers his envelopes and enclosures to its owner, the broker or the owner's mailing agency. The renter receives the post office receipt for the mailed matter.

Good list owners keep their lists productive by constant checking and weeding ("cleaning"). They will therefore guarantee accuracy between ninety and ninety-eight per cent, and will refund postage on every piece returned as undeliverable in excess of the two to eight per cent they have allowed for. They will also inform the renter or purchaser of a list of the mailing time, nature, and price of the merchandise last offered to those on the list, and other relevant facts about it.

Through rentals or purchase, therefore, your list can bring in subsidiary income. If you do this through a list broker, take care to use one who is well established and reputable. And do not sell or rent your list indiscriminately to all comers, unless you are finished with it and no longer intend to do business with it yourself. You would not want your list to get into the hands of a competitor, or to be used for the promotion of a product offensive to your customers. The pulling power of a list has often been damaged, at least temporarily, by offers that irritated the prospects or made them suspicious.

You can find the names of list brokers in the classified telephone directory under the heading of "Mailing List."

THE WELL-TENDED LIST

To get the most out of your list—

Keep it orderly. Classify it so that customers are separated from prospects; arrange each of the two classifications geographically to take advantage of postal rate regulations and geographical conditions, and to enable you to synchronize mailings; and make as many other classifications as are practicable—by industry, trade or profession; by age, sex, buying power as indicated by credit ratings; by responsiveness as indicated by previous purchases, etc.

Keep it fresh. Because of death, bankruptcy, removal, and other unforeseeable contingencies lists undergo an average annual mortality of twenty per cent. Therefore it is advisable to check your list regularly.

Some houses make such checks semi-annually. Some do it by sending inquiries to the addresses whether they wish to have their names retained on the list and, if so, to verify the address. Others examine sales records and drop those who have not responded for a certain period, say a year. Others make a mailing both for the purpose of checking the list and of testing the elements of a projected mailing.

Returned mail is used as a checkup. For that purpose a "Return Requested" mark is used on the mailing pieces.

The Post Office makes a minimum charge for the return of third-class mail. This serves as a check on the accuracy of your list and furnishes the addresses of those on the lists who have moved away.

To obtain the new address, print below the return address in the upper left-hand corner of the envelope "Return Requested." If a forwarding address has been left with the post office, you will receive the information on the returned third-class mailing piece.

Since Americans have a notably high mobility rate, you will have to weigh the advantages of a highly accurate list against the comparatively expensive method of keeping it accurate. If five per cent of a list of 100,000 names have moved, it will cost you at least $400 just to get the new addresses.

TEST MAILINGS

In large mailings it is advisable to test about 10 per cent of the list to be used. The test may be used to decide a variety of questions. Is the product salable through mail? If the tested response falls below a certain figure which allows no profit margin, there is no point in completing the mailing.

The tests may be designed simultaneously to answer such other questions as: "Is the price right? Is the copy right? Is the paper the right color? Is the ink the right color? Is it better to use stamps or printed indicia? Is it better to offer a booklet free or to make a small charge for postage and handling? Is it better to ask the buyer to pay postage and handling costs and to quote a lower price, or to absorb these costs in a higher price?"

The tests are conducted by sending out different letters and correspondingly different enclosures, the responses to which answer the questions. The elements that have brought the best responses are then incorporated in the material sent in the final mailing.

Even if the tests warrant further mailing, and all the approved elements have been used, many mailers do not plunge into the total mailing at once. They do it in batches of 10,000, let us say, so that, in the event of some sudden change in the situation, losses may be minimized. It has sometimes happened that a late summer or a late winter, or an unaccountable shift in taste, or alarming headlines in the news have adversely affected sales and responses.

Testing for sales response is quite simple. Suppose the manufacturer of a $5 article wishes to test a 25,000 name list. Mailing costs, including copy preparation, printing of enclosures, stationery, postage-prepaid envelopes, cost of list and postage come to $72 per thousand. Suppose the orders from the 2,500 names tested come to 125, for a total of $625. Suppose manufacturing costs of the article is $180 and shipping costs $20. Total costs, then, for the test mailing come to $380. This sum, subtracted from the total returns of $625, leaves a profit of $245 or $1.96 per order. That test would be a green signal.

THE SALES LETTER SERIES

Most direct-mail campaigns involve a series of letters. Sometimes the first letter is sent only to draw inquiries, the answers to which are expected to produce the sales. In any case, if the first letter does not make the sale, successive letters are sent. Especially in the case of expen-

The RIKE-KUMLER Co.
DAYTON 1, OHIO

Dear Customer:

Because we always try to bring you top values ...

... we are happy to tell you of a special arrangement made with the publishers of LOOK -- an arrangement that brings LOOK to our charge account customers at just _half the single copy price!_

Month after month, thousands pay $3.50 for a year of LOOK (26 issues), but RIKE'S can now offer you personally the special money-saving rate of -

18 MONTHS (40 ISSUES) OF LOOK FOR ONLY $3.00

This is the lowest price at which LOOK has been sold in many years, and not only does it bring you a 50% saving on the single copy value (bringing you a saving of $3.00) ...

... but it also assures you of receiving LOOK regularly every-other-Tuesday for a year and a half -- 40 big issues that your entire family will enjoy.

You will find that LOOK keeps you well-informed .. that LOOK takes you behind the scenes .. gives you the background of vital events .. tells in pictures how they affect you, your home, your family, your friends.

So we suggest that you take advantage of this offer right now!

We at RIKE'S believe you will like LOOK -- that you will find it entertaining, informative, and well worth the cost -- but, in any event, you are protected by the publisher's MONEY-BACK GUARANTEE ...

    ... a guarantee that makes it possible for you to obtain a
    full refund _at any time_ on the unused part of your order.

LOOK's regular rate is $3.50 a year (26 issues), and this offer of 40 issues for $3.00 is available to our customers. The special price will not be made to the general public.

So please mail the certificate NOW -- _while this offer is still in effect!_

Cordially yours,

Cornelia

Cornelia,
Your personal shopper at RIKE'S

C:LD61

P. S.   Because RIKE'S is _the only store_ in Dayton which can make this offer, the publishers have requested that the enclosed certificate be made non-transferable (except to members of your own family).

Fig. 23. Using hanging indentations and other attention-getting typographical devices, this letter offers to charge account customers a half-price subscription to a national magazine.

NEWSWEEK BUILDING • BROADWAY AND 42ND STREET
NEW YORK 36

October 21, 19

Down in the Gulf South - which includes the area around
Mobile and Pensacola - United Gas is helping to open a
whole new region for industrial development. And, United
Gas is telling business and industrial America about the
Alabama-Florida region in this NEWSWEEK advertisement on
page 21.

The United Gas ads...a smartly designed full page 2-color
series...has helped to spread the news of the rapidly expanding Gulf South area.

NEWSWEEK reaches the nation's top business and industrial
leaders - the important decision-makers - the men with the
authority to decide on new plant locations. The United
Gas ads give NEWSWEEK's readers the green light...bringing
them interesting, informative material that has served to
build good-will and prestige for your company as well as
draw attention to the Gulf South section.

Very truly yours,

Arthur Windett

Arthur Windett
Advertising Director

AW:ss

THE MAGAZINE OF NEWS SIGNIFICANCE

Figures 24, 25. Letters to advertisers, affirming the prestige and good-will value,
as well as other values, of such advertising promotion.

Newsweek

NEWSWEEK BUILDING · BROADWAY AND 42ND STREET
NEW YORK 36

January 6, 19

A brand new advertising campaign for CONSOLIDATED
ENAMEL PAPERS appears on page 14 of this issue of
NEWSWEEK. Here's a voice of the turtle message
that makes economic sense...the reasons why CON-
SOLIDATED ENAMELS add up to an important saving
for paper buyers.

NEWSWEEK's more than 900,000 well-informed readers
include the top executives from coast-to-coast --
more than 57.8% of these busy businessmen exert
important influence on company buying policy.
CONSOLIDATED's ads in NEWSWEEK and the other news-
weekly publications help to reach your important
customers and prospects and pre-sell them on this
unparalleled value in enamel papers.

NEWSWEEK makes your selling job a lot easier by
familiarizing your contacts with the CONSOLIDATED
story...be sure to take advantage of CONSOLIDATED's
heavy 1954 advertising promotion and put NEWSWEEK
to work for you!

Sincerely yours,

Arthur Windett

Arthur Windett
Advertising Director

AW:ss

THE MAGAZINE OF NEWS SIGNIFICANCE

Fig. 25

640 FIFTH AVENUE · NEW YORK 19, N. Y. · PLAZA 9·1000

November 25, 19

Dear Sir:

The December issue of The American Magazine enclosed, will be on the newsstands from November 27th to December 31st.

Your newest "Man of Distinction" advertisement appears on the 3rd cover and will be pre-selling LORD CALVERT for 5 full weeks during the holiday gift-giving and entertainment season.

That means extra-long selling time for LORD CALVERT. It means extra sales and extra profits for your licensees, many of whose best customers are among The American Magazine's 10,230,000 devoted readers.

Tell your retailers that by featuring and displaying LORD CALVERT with your 3 luxurious velour-finish gift cartons and special "Man of Distinction" greeting cards, they can cash in on the extra sales and extra profits this ad is sure to produce.

Sincerely yours,

E. R. Chenoweth
Advertising Sales Manager

Figures 26, 27. Letters to advertisers emphasizing the economic value, and calling attention to other values, of magazine advertising promotion.

THE **American** MAGAZINE

640 FIFTH AVENUE · NEW YORK 19, N. Y. · PLAZA 9-1000

March 9, 19

Dear Calverteer:

Month after month LORD CALVERT keeps telling The
American Magazine's 10,230,000 readers that Custom
Distilled LORD CALVERT costs a little more
                    tastes a little better
                    adds a little more pleasure.

A distinctive theme for the "Whiskey of Distinction"
with just the right sales appeal for readers of The
American Magazine who want a little better
                    live a little better
                    can afford a little more.

And you can be sure they'll see LORD CALVERT'S advertising because, in comparison with other magazines,
The American Magazine receives more reading sessions.

Here's a combination that's hard to beat. Be sure
to bring it to the attention of your licensees and
show how it means extra sales and extra profits for
them. Urge them to display LORD CALVERT prominently
and cash in on the "Pretty Special" LORD CALVERT ad
which appears in the March issue of The American
Magazine ... and leave blotters with your best
customers.

                    Sincerely yours,

                    E. R. Chenoweth
                    Advertising Sales Manager

Fig. 27

sive articles reliance is placed upon a series of letters.

As many as ten mailings are sometimes made, though most direct-mail people feel that more than six will not pay off. Each letter in the series is prepared in advance so that it may be sent in proper succession and for delivery on a predetermined good mail day to prospects remaining unsold.

The opening letters usually stress the desirability of the article and offer samples or free inspection. The next mailings may intensify the appeal with testimonials and guarantees. The concluding mailings may offer further inducements—special price, deferred payments, etc.

A method called "The Wear-Out Series" continues the series only as long as returns justify it. Thus, if the returns of the fourth letter, for example, show no profit margin over costs, the series is discontinued.

In sales correspondence, however, whose purpose is to solicit the trade of new dealers, the campaign is never-ending. One large company analyzed the record of 350 of its best customers to determine how many years of correspondence it had taken to get the accounts. The analysis showed that 52 had been booked the first year; 82, the second year; 33, the third year; 10, the fourth year; 3, the fifth year; 8, the sixth year; 29, the seventh year; 2, the eighth year; 11, the ninth year; 14, the tenth year; and 70 in more than ten years. Data was inconclusive for the remaining 36.

Sales correspondence for dealer trade is never-ending.

POSTAL INFORMATION

Since the mails constitute one of the key tools of the direct-mail business, it is wise, of course, to know that tool. It is strongly recommended, therefore, that the *Postal Manual* be kept on file and regularly consulted. You may purchase the *Postal Manual* from the Post Office Department, Washington, D.C. 20260.

First-Class Mail consists of sealed mail—letters or parcels that the sender will not permit the Post Office to open for inspection. Unsealed correspondence, letters, or parcels also go under the first-class rate if they contain writing, typing, or carbon copies. Parcels of merchandise containing a single invoice can, however, go fourth-class. First-class mail can be registered, certified, or sent C.O.D., but cannot be insured. Rates for first-class are 6¢ an ounce or fraction in the United States.

First-class mail gets the best response in direct-mail appeals because, being sealed, it appears to be a more personal communication.

Post Cards, private mailing cards, or other cards within the accepted limits (3″ × 4¼″ to 4¼″ × 6″) take 5¢ postage. Double cards—original and detachable return cards—take 10¢ or 5¢ a card. Cards outside the given dimensions require 6¢ postage at the letter rate. Without plainly marked designations such as "Post Card" or "Private Mailing Card" or "First Class," cards that do not carry writing will be classified as third-class mail.

Air Mail rates are, currently, 10¢ an ounce or under for letters, and 8¢ for post cards.

Second-Class Mail includes newspapers, magazines, and other periodicals that carry notice of second-class entry in the publication. The rate is 2¢ for the first two ounces or under, and 1¢ for each additional ounce or fraction. Second-class mail may be registered if postage at the first-class or air mail rate is affixed.

Third-Class Mail includes circulars and other printed matter (except second-class publications, proof sheets, or corrected proof sheets with manuscript accompanying them). It also includes merchandise, farm and factory products, etc. The weight limit is 16 ounces and the rate is 4¢ for the first two ounces and 2¢ for each additional ounce or fraction.

Third-class mail may be sent in bulk at special rates. At least 200 identical pieces must be mailed at one time. Third-class mail (but not bulk-rate mail) may be insured or sent C.O.D.

Fourth-Class Mail (Parcel Post) includes printed matter and merchandise that weighs over 16 ounces. Sealing of Parcel Post is permitted.

Book Rates are 16¢ for the first two pounds and 6¢ for each additional pound, provided that no advertising matter other than incidental announcements of other books are enclosed. Complete books of 24 pages or more, if at least 22 pages are printed, are classified as books for this purpose. Third-class bulk mailing of books permits 200 identical pieces or weights of 50 pounds of separately addressed pieces mailed at one time, at the rate of 12¢ a pound.

IMPORTANT SECTIONS OF POSTAL LAWS

Section 134.22. Direct mailers should be acquainted with this section of the *Postal Manual* dealing with bulk rate regulations.

Section 134.22 permits mailing third-class matter in bulk at pound rates. Printed indicia may be used. This requirement applies also on mailings carrying the minimum per-piece charge. Bulk mailing saves stamping and metering time and labor.

Permits for this privilege are obtainable at the local post office by filing an application form and paying an annual $30 fee plus a $15 imprint fee if printed indicia are used. The assigned permit number is incorporated in the standard indicia form and printed on envelopes, labels, wrappers, etc. Hand stamping the indicia instead of printing them is permitted also.

Third-class matter mailed in bulk must be presented in quantities of at least 200 identical pieces. These must be separately zip-coded and presorted by zip codes.

Each mailing must be accompanied by a statement on Form 3602, filled in and signed by the permit's owner, showing the permit number, the class of the mailing matter, the number of pieces, and the weight of single pieces. On third-class matter paid at pound rate the mailer's statement must show the number of pounds for mailing.

Matter bearing permit indicia must not be distributed otherwise than through the mails and may not be mailed at a post office other than the one shown on the indicia. Otherwise the permit may be revoked.

Precanceled stamps and postage-metering indicia are also permitted in bulk mailing. No charge is made for the permit to use precanceled stamps in bulk mailing, but some special conditions must be met. Postage must be paid for by the piece instead of by the pound, and the mailing cost is determined by weighing at the post office. Conditions for postage-metered indicia are identical except that the words "Bulk Rate" must be incorporated in the metered design. Postage-metering machines may also carry an imprinted advertising message as part of the design.

Section 131.23. This permits return of business-reply mail without prepayment for detachable cards or postage-guaranteed envelopes. Postage is paid only on matter mailed back by prospects. They go first-class and must follow these conditions:

Business-reply cards must be within the maximum 4¼″ × 6″ and minimum 3″ × 4¼″ sizes for the minimum rate.

Cards and envelopes must bear printed indicia. Cards may be prepared as reply portions of double post cards or as folded cards or as inserts.

Colors may be used, but light colors for address readability are preferred.

Permits are granted, without charge, on application. Business-reply envelopes cost 8¢ each: 6¢ regular postage plus 2¢ for the extra service. Cards cost 7¢; 5¢ plus 2¢ for the extra service.

Form 1510. If a cash remittance is lost in the mail or a valuable mailing is claimed as not received by the customer, Form 1510 can be used for tracing.

C.O.D. Orders. Form 3877a, for which there is no charge, is used for C.O.D. orders. The post office assigns a series of numbers to the applicant and the money order that the post office sends to the mailer in payment of the C.O.D. charge will show this number in the space usually used for the name and address of the money order purchaser.

Reaching Box Holders. The Post Office makes available a simplified form for reaching post-office box holders and star-route box holders. This makes it unnecessary to include the name and box number. All that is required is to print on the envelope, label, or wrapper the name of the post office and the state or the words, "Postal Patron, Local."

GOVERNMENT REGULATIONS

Direct mail business falls under regulation by the following government departments or bureaus:

The Federal Trade Commission, which protects the law-abiding businessman against unfair competition, and the consumer against fraud and misrepresentation;

The Foods, Drugs and Cosmetics Administration, which inspects products offered for sale, and tests samples in its laboratories to see that they meet claims made for them and that they are no hazard to health;

The Post Office Department, which acts to prevent lotteries and the circulation of fraudulent or obscene matter.

THE **American**
MAGAZINE

640 FIFTH AVENUE · NEW YORK 19. N. Y. · PLAZA 9·1000

February 26, 19

HERE'S NEWS ... BIG NEWS!

The attached advertisement is another indication
of how THE AMERICAN MAGAZINE is moving ahead on
all fronts.

For the first quarter of the year, THE AMERICAN
MAGAZINE again reports significant gains in
advertising space and advertising dollars:

    <u>1st Quarter 1954 vs 1st Quarter 1953</u>

    ADVERTISING LINAGE UP 10%
    ADVERTISING INCOME UP 15%

Compare gains in advertising space and dollars
for this period with those estimated by any
other general family magazine!

    Sincerely yours,

    E.R. Chenoweth
    Advertising Sales Manager

Fig. 28. Letter to advertisers pointing up in a highly concrete way the specific economic advantage of magazine advertising promotion.

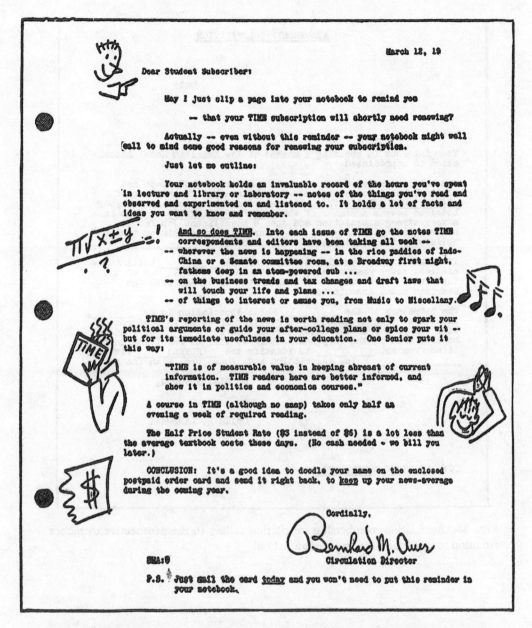

March 12, 19

Dear Student Subscriber:

May I just slip a page into your notebook to remind you

-- that your TIME subscription will shortly need renewing?

Actually -- even without this reminder -- your notebook might well call to mind some good reasons for renewing your subscription.

Just let me outline:

Your notebook holds an invaluable record of the hours you've spent in lecture and library or laboratory -- notes of the things you've read and observed and experimented on and listened to. It holds a lot of facts and ideas you want to know and remember.

And so does TIME. Into each issue of TIME go the notes TIME correspondents and editors have been taking all week --
-- wherever the news is happening -- in the rice paddies of Indo-China or a Senate committee room, at a Broadway first night, fathoms deep in an atom-powered sub ...
-- on the business trends and tax changes and draft laws that will touch your life and plans ...
-- of things to interest or amuse you, from Music to Miscellany.

TIME's reporting of the news is worth reading not only to spark your political arguments or guide your after-college plans or spice your wit -- but for its immediate usefulness in your education. One Senior puts it this way:

"TIME is of measurable value in keeping abreast of current information. TIME readers here are better informed, and show it in politics and economics courses."

A course in TIME (although no snap) takes only half an evening a week of required reading.

The Half Price Student Rate ($3 instead of $5) is a lot less than the average textbook costs these days. (No cash needed - we bill you later.)

CONCLUSION: It's a good idea to doodle your name on the enclosed postpaid order card and send it right back, to keep up your news-average during the coming year.

Cordially,

Bernard M. Auer

Circulation Director

BMA:0

P.S. Just mail the card today and you won't need to put this reminder in your notebook.

Fig. 29. Hanging indentations, marginal illustrations, ruled notebook paper, and other devices allow the copywriter to develop the analogy, brightly and wittily, between the magazine for which a renewal of subscription is being sought and school-study and preparation. In addition to the inducement of the special student offer, those virtues of the magazines are emphasized which most immediately correspond to students' needs and interests.

```
                    MEMBERSHIP SOLICITATION


                                     Date


      Dear _____

      Your interest in becoming a member of the American Hotel Associ-
      ation is appreciated.

      The American Hotel Association is a federation of state and
      regional hotel associations.  This means that in the case of
        (NAME OF HOTEL & CITY) , it would first be necessary for your
      hotel to become a member of the (STATE ASSOCIATION) .  This is
      a very strong association and does a magnificent job for its
      members in legislative and all other matters pertaining to the
      welfare of the hotel business in the State of _____.

      Immediately upon becoming a member of the _____ Hotel Asso-
      ciation, every member hotel is entitled to the full use of the
      facilities and services and identification of and with the
      American Hotel Association.

      The Secretary of the _____ Hotel Association is Mr. _____,
      located at (STREET ADDRESS AND CITY) .  If it is in conformance
      with the policy of our hotel association in _____, I am
      hopeful that in the very near future we will be receiving instruc-
      tions from Mr. _____ to identify the   (HOTEL)     with the
      _____ Hotel Association and, therefore, with the AHA.

                                     Cordially yours,


                                     ORION E. LANDMARK



      CC:  (NAME OF SECRETARY)
```

Fig. 30. Association membership solicitation calling to the prospective member's attention some of the advantages of affiliation.

TIME

840 NORTH
CH

YOUR SUBSCRIPTION
EXPIRES THIS MONTH

February 5, 19

Dear TIME Subscriber:

You might call this a "double last chance" letter.

For it's my last chance -- before your TIME subscription
expires this month -- to remind you of TIME's bargain longterm
renewal rates. And it's your last chance to renew that subscription without missing any copies!

I hope you've been reading TIME much too long now to be
willing to miss any of

TIME's clear roundups of each week's important news ...

The TIME Cover Stories that introduce you to so many
fascinating people ...

TIME's sprightly accounts of the worlds of books, music,
medicine, art, science ...

-- and all the other things that make "TIME night" a
special event each week.

So won't you please sign the enclosed card and fly it back
to us at our expense today --

For only if we receive your order by return airmail can we
keep TIME coming each week without a break in your subscription!

Cordially,

Bernhard M. Auer

Circulation Director

BMA:P

Fig. 31. Prominent reminder and hanging indentation are used to solicit
renewal of subscription and to call attention to some of the magazines most
attractive features.

CHAPTER FIVE

CREDIT LETTERS

In most business concerns credit and collections are the responsibilities of a single department. This unified control is logical because the two functions are closely related. The manager of such a department, if he follows a careful credit policy, reduces collection problems to a minimum. Moreover, he makes the process of collection an extension and illustration of his credit policy, so that the act of collection educates the delinquent customer and becomes a preventive measure against potential further delinquency.

In collection letters it is better to use the department designation of "Credit Department," or the identification of the writer as "Credit Manager," rather than "Collection Department" or "Collection Manager." Only in the very last stage, when pressure must be resorted to, should the relationship be thought of as other than a credit relationship.

USEFULNESS OF CREDIT

Sometimes, under the strain of harassing credit problems, some businessmen sigh for the return of the supposed good old days when practically all business was on a cash basis and there were no "headaches." But then the glory of the American standard of living, which is virtually based on credit, would have to be sacrificed. The modern, American way of business would be inconceivable without credit.

Credit makes possible the diversity and volume of modern American business. Credit facilitates every type of business, but it is particularly essential in merchandising. It enables the merchant to carry a larger and more varied stock than he would be able to on a rigid, cash basis. It makes possible greater and more diversified services to customers.

Once restricted to the wealthy, credit has become a convenience available to the man in the street, through the spread of installment buying, loan banking, and other measures. Almost all major department stores and retail mail-order houses have charge-account facilities, and through the use of credit cards such as those issued by Diners' Club and American Express it is possible today to buy on credit almost anything from a flower corsage to an around-the-world trip. Credit is now part of the American system at every economic level.

CREDIT RISKS

Most people are honest. That is the lesson of credit buying. Those who aren't are too few to discourage the adoption of credit systems. And the borderline cases are kept in line by the pressures of our business-minded society, which makes the loss of credit standing in the community too distressing to be risked. Therefore it is enough, today, for a person to be employed and to be able to present the names of his employer, doctor, minister, or other reputable persons in his community to obtain credit for a large variety of transactions.

Naturally, easing of credit has complicated the tasks of the credit manager. His problems are no longer as simple as in the past when little

TO. NATIONAL BANK COMPANY
OF NEW YORK

BUDGET-LOAN APPLICATION

This application dated _____ 19___ is submitted to obtain a loan of $ _____ for _____ months, payable on the _____ day of each month for the purpose of:

PERSONAL

Name _____ Date Birth _____ Are you a Member of { National Guard— Reserve Forces— Draft Status } Active — Inactive

Single ☐ Married ☐ Separated ☐ (Name of Wife (or Husband)) _____ No. of Dependents _____

Home Address _____ Apt. No. _____ Tel. No. _____

Rent ☐ Lease ☐ Own ☐ To Whom Paid _____ (Name) _____ Yrs. ___ Mos. ___ Amount Paid $ ___ ☐ Weekly ☐ Monthly

Previous Address _____ No. Years ___ Year and Make of Car Owned (Address) _____ License No. _____

Nearest Relative Not Living With Me (Name) _____ (Address) _____ (Relationship) _____

EMPLOYMENT OR BUSINESS

Employed by ☐ Self employed ☐ (Firm Name) _____ Dept. ___ Position _____

Address _____ Yrs. Tel. No. ___ Mos. ___ Name of Superior _____

Kind of Business _____ Salary $ Commission $ ___ ☐ Week ☐ Month ___ Name of Superior _____

Previous Employer _____ (If less than 2 years in present position) (Address) ___ No. of Yrs. ___ Name of Superior _____

Other Income $ ___ Month Week Source _____ Other Wage Earner? ___ Name _____ Age ___ Relationship _____

Name and Address of Employer _____ Tel. No. ___ No. Yrs. ___ Salary $ ___

ARE YOU PRESENTLY INDEBTED?
IF YES—LIST DETAILS   IF NO—LIST DETAILS OF OBLIGATIONS PAID WITHIN LAST 3 YEARS

Name	Address	Date Incurred	Original Amt.	Present Bal.	Amt. Mo. Pyts.	Amt. Past Due

ARE THERE ANY JUDGMENTS RECORDED, OR GARNISHMENTS OR OTHER LEGAL PROCEEDINGS PENDING AGAINST YOU?   If yes, explain _____

HAVE YOU EVER BEEN SUED?   If yes, explain _____

Business Reference (Name) _____ (Address) _____ Date of Last Transaction _____

Are you at present a Co-maker on any loans? ___ For Whom? ___ At What Bank? _____

Bank with (Name) _____ Branch (Address) _____ ☐ Checking ☐ Savings

Amount Life Ins. ___ Cash Value ___ Amt. Borrowed Against ___

As security for this loan I offer the collateral listed on reverse side.
If loan is granted on basis of this application, you shall be entitled to take in advance interest computed at a discount rate of not more than .00932 per month on unpaid principal balances deducted in advance. You are authorized to pay proceeds as follows:—
☐ In hand ☐ Credit my account ☐ By ordinary mail at my risk to me or to following persons or companies:—

(Name) _____ (Address) _____ (Amt.) ___

(Name) _____ (Address) _____ (Amt.) ___

Customer desires to do business with _____ (Address) _____ Branch ___

You are authorized to deduct monthly payments from my savings or checking account with you until this loan is paid in full. Yes ☐ No ☐
I certify that I have read the foregoing answers and have noted the above answering check marks and that they are true and correct and are made for the purpose of obtaining credit, and that you are entitled to rely thereon without obtaining further information, and that this is not to be construed to restrict in any way any investigation you wish to make. If this application is not approved, I authorize you to return the note by ordinary mail at my sole risk and to retain the application for your records

x _____

Fig. 32. Application to a bank for a loan, for personal or business reasons. This form, with perhaps few and minor variations, is a standard one used by most banks for this purpose.

more was necessary than to examine the financial statement of the applicant for credit and to look up his listing in a credit-rating directory.

REQUESTS FOR CREDIT

Usually the request for credits is incidental; it is frequently part of a first order given to a salesman. When the salesman turns in the order, the credit manager of his concern begins making credit inquiries, as will be explained later in this chapter.

Sometimes orders are mailed in by a customer, responding perhaps to trade advertising or a catalogue mailing. Such orders are usually accompanied by letters requesting credit, such as the following:

Dear Mr. Bingham:

Please open an account for us with the attached order for a dozen of your new line of fans as advertised in the current *Electric Age*.

The three references listed below include an officer of our bank and two merchants in this city. I am sure they will supply you with such information as you may require relative to our financial status and record.

I believe we can do well with this merchandise, provided that we can have time for proper display and other promotion, in which, we understand, we will have cooperation from you in dealer helps and cooperative advertising. Your completing your credit investigation as early as possible will be to our mutual advantage.

Yours truly,
A. B. Sutton

Below is a letter requesting credit, from a customer who had hitherto bought for cash:

Dear Mr. White:

It is over a year now since I started in business. At that time you explained that, in view of my restricted capital and the fact that this was my first business venture, you could not see your way clear to extending credit to me. You offered assistance in other ways, such as various dealer helps, cash discounts, and advice which I found very helpful and for which I take this opportunity again to express my appreciation. You also expressed confidence, at that time, that I would soon establish myself in this field. You knew of my experience in it and you were kind enough to express a good opinion of my ability and earnestness. You suggested that when I judged my business to be sufficiently well established, I should again apply for credit.

I think that time is here. Your records will show that my business with you has steadily increased. I have a fine list of customers, including, now, some of the most substantial houses in this city and a growing clientele in neighboring communities.

The ———— Bank, which carries my account, will be glad to furnish you whatever information you consider necessary and you may also refer to the following business concerns:

———————

———————

———————

My further business growth now requires credit. The expansion I am planning is conservative and fully justified by the business situation in this community. I shall therefore appreciate your extending a line of credit consistent with my progress, my capital investment, and your past experience with me. I look forward to a prompt reply and, I hope, the continuance of a pleasant and mutually profitable relationship.

Yours sincerely,
A. M. Hopkins

CREDIT INFORMATION

The information sought in credit investigations is often derived from various sources and covers personal as well as financial data. The sources may include the salesman's judgment, reports from the applicant's bank, and confidential information from other businessmen in his community. The data should include the applicant's prospects for expansion, the trade situation in his community, his previous business activities, an idea of the way he conducts his business, his record for meeting his bills, etc. It must also include personal data. Obviously, an applicant who is known to drink heavily, or who plays the races, or who lives extravagantly, is not so good a risk, other things being equal, as a more sober type of person.

Even a financial statement may require a little scrutiny as to what may be behind it. A businessman with small capital may be a better risk, when other factors are taken into account, than a man with a much larger capital. The man with small capital may have accumulated what he has by his own enterprise and exertion; the man with large capital may have acquired it by sudden inheritance. In the latter case it would be advisable to look into his past record. Large capital can melt fast under poor management.

Also a previous failure should not necessarily rule out a credit applicant. The circumstances of the failure should be looked into. For example, the shutting down of a large plant in a town with few industries may force even the most efficient merchants into bankruptcy. Furthermore, many merchants have learned business lessons the hard way, through failure, and have as a result become better businessmen and, consequently, better credit risks.

Other factors to be considered are whether the credit applicant's community is experiencing growth or decline, whether the competition he faces is heavy or light, whether the community has few industries or many. For example, in a town that is mainly given over to textile manufacturing, a drop in cotton prices or sales will affect merchants more drastically than the merchants of a town with more diversified industries.

In considering a credit applicant's capital, it is not enough to be told the gross amount. The wise credit manager will wish to have a breakdown of the applicant's capital resources. How much of it consists of bank deposits? How much of it is in secured notes? How much of it consists in accounts outstanding, stock values, plant and fixtures, real estate, etc.? The credit manager will want to have an understanding of the fluidity of the various properties. For example, a firm with a large proportion of its undeposited capital in marketable goods is a better credit risk than a company with a large proportion of its undeposited capital in the less readily convertible form of real estate.

As far as possible, the reported assets should be analyzed. How many of the accounts outstanding are long past due? How many of these accounts are secured by good notes? Are the notes held in a farming community? If so, then the season in which they may have to be called in becomes important. Such notes are better in the harvesting season than in the planting season.

How are the assets distributed? Are the credit applicant's investments of a kind that may be converted readily and without loss, should the need arise?

GRANTING CREDIT

It should be clear from the foregoing that to extend credit without the most careful credit investigation and without the closest analysis of the ascertained facts would be to invite trouble. Laxness here only serves to encourage laxness in the customer. If the latter feels free to order whenever he feels in good spirits, he is likely soon to be overstocked. Then he will be unable to meet his obligations, and the careless creditor will be confronted with a problem caused by his lack of caution. A "soft" credit policy can be a disservice to the customer, who is left with a damaged credit rating.

Careful credit relations can educate the customer. He is thereby unobtrusively guided into wise buying, the avoidance of overstocking, and the enjoyment of a consistently high credit rating.

CREDIT LETTERS

A good credit policy operates with the aid of effective credit letters. In these the first essential is tact. Businessmen are naturally sensitive about their credit standing. Clumsy inquiries can give needless offense. As far as possible, let the customer feel that the questions you ask him are intended to help you give him better service and protection against over-buying.

Firmness and consistency are also very important. Be conservative as to promises. It is better for a customer to be pleasantly surprised by unexpected concessions later than to have great expectations and be disappointed.

THE CREDIT INQUIRY

The first step is a letter requesting information from the credit applicant.

Such a letter may be of two sorts—an individually written letter or a form letter. As in all business correspondence, individually written letters are preferable. Sometimes, however, the volume of correspondence makes this impractical.

In either case receipt of a new order should be gracefully acknowledged. Pleasure should be expressed over gaining the new account along with a reference to the hope for mutually pleasant and profitable business relations. The letter should include a clear and precise state-

ment of terms. Then, as a necessary preliminary to filling the order, a financial statement should be called for, to be returned promptly, in order that there be no delay in the shipment of the goods. This request is made, however, only when your firm does not check credit through an established credit rating agency.

While waiting for the applicant's reply, the credit manager will assemble and analyze all the information he can secure from other sources. He will get the salesman's opinion of the applicant. To the extent that the order or the prospective customer's situation warrants it, he will apply for additional information from the pertinent bank, from credit associations, from businessmen in the community, etc.

Below are samples of credit inquiry letters. The first is a letter to the credit applicant:

Dear Mr. Miller:

I thank you for your order of October 20 which our salesman, Mr. George Burns, has just turned over to us. It is a pleasure to add you to our list of customers. I feel confident that you will be satisfied with our line and with our services, which include a considerable amount of cooperation in the form of displays and various sales helps and analyses of trends and merchandising methods. Mr. Burns' report is such as to lead us to believe that such efforts with you will not be misplaced.

As Mr. Burns has no doubt already informed you, our terms are (state terms precisely). However, before we can open an account for you, certain routine but necessary information will be required. Please fill out the enclosed form and return at your earliest convenience.

The goods you ordered are among our best sellers. We should like to get them to you without delay because they will be good items for your holiday trade, and your prompt response will be of benefit to us both.

With best wishes for a prosperous holiday season, I am,

Yours truly,
Francis Pell

Gentlemen:

We shall appreciate a prompt reply to our request of
June 14 for a recent financial statement.

We should very much like to proceed at once with your
order; and your attention to this matter will help
facilitate the completion of the transaction.

If the financial statement is not now ready, will you
please notify us as to when we may expect it.

Very truly yours,

Fig. 33. A Credit Department's request for the prospective customer's financial statement. It is to be observed that here, too, the writer employs the "you" attitude; the financial statement will serve the customer's ends, by facilitating shipment of the requested order.

Letters to the applicant's bank should go directly to its credit manager, giving his name and title if these can be conveniently obtained. Be accurate about the applicant's name and address. State the purpose of your investigation frankly. Also be precise about the information you desire. Don't leave it to the other person to guess what you want to know. Questions asked in general terms will be replied to in general terms, and you may be obliged to send additional inquiries with all the irritations, embarrassments and delays that such fumbling involves. If you are making other inquiries in town, let the bank know. In all such inquiries, give assurance that the information you receive will be held in strictest confidence. Also never fail to offer to reciprocate, at any time, with information you may be able to give. Send the letter out under your signature and with a clear indication of your position in the firm.

In certain cases your bank may be willing to conduct a credit investigation for you. But ask for such services sparingly. The bank, naturally, will balk if you make it appear that you intend to use them as your credit department.

The information usually sought in a credit inquiry to a bank includes the following:

How long has the bank had the applicant's account? (If a short time this may indicate a tendency to change banking connections, in itself an unfavorable sign.)

What is the applicant's line of credit. Is it granted on an open or a secured basis? If accommodation has been granted on secured promissory notes, what have been the amounts and how frequent have been the loans? (Indicate in your letter, that you will appreciate a reply in general terms if there is a reluctance to give exact data.)

Are balances commensurate with the line of credit? It is generally expected that an average balance of twenty per cent of the loan will be maintained. Where the balance falls below that figure it would generally be considered unfavorable to the applicant's credit standing. The bank may not be willing to give exact data here, too, but may give the applicant's average balance.

Does the applicant settle his loan periodically? An affirmative answer to this question would be a good sign.

What is the bank's opinion of and attitude toward the applicant?

Does the bank's record of the applicant's cash deposits tally with the figure given in his financial statement? Small discrepancies should be expected because of outstanding checks. But if the difference between the two figures were considerable, suspicion would be justified.

Other information may be sought for at the same time from references furnished by the applicant and from credit associations operating in the applicant's community. The credit associations that have been formed for that purpose have been a boon to American business. San Francisco has the honor of being the pioneer community in this field. The first American credit association was formed there in 1877 by the city's Board of Trade. This type of organization has been established in almost every sizable business community in the country. Most credit managers, today, are members of the National Association of Credit Men and avail themselves of its many useful services.

The following is an example of a credit inquiry sent to a businessman named as a reference by a credit applicant:

Dear Mr. Gray:

Mr. Arthur Wallace of your city (if a large city, give his address) wishes to open an account with us and has given us your name as a reference.

We shall be grateful to you for any information you can give us regarding his business and for your opinion of his reliability and his business prospects. Such information will be treated in utmost confidence. Be assured, also, that any time in the future, if we can reciprocate with similar information, we will do so gladly and promptly.

Sincerely yours,
Abraham Addis

The following is an example of a more detailed inquiry letter to the applicant's bank:

Dear Mr. Sparkman:

We understand that you have had dealings with Mr. William Strand who wishes to open an account with us, and that you are therefore in a position to furnish information helpful in determining a line of credit for him.

We shall be grateful to you for answers to the questions listed in the attached form and for your general opinion as to Mr. Strand's character, habits, and business ability and the financial standing of his business. We will, we can assure you, keep whatever information you give us in strict confidence. And we also wish to assure you that we will gladly reciprocate with similar information on any occasion you may desire it.

Since the merchandise Mr. Strand wishes to order is seasonal, we should like to act on his credit status as quickly as possible. We would, therefore, appreciate an early reply, for which we enclose an addressed envelope.

Yours sincerely,
Clifton Avery

Below is the attached inquiry form:

Re William Strand (Firm name, address and date)
Is he now a customer of yours?

. . . .

How long has he done business with you?

. . . .

What credit do you extend to him?

. . . .

Does he earn cash discounts?

. . . .

If not, does he make prompt payments when due?

. . . .

If he asks for extensions, how often does he do so and for what length of time? (A general answer will be satisfactory.)

. . . .

Unless this is against your policy please state how much he currently owes you; and of this sum is any amount or percentage past due? (A general summary will be satisfactory if exact figures cannot be given.)

. . . .

Would you consider your business relationship with this applicant a generally satisfactory one?

. . . .

Have you any reason to suspect that this applicant's business situation has changed and that he is not so good a credit risk now as he was formerly?

. . . .

Please furnish any other data that might have bearing on this applicant's credit position.

. . . .

The following is another type of inquiry letter that may be sent to a reference furnished by the applicant:

Dear Mr. Furness:

Mr. Oscar Dahl, who is seeking to open a credit account with us, has included your name in his list of references as a concern he has been doing business with. We shall be glad to have from you any information that will help us obtain an estimate of his reliability.

Will you be good enough to inform us about his payments? Are they regular and prompt? What is your judgment of his present financial position? Is it better or worse than when he began to do business with you? Are his business prospects favorable? Is the general business situation in his city favorable?

Please rest assured that any information we receive from you will be kept in strict confidence. And, of course, any time we may be in a position to reciprocate, please call on us.

Mr. Dahl is pressing us for the earliest possible delivery of the goods he has ordered. We would, therefore, appreciate a prompt reply and are enclosing an addressed envelope for your convenience.

With thanks for your consideration of this matter, I am,

Yours sincerely,
D. A. Barlow

The following is a specimen of an answer (favorable) to a request for credit information:

Dear Mr. Barlow:

We are happy to answer your inquiry about Mr. Dahl immediately and favorably. As he has correctly informed you, we have been doing business with him for the past three years. In all that time our relations with him have been consistently and entirely satisfactory. He has met every invoice promptly. Our records show not a single past due payment.

We have no reservations in recommending Mr. Dahl.

Yours sincerely,
Howard Furness

The answer (unfavorable) may take the following form:

Dear Mr. Barlow:

In answer to your inquiry about Mr. Edward Brooks as a credit risk I am sorry to inform you that my reply must be in the nature of a warning.

Even his statement that he has been doing business with us for three years is characteristically inaccurate. Our relations, it is true, are in their third year, but the third year has barely begun. He would have been more correct to say that he has been doing business with us for two years.

They have not been pleasant business years. After seven months' experience of delays in payment and indifference to our correspondence we were obliged to withdraw credit privileges from him. Since then his dealings with us have been on a strictly cash basis. Only threats of legal action secured settlement of past due accounts.

Frankly, we are mystified by Mr. Brooks and his business behavior. His continuing with us on a cash basis for so long has surprised us. The amount of business he has given us has been considerable. This would suggest that his financial position is actually not a bad one. Perhaps other houses may succeed where we failed—by educating him to a better way of conducting his business.

Our own opinion, however, is that a firm that undertook such education would require much patience and would be taking risks. We prefer not to hazard it.

Yours sincerely,
A. V. Laidlaw

LETTERS GRANTING CREDIT

Letters granting credit should open with an expression of satisfaction over the information received either from the applicant or from his references.

A department store approving a charge account sent this letter to the applicant:

Dear Miss Perkins:

We are happy to tell you that our check of the references you named in your application for a charge account was completely satisfactory. You are to be commended on the high esteem you have won, and we are pleased to welcome you as one of our charge accounts. Your listing has been entered and you may phone in orders today if you wish. Incidentally, telephone orders will receive as prompt and courteous attention as you may expect when shopping in person.

For any special problems such as matching or choosing gifts for difficult cases we have a person, experienced in out-of-the-ordinary shopping, who is always ready to help you. Her name is Miss Genevieve Adams, and you may call on her at any time.

Also, as a charge account customer, you will receive advance notice of events valuable to shoppers. When new styles come in, you will be informed several days before the general announcement is published. Similarly, when we hold a sale, you will be told in time to make a first selection. We are happy to be able to extend this service to you right now. There will be a forty per cent markdown on better slips this coming Friday. You can have a choice of them tomorrow or the day after before they are put out for public sale.

In regard to terms, our practice, as you have probably already been informed, is to send out statements to reach customers the first of the month, for payment within that month. This has proved to be most satisfactory to our customers.

If you have any questions don't hesitate to ask any department head. I shall be happy to have you call on me if you have any question about methods of payment or terms of payment, etc.

Once more, we welcome you to all the services this store has to offer.

Yours sincerely,
Arthur E. Ives

A letter from a manufacturer or a wholesaler to a dealer, expressing satisfaction with the information received from him or from his references, should state in one of the first paragraphs that the goods ordered are being shipped. That information, after all, is what the applicant most wants to hear. It is the most concrete evidence that credit has been granted. The information should include the exact time and means of shipment.

The letter should also, of course, have a plain statement of terms to prevent any later possibly disagreeable misunderstanding. There is no harm, at this point, in putting in a word about the value of prompt and regular payments for a mutually pleasant and profitable business relationship.

Nor is any harm done in introducing a sales talk on the articles ordered. It will provide the opportunity to emphasize such special cooperation as your firm offers in the way of dealer helps, shared advertising costs, sales suggestions, and other services. This kind of practical assistance builds up confidence in you and in your merchandise and induces the customer to push it. Here's an example:

Dear Mr. Whitaker:

We thank you for sending us your financial statement promptly. We have been thereby enabled to fill your order at once, since the infor-

mation in the statement was entirely satisfactory. The goods were shipped this morning via Jersey Central and should reach you within two days. We are happy to welcome you among our accounts which, we take pride in saying, are a select business group.

Your special order for ten dozen assorted pairs of our new Two Timer Sport Shoes indicates your alertness to buying trends. This style is proving one of the best we have ever offered, because people want ruggedness built into sport shoes without detracting from the outer details of good appearance.

We are looking for dealers who see all the possibilities of this line and are ready to push it in their community. If you would undertake to do this in your city, we shall be glad to furnish you with special dealer helps, to share on a liberal basis in the cost of advertising in local publications, and also to put before you a novel merchandising plan that has brought unusually good results to every dealer who has tried it. Please let us know at once if you are interested.

Our Mr. Shane, when he last called on you, probably told you on what terms we extend credit. Invoices are sent with each shipment and the terms are 2/10 net thirty days. No cash discount will be allowed on payments received after the ten-day discount period. In any event we shall expect payment in thirty days. We are sure your own business experience will favor strict adherence to terms.

If I can be of service in any way, please do not hesitate to call on me.

We look forward to a long and pleasant business relationship with you.

Yours sincerely,
Edwin Davenport
Credit Manager

SAYING "NO" GRACEFULLY

On occasion the business letter must convey a refusal—a refusal to extend credit, to lengthen terms, to submit a bid, to grant a discount, to make an adjustment, or to contribute to a cause. In practically every case, your object is to say "No" in such a way as to retain good will.

Here are six suggestions that will help you:

1. Answer Promptly. An immediate response makes a favorable impression. It is also more considerate because it gives the inquirer more time to make alternative arrangements.

2. Be Friendly. A refusal can be friendly, tactful, and courteous. It is not necessary to slam the door in a customer's face. As one writer puts it, "If you must shove away business, hold the customer's hand as you shove."

3. Explain Why. Early in the letter, make clear the reasons for your refusal. Be as definite as you can. "It's against the company policy" is vague and annoying. Put your explanation on a believable, frank, man-to-man basis, if you want the customer to accept it without resentment. By implying, "I wish we could, but . . ." you will soothe his ruffled feelings.

4. Emphasize the Positive. If there is some angle of your refusal letter which permits a positive action or affirmative answer, put the emphasis on that angle and soft-pedal the refusal. For example, if you can grant an alternative, start your letter with, "I am glad to say that we can . . ." and put the refusal at the last, rather than starting with the refusal and then offering the alternative. You will readily understand the psychological advantage of this procedure.

5. Don't Overdo the Apologies. A courteous explanation is more convincing than profuse apologies.

6. Make It a Sales Letter. If you can't grant what the customer wants, don't simply say so and sign off. This type of letter is no exception to the rule that every business letter should be a sales letter. Add a positive wish to be of service in some other direction, despite this refusal.

Every person who writes letters can acquire the art of saying "No" gracefully. It takes a little effort and thought, but once mastered will help you all through life, not only in writing better letters but in all your relations with people.

LETTERS REFUSING CREDIT

Dear Mr. Landis:

Mr. Aswell, our representative in your territory, recently turned in your order for six dozen assorted tires, for which we thank you, along with your request that we open a credit account for your firm.

As part of the customary credit investigation undertaken in such cases we asked you for a financial statement and other information. On the basis of the information received, we regret to say that we must defer granting you a line of credit at this time.

Our judgment is based mainly on your present limited capital, and the short time you have had to establish your business.

Where we defer opening an account, we suggest a period of doing business on a cash basis and watching further developments. We would welcome your business, remittance with order or C.O.D., as a tentative arrangement.

If there are factors in the situation which have escaped us or to which you think we have given the wrong weight, please write us. Better still, if it suits your convenience, call on us here in person. We will be glad to have any facts that will justify reconsideration of this matter.

We trust you can see our position, and we shall be pleased to cooperate with you in every way consistent with our credit policy.

Yours sincerely,
James B. Kennedy

LETTER SUSPENDING CREDIT

Dear Mr. Hancock:

We thank you for your order which we received in this morning's mail. It is being prepared for shipment but there will be a small delay. We regret this delay because we like to give as prompt service to our customers as possible.

The delay is occasioned by the fact that there are three months' bills outstanding in your account. It will be necessary to hold up shipment on this order pending settlement of these past due bills.

We have shipped you two orders since your first past due bill. We thought this was an oversight that you would correct as soon as it was called to your attention. However, although several statements have been sent you, these bills remain unpaid.

It is our policy to suspend credit in all cases where past due bills have been allowed to run this far. We therefore request that you send us a check in settlement of the account, by return mail, so that your order may be filled without further delay.

Yours sincerely,
Anthony Wright

CHAPTER SIX

COLLECTION LETTERS

A credit manager should not ignore even the first deferment of payment, no matter how prompt and regular a customer has been theretofore. The very fact that the deferment is unusual is a sign that something may be amiss. It is better to find it out at once.

Deliberate delinquents are few, patience and consideration should be shown in nearly every case and all through the collection procedure. The first steps, especially, should be obvious, routine measures that can give no offense.

If the response—or rather, lack of response—to these first steps indicates a collection problem, do all you can to get whatever information is available. It will be valuable in forming a realistic judgment on the delinquent's readiness and capacity to pay.

It will be important to learn more than his immediate financial position. His personal situation or local business conditions may affect both his present problems and his prospects for the future.

However, it is only a very exceptional case that should permit letting things slide. The fact that he is being dunned usually moves the debtor, psychologically, a step closer to paying.

As noted before, avoid using the term "collection" until the final notice of resort to legal action. Instead of "Collection Department" or "Collection Manager" use "Credit Department" or "Credit Manager." For as long as possible let the procedure be thought of as part of the credit relationship.

TYPES OF APPEALS

In collection letters almost any basis of appeal is used. Which it should be will depend on the particular case. The appeals most generally employed are to pride, self-interest, the sense of fairness and mutual good will, and—as the last resort—fear. More than one appeal may be, and usually is, used in each letter; and the appeal used is seldom exhausted in one letter. Up to three letters may be used, the successive letters striking stronger on the chosen note.

Generally the first letter respects the customer's pride and self esteem. Its purpose is to "save face" for the customer, while drawing his attention to the unpaid bill. The suggestion that the bill has been "overlooked" is the commonest of the face-saver expressions.

The appeal to self-interest usually involves references to the customer's credit standing. Because of its importance to a business man, the suggestion that his credit standing is being jeopardized by his failure to pay is often enough to extract payment from him. Other self-interest appeals include references to discounts and premiums, these will be taken up later.

In the appeal to the customer's sense of fairness and mutual good will, appeals to his pride and self-interest are usually combined or implied. Fair dealing is one of the elements in a business reputation. Anything that reflects doubt on it would injure business standing.

THE NECESSITY FOR CAUTION

Fear is the most effective of all appeals, yet the one that should be most sparingly used. The best collection procedure is the one where it is the least used. It should be turned to only as a last resort. Barring exceptional cases, the aim of the collection procedure is to keep the account while collecting the debt. This objective becomes close to impossible after the use of threats. Fear almost always destroys good will.

There are other reasons for caution in the use of threats. If anything in them can be construed as extortion or blackmail, an enraged and unreasonable debtor—and debtors are often harassed beyond the point of calm and reason—may use such an expression as grounds for a lawsuit. Also, never threaten criminal prosecution; confine your threats to civil action. During your collection-letter series avoid anything that the customer may allege to be damaging to his business reputation. Damaging postcard notifications or letters stuffed into window envelopes in such a way as to expose some tell-tale phrase may be used as grounds for libel suits.

THE "YOU" ATTITUDE

As in other forms of business correspondence the "you" attitude is most desirable in collection letters. The function of these letters is to appeal to the customer's reason or emotions, not to express the creditor's apprehension. Letters that are obviously written by the creditor to relieve his feelings may be worse than ineffective—they may offend the customer instead of persuading him. And if it comes to court action such letters do not do the creditor's case any good when read into the evidence.

Therefore the creditor should avoid blunt, impatient or sarcastic expressions. These reflect anger or anxiety instead of the reasonableness and confidence that get the best results. A patient and considerate attitude is not only more effective but, actually, more just.

Most people, as we have already noted, are honest. If they weren't the credit system would collapse immediately. If payments are not met on time, it is usually not because the debtor does not choose to. He is kept from doing so by difficulties for which he deserves cooperation; or by poor business policies which the creditor is often able to correct by good advice, to his own subsequent advantage.

So, before putting the "squeeze" on in any collection-letter series, make sure that the delinquency is not due to something that calls for leniency. The customer may be reticent, and it may be necessary to find it out from other sources. If you learn that he has had illnesses in his family or other misfortunes, your consideration at such a time will more than pay off in good will.

The letters printed below illustrate the use of different tones and approaches.

Letter where leniency was applied:

Dear Mr. Vance:

We have just heard from our Mr. Howard Jamison, who calls on you, of your wife's operation. We were glad to hear that the operation was successful and that Mrs. Vance is now recuperating satisfactorily. We realize that this must have put you to considerable expense and therefore we regret that we were not informed of it before a reminder of your outstanding bill was put in the mail. Please do not let it give you any concern. We know that you will attend to this as soon as you are in a position to do so. We are satisfied to wait until you find yourself able to make the payment without strain.

With best wishes for Mrs. Vance's early recovery, I am,

Sincerely yours,
Albert H. Jackson

A debtor answers a collection letter by requesting an extension:

Dear Mr. Butler:

I am immediately answering your letter about my overdue account. I wish to assure you that I recognize my obligations and have no intention of evading them.

When I wrote you before that I was in temporary financial straits I did not go into details. That was partly because I found it painful for me to do so, and partly because I thought that you would bear with me in consideration of my good past record. But it is always best to give full and clear information.

What I omitted to tell you was that I and two other members of my family became seriously ill at the same time. I was obliged to leave my store in the care of an inexperienced person and sustained some losses. One of the illnesses required hospitalization and surgery, and the costs were high.

But I am now back in the store and things are in order again. It will be a couple of months, however, before I will be able to settle all outstanding accounts. So I am asking you to grant me additional time.

For corroboration of these facts I refer you to the Polyclinic Hospital or to Dr. Clyde Mahan (address).

Sincerely yours,
Richard Llewellyn

Response to an explanation for late payment:

Dear Mr. Llewellyn:

We appreciate your prompt and full explanation of your situation. I wish you had told us this before so that we might have spared you the embarrassment of the second letter we sent you. We hope you and your family are now fully recovered. We have every confidence in your will and capacity to meet your obligations. If we seemed insistent on having an explanation, it was only to have the information necessary to take the right course. If it had turned out, for example, that our merchandise was in any way unsatisfactory, we might have considered making some adjustment. In view of

what you tell us we are, of course, granting you the extension you ask for.

Sincerely yours,
H. H. Butler

INDIVIDUAL LETTERS

Wherever possible collection letters (except routine notices of lateness) should be individually composed letters suited to the special requirements of each case. Where form letters are used because of the volume of the necessary correspondence, the letters should be individually typed. If the recipient of a form letter recognizes it as such, he is less likely to give it his attention than if he thinks it is an individual letter. Therefore change form letters periodically (many firms change them every three months) so that, if the series has to be repeated, a customer does not get the same letter the next time he misses payment.

THE COLLECTION LETTER SERIES

Common practice in collection procedures involves three steps. First comes the formal notice that the account is past due. Then the personal correspondence urging payment. Finally the series of "pressure" letters.

The number of letters used in each step may vary. The formal notices may run to three, the personal correspondence to four, the "pressure" letters to two. Not only the number of letters but the intervals between them may vary according to the case and circumstance. There will be more letters and longer intervals between them with good payers than with those whose records are poor.

THE FORMAL NOTICE

If the routine monthly statement, the first formal notice, is not paid in time, a duplicate statement is sent with some note such as "please remit," or "past due," typed over it conspicuously, or on a small piece of paper clipped or stapled to it. Some firms use a message that is a little more elaborate. But the message is purposely kept impersonal, and has no salutation or signature. The intent is to suggest a mere bookkeeping formality. The slips used are printed or otherwise mechanically reproduced and carry some message (with blanks to be filled in) such as:

Invoices of the following dates .... amounting to $.......... now past due. We should appreciate your giving this your prompt attention.

Where salutations and signatures are used, the salutation is general and the signature is typed, not written, e.g.,

Dear Sirs:

Your account for .... (give month) in the amount of $.......... is now past due. Please give this matter your attention.

Signature (typed)
Position

THE FIRST PERSONAL LETTERS

When a succession of routine formal notices fails to bring payment, a series of personal letters is the next step. These should be the "face savers" already mentioned. They should be courteous, respectful messages that avoid any ruffling of the recipient's self-esteem.

From a department store to one of its charge customers:

Dear Miss Bliss:

In this busy town and in these hurried times it is difficult not to forget or overlook some necessary things. That may be the reason you have not yet settled your March account. If you will look through your papers, you will find two previous notices. The amount due is $42.64.

We should like to get our accounts up-to-date and should therefore appreciate receiving your check in the next few days, preferably by return mail if possible. We enclosed a stamped and addressed envelope for your convenience. If you find yourself unable to make this payment immediately please use the envelope to tell us when we may expect it.

Sincerely yours,
Anthony Drake

From a manufacturer to a dealer:

Dear Mr. Avery:

It may be that your check is already in the mail. If so, please ignore this letter. We send it only because it is so unusual for you not to meet your monthly invoice promptly. We trust that the previous notice we sent you was mislaid or overlooked and that you will welcome rather than resent a reminder.

Sincerely yours,
John V. Scott

Another manufacturer-dealer letter:

Dear Mr. Alvin:

Probably you have overlooked our last duplicate invoices. Or they may not have reached the right person in your organization. This is a third reminder. We are sure you appreciate the importance of keeping our accounts and your credit in order. We look forward to seeing, in the next few days, your check settling this overdue bill.

Sincerely yours,
H. A. Alexander

SALES TALK IN COLLECTION LETTERS

To include a sales talk in a collection letter has a double value. It performs its sales function, of course; and it helps soothe any irritated reaction over being dunned. These purposes are accomplished by implying in the sales talk that you have confidence in this customer and wish to keep on doing business with him. It may be advisable to give the impression that sales talk is the chief reason for the letter. In that case the sales talk should be its first item with the collection notice seemingly added as an afterthought. Where the collection appeal is to be stressed, have the sales talk come second. Examples:

A store to a charge customer:

Dear Miss Evans:

Our new spring dresses have just come in. They are being assembled for display. You and other good customers will be invited to a preview to take your pick if you wish. We think they are our most stunning spring collection in years. Next Tuesday morning is the date, at the Salon, and we hope you will be able to be there.

To avoid bothering you with another letter, may we take this occasion to remind you that your account has become overdue. The amount outstanding is $34.40. The duplicate statement mailed to you has probably been mislaid. We should appreciate your giving this your attention in the next few days.

Sincerely yours,
Frederick Peterson

A manufacturer to a dealer:

Dear Mr. Sands:

We are anxious to bring our books up-to-date and we find that in your account there is still outstanding the July bill for $54 about which we wrote you last September 2. We would appreciate your giving this your prompt attention.

The enclosed circular describes a new carving set which we are featuring for holiday sales. You probably have noticed the trend toward useful gifts in holiday buying. With Thanksgiving and Christmas on the way, this unusual set, reproducing a famous Swedish design, is bound to be a fast seller. Details of material, construction, and design are given in the circular so that there is no need to go into them here. What we want to emphasize is the dealer helps we provide on orders of a dozen or more. These include a handsome metal display rack

and a novel, accordion-fold circular in four colors, a copy of which is enclosed. We feel certain it will be a tonic for your holiday sales.

Sincerely yours,
Angus Richardson

THE REASON WHY

After the duplicate statements and the "face saver" letters have been sent, the ensuing collection correspondence should ask for payment or the reason for the delay. Some houses do this in their very first letter. It is important to get an explanation from a debtor because that is often the best information you can have about his situation and particularly his state of mind. Secondly, by asking for a reason for the delay in payment you show a desire to be considerate and reasonable.

Frequently the debtor has a good reason, and when you know it, you can help him. He, or someone in his family, may have fallen ill; he may have lost his job; he may have had a fire or other accidental losses; he may have been hit by some economic disaster in his community or region such as the shutdown of a large mill from which local people draw their livelihood or a drought and destruction of crops. Or he may have some grievance against your concern. Perhaps the goods he received are not moving, and he believes that your representative oversold him. Perhaps some request or complaint he has made was handled too tactlessly and has left him resentful.

In any case, once you have managed to get him to give a reason, the ice is broken. If he is in real trouble, you can grant him an extension, give him some other assistance, or take the steps you may consider necessary to salvage what you can. If he has a grievance, you can adjust it and regain his good will. If it turns out that the goods he bought are not moving you may let him return them. It would be better, how-

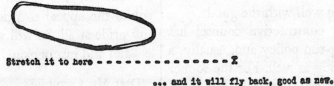

Look America's Family Magazine

110 TENTH STREET • DES MOINES 4, IOWA

Dear Friend of LOOK:

Here is a common, ordinary, garden-variety rubber band.

Stretch it to here - - - - - - - - - - - - - - - X

... and it will fly back, good as new.

But stretch it to here - - - - - - - - - - - - - - - - - - - X

... and IT MIGHT BREAK!

Similarly, a credit arrangement - such as the one which you and I made on your LOOK subscription - has elasticity ... up to a point.

Seriously won't you please send in your remittance today?

Sincerely,

Lester Suhler

Lester Suhler, for
LOOK, America's Family Magazine

ZS:keh

P. S. We will resume service immediately upon receipt of your remittance, and you will, of course, receive the full number of copies necessary to fill out your subscription.

Fig. 34. Often devices, such as graphic reminders, are used in collection letters, particularly in letters of this sort, where an amiable tone is clearly indicated. Such a tone frequently evokes the desired response, where a harsher one just as frequently fails.

ever, once you know the difficulty, to try a more positive approach. See what helpful suggestions you can make. In some cases what is needed is simply to show the customer how to operate the article. Often, then, he takes pride in demonstrating it to his customers and is soon making sales with it.

Some firms find it worthwhile to send special representatives to delinquent customers' stores to inspect them and to see what improvements can be made in their sales techniques. They may make suggestions with respect to lighting, stock display, merchandise promotion, and even accounting methods. They may describe and analyze methods used by other stores that are doing well with the goods.

This process of constructive counsel has proved a good long-run policy and, usually, a good short-run policy as well. For the sooner the goods are converted into cash by improved store operation, the sooner outstanding accounts are paid.

The attempt to have the customer explain why he is delinquent in payments should be continued up to the last letter in the correspondence—the blunt question. Examples:

Dear Mr. Cott:

We were hoping it would be enough merely to send you a duplicate statement of your amount due. The amount is $40.50. We have carefully examined our records for possible error in our billing and have found none. But if you know of any error will you please inform us.

We should appreciate your settling this matter promptly or informing us of any reason you have for delaying it.

Yours sincerely,
E. R. Bowles

Dear Mr. Apthorp:

This is our sixth letter seeking settlement of your account for $200, now six months past due. In each letter requesting payment we have also asked you to give us some explanation which might enable us to help you. We are still ready, if there is a reasonable explanation, to discuss with you measures that might be mutually advantageous. We should still rather do that than turn to the last resort—legal action.

However, if we do not hear from you within the next ten days, you will leave us no alternative but to turn the matter over to our attorneys for action.

Very truly yours,
Stewart V. Ames

THE APPEAL TO FAIR PLAY

Generally the appeal to fair play also involves the appeal to pride. If the debtor has any pride at all, he will wish to be thought of as a fair and just person. Some examples:

Dear Mr. Cartwright:

When you purchased the automobile from us, we gave you the best machine we had at a price you yourself said was a bargain. We extended credit to you without red tape when you presented satisfactory references. The payments arranged for were set low enough for you to be able to meet them conveniently. When repairs were necessary, we took care of them the same day you notified us. You can't say we have not done our part.

Consequently, we cannot understand why you are not doing your part. You are now three payments behind and have not even answered our notices. You have not seen fit to make an explanation, as we requested, so that if you had any reason for deferring payment we could give it proper consideration and do what we could to help out.

We believe that we have been fair with you. Don't you want to be fair with us?

So let's have the check or the explanation by return mail. We enclose a stamped addressed envelope for your convenience.

Sincerely yours,
L. M. Cole

Dear Mr. Frey:

We are sure you would agree that mutual understanding and consideration are the core of good business relations. When we filled your order four months ago we shipped the goods the same day to assure you ample time for display for the holiday trade. Shouldn't we expect the same consideration from you? Your bill for these goods is now three months past due. We have not even had a reply to our notices and letters. You surely understand how necessary prompt remittances are to the proper running of a business.

We shall therefore expect an answer, this time, by return mail. If you cannot send us a check we shall appreciate a note as to when we may expect it, or a reason for your deferment of payment.

Sincerely yours,
Maurice Sidney

THE APPEAL OF SELF-INTEREST

The strongest appeal to self-interest is one that touches, at the same time, on pride and danger—the hint or outright comment that continued failure to pay may affect the delinquent's credit standing. But such an appeal is more effective with merchants than with retail customers, for the latter can always return to a cash basis in making their purchases. However, even housewives may be anxious about their financial reputation in the community and, therefore, a dealer in home appliances used this appeal:

Dear Mrs. Cathcart:

When you purchased your washing machine from us, you gave as your references the Rev. Walter J. Arnold, Dr. Benjamin Humphrey, and Mr. Edward Reiner. Their replies to our inquiries indicated that you are held in high esteem in your community. We should like to avoid doing anything to lessen that esteem. However, unless you answer our letters requesting an explanation, at least, of why you are not making the payments agreed to, we shall

have to seek information on this matter from the persons you referred us to.

If you are withholding payments because you feel we are at fault in some way, please let us know. If you are in temporary financial difficulties we shall be glad to discuss the matter with you.

In any case a prompt reply from you will make it unnecessary for us to go to anybody else for the information we need to have.

So please let us hear from you within the next ten days, for your benefit and ours.

Sincerely yours,
Thomas Chaplin

With business men the suggestion of harm to their credit rating is more effective. Businessmen, today, could not carry on without credit; consequently, they will go far to avoid any damage to their credit standing. Appeals to their self-interest on that score are, therefore, generally effective. An example:

Dear Mr. Dever:

A firm with which you are seeking to open an account has inquired about your credit standing with us. We should like to report a good credit record for you, and up to this month we would have been able to do so unhesitatingly. But you have allowed a bill to go unpaid for the fourth month, as of today, and under the circumstances it would be difficult for us to assign the highest credit rating to you, as we should prefer doing. However, if we receive your remittance by return mail we shall be glad to render a favorable report, since this is the first time you have allowed your account to become overdue to this extent. We feel sure that you value your business reputation enough to take prompt and proper action to preserve it.

Sincerely yours,
Howard Henderson

DISCOUNTS, PREMIUMS, ETC.

A more positive appeal to self-interest is the offer of discounts or premiums. These are rather risky because they may weaken the debtor's sense of responsibility to the creditor. To reward somebody for carrying out his obligations is to tempt him into subsequent delinquency. Spoiling customers is as easy as spoiling children. However, businessmen sometimes feel it expedient to make such an appeal. Examples:

Dear Mr. Hollander:

We are breaking a rule in making you this offer. We know that you were disappointed when we disallowed the 2% cash discount you took when you paid your last bill after the ten-day period for which we grant cash discounts. However, since you state you were given that privilege by other concerns and have become accustomed to this practice, we have decided to make an exception in your case. If you meet your current bill before the end of the month, we shall allow the 2% cash discount.

Sincerely yours,
Walter P. Sims

Dear Mr. Hopkins:

We realize that you would not have allowed your last bill to go unpaid so long unless you were under some extra heavy burdens. We should like to help you so far as we can. We therefore propose the following:

We will allow you a five per cent discount from the amount due if full settlement is made within the next ten days. If you cannot manage that, we will accept fifty per cent in payment now, the rest to be paid within ninety days. We make this offer because we want to arrange a settlement that will be most convenient for you and because we are anxious to bring our outstanding accounts up-to-date. We should appreciate an immediate settlement on one basis or the other and look forward to your prompt response.

Sincerely yours,
George Ayer

Dear Mr. Toole:

We are sure you have overlooked your last payment for your record player. We cannot believe that you are deliberately disregarding

your contract and are ready to risk losing the instrument that is giving you so much pleasure. So we send this note as a reminder—and also as a notice of an opportunity you will probably want to take advantage of.

Perhaps you have found the successive monthly payments a bother. We note that there are only three payments left to make. Wouldn't you like to settle the outstanding payment and the next three at one time, now?

We should find it convenient, too; and we propose to pass on our savings in bookkeeping and other operating costs, to you, in the form of a gift album, one of those listed in the enclosed circular. But you must act at once. This offer will be withdrawn if we don't hear from you within the next ten days.

Please use the enclosed stamped, addressed envelope. Put your check in it and in a day or two you will be enjoying your choice of one of these wonderful new albums.

Sincerely yours,
Anthony Delisio

HUMOR

Debtors have been known to melt under the warmth of a smile. Humor is often used, for that reason, in collection letter series. But this appeal has its dangers. If the joke falls flat, the reader of the letter may feel put upon, or contemptuous, and less disposed than before, to make a settlement.

Elbert Hubbard, one of the most successful mail-order booksellers, used to close many of his collection letters with "Come, partner, dig; it will take only a minute, and God knows, I need the money."

Another creditor's humorous appeal took this form: On the covering letter accompanying a duplicate statement a piece of string was attached with scotch tape; a stamped, addressed envelope was also enclosed. The letter read:

What's the string for?

To tie around your finger to remind you to settle that past due bill.

What's the envelope for?

To save you the bother of going around with your finger tied up.

Just put your check in the envelope, and it will be all over. Then we'll both be happy.

THE "PRESSURE" LETTER

As we have already observed, "Pressure" letters in collection series should be avoided as long as possible. With customers who are not in business themselves and have little knowledge or experience of the law, a hint of legal action is often sufficient. Example:

Dear Miss Hart:

Please give this letter your attention. It is important to you. According to our records this is our fifth notice to you regarding your unpaid account for $63.00. In our last letter, sent exactly a month ago, we asked for payment or at least an explanation of the delay. That letter, like the others, has not been answered. Since you are not willing, for some reason, even to give an explanation, we may have to turn to legal means. This letter is to give you final notice that if we do not hear from you within the next five days, we shall be forced to take another course of action.

Very truly yours,
Vernon Pritchard

In warning letters to businessmen delinquents it is best to be precise and direct.

Dear Mr. Andrews:

We have had no answer to our three recent letters to you. In these we asked for at least the courtesy of a reply and some explanation.

Would you really prefer that we take legal action? We would rather spare you the additional expense involved, not to speak of the trouble and embarrassment.

This is our notice to you that unless we hear from you within the next five days we will put the matter in the hands of our attorney.

Very truly yours,
Bertram G. Phillips

It is important, let us repeat, not to make such a statement **unless you actually mean to carry it out.** If Andrews gets no summons after the five days' warning, he will feel still more inclined to evade payment.

THE MASKED REQUEST

Before proceeding to formal statements of legal action some concerns send out a final letter under the signature of a person whom the debtor has not heard from before and on stationery other than the firm's letterhead. To some debtors this suggests that the matter is already in the hands of a collection agency and they had better hurry to settle up.

Another device frequently employed with success is a request for payment made by telegraph or telephone.

DRAFTS

Under certain circumstances, drafts can be used to effect settlement. The draft serves the same function as a C.O.D. collection. It can be attached to the bill of lading for goods delivered on a new order from the delinquent customer. The invoice and attached draft are sent to the customer's bank, which is thus called upon to act as the creditor's agent to make the collection.

Since resort to the draft means making public to the business world that the customer's accounts are not in order and, therefore, that his credit standing is in question, threat of using the draft is occasionally sufficient to get him to pay up. However, this device must be used with care, since the customer may be antagonized by the change in shipping procedure and may, in fact, refuse to accept your shipment.

INSTALLMENT COLLECTION LETTERS

Collecting from delinquent installment buyers involves somewhat different procedures from those used in manufacturer-dealer, whole-saler-dealer, or store-charge customer relations. With installment buyers it is particularly important to secure an overdue payment in such a way as to ensure subsequent regular payments. Also, it is much more important to secure payment as quickly as possible.

In other business situations, relations will continue, in most cases, but in installment delinquencies, if the matter drags on very long, the customer is likely to let the goods be repossessed. This means no profit, for the profit is in the last payments; or even a loss, for second-hand goods seldom fetch fair prices.

For the same reason it is important to be extra tactful since irritated customers often ask for an article to be taken back, to express their resentment. And again, for that reason, it is wise to inject a little sales talk into the collection letters. Remind the customer of the services he is getting from the article. Let that be in his mind when he considers the idea of parting with it.

First, then, when a payment is skipped, don't let it slide. Send the routine reminder in a week or ten days and mark it "second notice." Secondly, avoid ruffling the customer's feelings. If the second notice is ignored, send a mild letter. Show interest in his situation; ask to be told if anything unusual has occurred that is keeping him from making his payments. Speak of the value or enjoyment he is getting from his purchase. Follow with three more letters, if necessary, each one a little more urgent than before. Avoid threat of collection through a collection agency as long is possible.

Example of an Installment Collection Series:

Dear Mrs. Haskell:

We feel sure you must have overlooked last month's installment on your electric washer. That's so easy to do in these rushed times. One customer explained that since she got the machine her mind had become so free of thoughts about washing that she had forgotten the payments too.

Perhaps you would like to take care of this matter like other customers who have overlooked it. Since the delay brought them close to the date of the next payment, they paid the two installments together. Would you like to make the two payments now and save yourself bother? We shall appreciate an early reply.

Yours sincerely,
Vernon Adams

Dear Mrs. Haskell:

We didn't think a second letter, which means a third notice about the overdue payment on your electric washer, would be necessary. We felt sure we would find your check, or some explanation why you cannot meet installments, in the return mail. As in our last letter we suggest that you make the overdue payment and the current payment, which is now due, together, which would save you and us some bother.

If there is any reason for your withholding payment please let us know. Is any repair necessary in your washer? We want you to enjoy its wonderful services without any hindrance, and will attend to it promptly if that is the case. Or if it is some temporary financial embarrassment on your part, please do not hesitate to write us frankly about it.

Sincerely yours,
Vernon Adams

Dear Mrs. Haskell:

We cannot understand your not answering our previous letters—two letters and the customary reminder notice. Many of us fall into arrears sometimes; and it is an unpleasant experience for everybody. But it has never helped anybody to evade it. On the contrary it helps to have a frank discussion of any difficulty that may have arisen, as we urged you to do in our last letter.

Have we failed in any of the services you expected from us? If so, we want to know—the sooner the better.

We have letters from customers saying that they feel years younger since the machine relieved them of backbreaking strain of washing the old way. Isn't that worth making every effort to meet the overdue payments?

If you are too pressed to do so at the present time why not discuss the matter with us? We have had wide experience and may have some helpful suggestions to make.

Sincerely yours,
Vernon Adams

Dear Mrs. Haskell:

We hope it is not some deep trouble that keeps you from answering your mail. If so, a few words of explanation from you will be sufficient. But we must warn you that a failure to give us some explanation will force us to take a course of action we prefer not to take.

We hope that whatever has been the cause of your lateness in making payment is now over, and that you will be able to settle the installments due and be spared further embarrassment. We would like you to enjoy the use of your washer without troubled thoughts.

If you cannot make a payment, please reply by return mail; do not force us to take any action we, as well as you, should not like. All that is necessary to avoid it is to give us a prompt explanation.

Sincerely yours,
Vernon Adams

Dear Mrs. Haskell:

This is our final letter about the unpaid installments on your washing machine. We hope you will try to avoid the consequences that will come from ignoring it. It could mean trouble and possibly humiliation and damage to your credit, so that it may prove difficult for you to make subsequent purchases on terms. If you ignore this letter, we will have to take legal action. This will mean repossession of your washer and depriving you of all its conveniences and benefits. It will mean bother and anxiety and other troubles.

We would much rather not go to that length, for your sake and ours. We should prefer, as we have written you before, to discuss the matter with you and to work out some reasonable arrangement. You must make the decision, and

within the next ten days. If we do not hear from you before April 10, the matter will be put in the hands of a collection agency.

Sincerely yours,
Vernon Adams

COLLECTING BAD DEBTS

Sometimes a special situation arises which makes it advisable to forego legal action. The debtor is in such a bad financial position that no judgment against him would be collectible. Such debts need not always be written off. Circumstances may change; the debtor may return to solvency and be in a position to pay his debts. The alert creditor who watches for such changes will get his reward.

For example, industrial blight ravaged a large mining area. The pits were shut down and other industries in the district were affected. A certain company that had sold expensive household appliances found itself carrying hundreds of uncollectible accounts. After every collection measure had been tried, the company decided to give up further attempts and to wait.

For over a year they kept 626 debtor accounts on their books. Then local representatives of the firm sent in reports that business conditions were improving. Mines were reopening and all sorts of other businesses were starting up again. When the favorable reports continued, indicating a real improvement, the company decided to try to clear those 600-odd debts. They used a three letter campaign which was so successful that the story was written up in *Printers' Ink*, a business-promotion magazine. The three letters as reproduced in full, are printed below.

The first was sent to all the 626 debtors. It drew 262 payments for varying amounts of the debt. The second went to 460 of the debtors; it was sent to all those who had not replied, plus certain of the customers who had responded to the first letter but whose remittances were considered too small. This second letter drew 165 payments and 17 explanations from customers who replied that they were not yet in a position to repay but promised to make payments soon. The 363 debtors to whom the third letter was sent included, again, a group whose remittances were considered too small. This letter was stiffer than the first two; it hinted at a recourse to legal action, though it was still friendly in tone. It brought cash from 37% of those who had not replied to the first two letters.

These remarkable results are a tribute not only to the good business sense and psychological insight of the letter writer, but also to the innate honesty and fair-mindedness of the people of this country, the qualities that make our credit system the broadest, most flexible and most effective in the world. Most of the responses to the letters, particularly the first one, expressed appreciation of the creditor's consideration in waiting for better times before pressing for payment. Clearly here, as everywhere in the country, the great majority of people have every intention of fulfilling obligations they have undertaken. It is only in circumstances beyond their control that any considerable number of people default. The three letters follow:

Dear Mr. —————:

Yesterday our treasurer called me into his office and said: "Mr. —————, I see that ————— of ————— has not yet settled his account. In fact he has not made a payment on it since —————————, though I've written him several times. I did not wish to bring suit, for they've had pretty hard times in that section during the past year.

"Now, however, conditions are better there. I'd like you to write to Mr. ————— and ask him to clear up this account. We've been fair with him and I think you will find that he will want to be equally fair with us."

I thought I could do no better than tell you just what our treasurer said to me. We have waited a long time, you know. So I am going to ask you to write and let me know just what you can do for us.

Yours truly,
Assistant Treasurer

Dear Mr. —————:

I know it's the usual thing, when no answer is received from a "collection" letter, to pretend to believe the matter was overlooked by the other party.

But I'm going to be frank enough to admit that I believe the reason you didn't answer my last letter with a remittance was that you perhaps didn't have the money right then. Am I right?

You see, I'm taking it for granted that you feel just as we should feel if conditions were reversed. So I'm just appealing to your sense of fairness.

Don't you think it would be only fair to let us have what is due us after we've waited so long a time? Think it over, Mr. —————, and if you cannot possibly send us a check today, let me know when we may look for one. This little courtesy won't take much of your time, and we certainly will appreciate it.

With continued good wishes we remain

Sincerely yours,
Assistant Treasurer

Dear Mr. —————:

If a customer owed you $————— and for two years had paid nothing on it, how would you feel?

But now suppose you had known that customer had been up against hard conditions all that time, so you had put yourself in his place and decided not to appeal to the law to collect your money.

Then, when things picked up with the customer, suppose you wrote to him as man to man, asking him to treat you as fairly as you had treated him. Wouldn't you feel certain that as a businessman and as a gentleman, he would respond? Wouldn't you?

There are laws that regulate business, Mr.

——————. But the biggest thing that keeps business clean and above board is the fact that most men believe in the square deal. Business would go to smash if we couldn't depend on the sacredness of a commercial agreement.

That is all we ask of you, Mr. ——————, a square deal. You believe in that just as we do, don't you? Then let's settle this thing as between friends and gentlemen. A check from you by return mail would confirm our belief that you do believe in the square deal.

Earnestly yours,
Assistant Treasurer

STORE COLLECTION LETTERS

The majority of retail customers are women. Generally speaking, they are not as familiar with business procedures as men. They are accustomed to greater courtesies and special treatment. Therefore they react more sensitively to pressure than men, showing a greater tendency to flare up. In attempts to collect from such customers tact is especially called for.

If possible, it would be well to know when these customers get their pay or their allowances. Then billing can be done so that the bills will reach them at a time when they still have funds.

If collection letters become necessary, be sure to space out the letters to customers with previously good records at longer intervals than you do for the known poor payers. Thus, the series in the first case might extend over five or six months; but in the second case, though more letters should be sent, the intervals should be shorter and the entire period should not extend beyond three months.

The ten-letter series below, again reproduced from *Printers' Ink*, was successfully used by a department store. A few of the stubborn cases got all ten; but the majority had paid up by the fourth letter.

The first letter was a formal reminder, an unsigned, printed card without salutation:

A matter of routine—nothing more than the hope that you will now be glad to send us your check for $........, the amount of your (name of store) bill for the month of ....

The other letters follow:

We know perfectly well how quickly the months slip by, how sometimes, unavoidably, your usual practice of paying monthly may be overlooked, and we are quite sure that you will now wish to send us your check for your (name of store) bill for (month). The amount is $........

As you have always found in the past, we like to cooperate with all our customers; we know we can count on the same from them. It is in that spirit that this letter is writen. The fact that your name is on our charge account list is in itself a proof of our full confidence. The further fact that there has been a little delay, unusual for you, leads us to believe that there must be some mighty good reason.

Now we haven't the slightest disposition to press. Perhaps we can help, and we are wholly ready. If for any reason whatever you still wish to postpone this matter, tell us about it and we will gladly do all we can to help you.

* * *

There are always two sides to any question. To us, however, your side is the important one, and we are eager to do anything, everything within our power, to show our understanding and cooperation in every way; we hope you will attempt to do likewise.

Because of our fullest confidence in you, we opened your account gladly. There was the usual understanding that bills were to be paid monthly. We are not disturbed when an occasional month slips by. When we hear nothing for several months, however, we like to feel that there is some very good reason, and we want to know it because we want to help.

Now, won't you drop in or telephone us (give phone number) for a friendly, frank chat? Then we shall all be happy.

Unless, of course, it is now convenient for you to send us a check for the amount of your bill (give amount).

* * *

Is it quite fair?

There's your (name of store) bill for $..... dating back now .... months.

Here we are, having been all along, ready to meet you far more than half way. We have told you so four separate times. But not a word from you.

The way out is simple. All you have to do is merely tell us what your difficulty is, and you will see how pleasantly and cooperatively we shall make every effort to arrange a convenient method for you to do the thing we know you really want to do—namely, to get this (name of store) bill out of the way.

* * *

We can conjure up in our minds any number of legitimate reasons why an overlong delay in the payment of your (name of store) bill might be unavoidable. What we cannot reconcile, however, is your complete silence, especially when a mere word of good faith would have delighted us to make some arrangement that we feel sure would be fair to you.

The amount of your bill, now .... months overdue is $. . . . We have not tried to press you. We feel you would like to be as fair to us as we have been to you. We shall therefore appreciate a prompt reply as to what your intentions are in regard to clearing up this bill.

* * *

There's inevitably a breaking point!

It's that way with our patience sometimes. Don't, for your own sake, ignore your (name of store) bill a minute longer. Never mind our side of it; consider your side of it, your credit reputation, our pleasant relationship in the past, and the fact that we have been more than patient in reminding you of your long past due bill in the amount of $......... Your prompt remittance, in whole or in part, or an explana-

tion from you, will make possible the continuance of that pleasant relationship.

* * *

Do we, or do we not?

In other words, shall we adjust your (name of store) bill amicably or shall it be the other thing?

There are two choices, either your check for the amount of your long overdue bill of $..... or an arrangement that will assure us that this bill is to be paid.

We prefer the check. At any rate, after writing you so many times, we must insist on a prompt response so that we may know which course you wish to have us take. We'd prefer to settle this in a friendly way; the choice is now up to you.

* * *

This note requires an answer by return mail.

Do you intend to pay your (name of store) bill which is now .... months overdue? The amount is $.........

Remember, please—by RETURN MAIL!

Unless we receive your check on or before (set date), our attorneys will receive instructions to summon you to court.

* * *

Another series of letters, written by Louis Victor Eytinge, an expert in the business letter field, is reproduced from *Mailbag*. It has been used frequently, and with good results, after its initial remarkable achievement of 100% returns when tried out on 500 accounts overdue from six months to two years. The letters to three of the addressees were returned as undeliverable (removed without forwarding address). All the rest had made payments by the time the five-letter series had done its work. In this series a piece of string was used as in a letter quoted earlier.

Dear Sir:

Do you remember how, when you were young and your good folks sent you downtown after something, they were likely to tie a string around your thumb to make certain you would not forget?

Those were the happy days, were they not?

But—there's no reason why the days of NOW should not be as happy, and it is just as certain that some of us are prone to forget the little things of today.

Because of that we are sending you this little reminder—NOT TO FORGET TO PAY—the enclosed statement.

We hope you enjoy the smile in our letter and that we may have the pleasure of hearing from you promptly.

Sincerely yours,

—tie the string—
and you won't forget.

Dear Sir:

Willie's mother had just given her boy a lecture and told him that his every act was known to God—that God's eye followed him wherever he went.

Willie went down the street ashamed of himself, and his faithful Fido followed close behind. In a few minutes Willie turned into a lane, saw the dog, and then delivered himself "Aw, go on home and quit follerin' me. Ain't it enough to have God wid me all the time without you taggin' on behind?"

Now, we do not wish to be tagging on behind. We do not want to annoy you or bother you one bit—but—we do want to remind you that we have sent you, already, one copy of the enclosed statement and we should be pleased to have your prompt settlement.

When will you oblige us?

Earnestly yours,

Yes, that's a piece of the same string we sent you with the other letter. It will prevent your forgetting this time. USE IT.

Dear Sir:

Do you remember the story of Midas, the great king of ancient days? You know he was said to have the magic touch—that everything he touched turned to gold.

Now, if we had the touch of Midas, we'd not be writing this letter. We would not be insisting on payment of the amount you owe us, $.........

A contract is a contract and should be lived up to. If we give our word to the bank to pay, we have to be right there with the money at the proper time—and if we are not, the bank uses the law on us. All the business of the world would go to smash if we couldn't depend on the sacredness of a commercial agreement. And, in order that we may make our payments as agreed, we expect you to pay us the money due us. That's fair, is it not?

Frankly, if someone owed you the money due us from you for as long a time, and you needed it just as we do—wouldn't you go after it with all the power you could use? To be sure you would. Then please treat us as fairly as you would expect to be treated. Just give us the square deal.

We shall expect your prompt remittance of $........

Earnestly yours,

Dear Sir:

The other day down in the Justice's Court there came up the settlement of a collection case. One man originally owed but $28, but by the time the matter had been put in the hands of the lawyers—by the time the papers had been served and the case heard—by the time that attachments had been issued against the man's property—it cost him $85!

Haven't we been fair with you? We have written you several times, frankly, fairly, squarely and in a friendly way, for we DO want to be friends. But, if you will not take steps to even up that little matter of $........ WE SHALL HAVE TO PROTECT OURSELVES BY GOING TO LAW.

Frankly, what IS the matter? Why not come in and talk things over with us, face-to-face? We are not unreasonable—we shall be as fair to you as you are to us. If all cannot be paid at one time, tell us the exact conditions, and we shall be as considerate as possible under the circumstances.

But—in order to prevent legal proceedings—we shall have to have some evidence that you actually intend to do what is right by us.

We expect to hear from you promptly.

Sincerely yours,

Dear Sir:

We have had no answer to our letters.

We have registered this to make sure of personal delivery, so that in the event a suit has to be filed, the defense cannot be offered that you have not had sufficient notice.

You surely do not recognize the position in which you place yourself by your continued neglect to pay us the sum of $........, long due us. You are surely aware that grocers, dry goods dealers, and all other merchants are organized for credit protection. The debtor who does not pay his just debts is blacklisted by merchants, doctors, and other professional people—the very ones upon whom you may have to depend at critical times. You surely do not care to destroy your reputation for honesty. Then take care of this matter at once, for if it is still unsettled by the end of next week, our lawyers will act.

You know well that when a judgment is entered against a debtor, he is assessed all the costs and that these are often greater than the original debt—that all services, subpoenas, court costs, attachments, judgments, executions, and lawyer fees—all these are charged against you and your property when it is sold to justify claims. You will have to act quickly to save all this.

We are willing to do anything in our power to adjust this on a friendly basis. Your best course is to come into the office to see us. If for any reason this is impossible, then write right away, telling us what you'll do.

It is UP TO YOU to act NOW. Only ten days' time can be given. After that it will be the Law and its expense. Why not act now?

Insistently yours,

Dear Mr. Doe:

Thanks for your payment.

The $500 in your bank account looks good. I'd like to have an account like it myself. There's only one thing wrong; we want part of it in our bank account. This selfish attitude of ours is what caused the trouble.

You say your gas was turned off with "No warnin' ... no nuttin'." We mailed a bill on October 20, another on November 19, a delinquent notice on December 11, a final notice on December 18, and a 3 months' bill on December 19. "No warnin' ... no nuttin'."

After the final notice went out we started thinking about Christmas, Good Will Toward Man, etc., so we decided not to mar your Holiday Joys by turning gas off before Christmas. Did you say "Soulless Corporation"?

On January 2, just to start the New Year right, we sent out a shut-off order. Our man came back and said you weren't home, so naturally we decided you had gone down to pay your gas bill. By January 6, the horrible truth was evident -- you weren't going to pay. Mr. Doe, what was there left to do?

We certainly don't want to see you use up your annual leave paying gas bills. If you decide you don't want to use your checking account to pay our bills, I'm sure our friends at Boynton's Variety Store will accept your payments on Saturday.

We're sorry this whole thing came up, Mr. Doe, but we hope you enjoyed your vacation before the storm broke.

Fig. 35. Although concerned with collection of current and future bill payment, this letter also seeks to appease and placate an outraged customer, while affirming the justice of the company's actions. As you can see, it does so in a highly individual manner.

CHAPTER SEVEN

EMPLOYMENT LETTERS

THE JOB-HUNT

America is the land of ambition. Every year more than a million young men and women begin their careers. Millions of others, already in jobs, seek advancement. If their prospects where they are do not satisfy them, they look elsewhere. This means that even in "good times," the job-hunt is an active feature of the dynamic American life.

On the surface it appears to be a case of men hunting jobs. But America also remains the land of competition. Often, where there is a place to be filled, to make sure of getting the best man available, an employer will not leave it to the comparatively hit-and-miss process of interviewing applicants responding to a want-ad or sent in by an employment agency. He will use other, more selective methods.

WHERE THE JOB HUNTS THE MAN

In some cases the employer, seeking to fill an important post in his organization, will make an offer to a man employed by another company, when he knows that that man has been thinking of making a change. Or he will turn to a file of previous applicants for the position who left a favorable impression when interviewed. Or he may ask someone in the field on whose judgment he relies to recommend a suitable person.

Since these are the less numerous cases, we may dispose of them first, with some comment on the letter-writing principles involved in the correspondence in such cases.

PRINCIPLES

As in all business letters, the first principle is the "you" attitude. Put yourself, as much as you can, in the place of the man to whom you are writing. That will be your best guide.

To put yourself in his place will be easier if you know something about him. This is particularly important if you are making an offer to a man who is employed. It will be useful to know, for example, what will most appeal to him. More money will appeal to everybody, it is true; but there are those to whom security or prestige—a title like manager or Director or Vice-President—will be surer persuaders.

At the same time it is unwise to arouse unrealistic expectations. A man brought over by anticipations of periodic big raises or bonuses that are not likely to materialize; or of a status that cannot be guaranteed; or of posts and titles that are not likely to become available, will become discontented. And a discontented man is not the most efficient performer.

In other cases the matter is simpler. Since you can assume that the man you are writing to is interested and available, the offer of the job sufficiently carries out the "you" attitude.

For obvious reasons letters of this type should be addressed, wherever possible, to the individual's home rather than to his business office. Examples:

The Money Appeal:

Dear Mr. Marcus:

Please hold the contents of this letter in strict confidence.

Mr. George Owen, our credit manager, has been in poor health for some months now, and his physician has advised him to retire. This is a blow to us, for, as you must know, he has been with us many years. It will be hard to get along without him.

We asked Mr. Owen to suggest a successor and you were his first choice. He thinks very highly of your ability, that you could take hold in a short time, and that you would like it here.

We do not like to appear to be "raiding" another house, but Mr. Owen assures us that you have been considering making a change. He says that you are looking for a connection where the volume of business would make possible a higher financial return to you.

We believe that our salary offer will interest you. Please telephone me during the week, at your convenience, so that we may arrange for a conference on this matter.

Mr. Owen asks me to give you his regards and to say that he will get in touch with you as soon as he feels fit again for visits.

Sincerely yours,
Arthur Penner

The following are other types of letters frequently used in personnel correspondence:

The Security Appeal:

Dear Mr. Zachary:

About a month ago you applied for a position in our Sales Department. As this letter testifies, you left a fine impression on us here.

Our Western territory is now producing more business than one man can conveniently handle. Mr. Willner, our Western representative, himself suggested that we split up the area into two, something we felt would have to be done sooner or later. We have decided that we might as well do it now, and we would like to have you in charge of one of the divisions.

The West, as you know, is the fastest growing section of the country, in population and industry. The section we propose to put you in charge of is already producing business that can provide you with an income bigger than the one you indicated you would like to earn as a

start. The potential business which we feel confident you will develop should easily meet your further expectations.

What especially interested us in your interview was your expressed deire for a connection with an established concern, with stable products and tried business methods. We are certainly no "sticks-in-the-mud"; at the same time principles and methods that have kept a house in business for over a century have their value. One of them is that a good man and a good job stay together. Most of our people have been with us ten years or longer. It is because we think you have the same feeling about your work that we would like to have you with us.

Let us know as soon as you conveniently can whether you are in a position to join us. I shall be glad to get together with you to give you further particulars about what we have in mind.

Sincerely yours,
David R. Ainslee

Prestige Appeal:

Dear Mr. Henderson:

Our mutual friend, Mr. George Castle, thinks you would like to be associated with us; and from what he tells us we would like to have you here. At his suggestion we have looked into your record and find it as impressive as he said it was. We feel you can fit in with us effectively.

The word *Associates* in our name is not just ornamental. It describes how we work here. We are organized as advertising men, autonomous in the way we handle our separate accounts, but banded together for the convenience and economy of sharing a common staff, and the help we can give one another when needed, by way of advice and a timely hand, but always retaining our independent identities.

To give further formal acknowledgement of this independent status the associates in our organization are officers of the company. If you want to join us you would have the immediate rank of vice-president, and you would, of course, retain control of your accounts.

This is a rough idea of what association with us would mean. Suppose we get together and fill in the details.

Sincerely yours,
Carl Ault

Checking of References:

Dear Mr. Burton:

Mr. William Brown has applied to us for a position in our Shipping Department. We are checking on his references and on the employment record he furnished us. We shall appreciate any information you can give us about him.

Please inform us in what capacity and for what period he was in your employ; and for what cause employment was terminated.

We enclose a stamped, addressed envelope for your convenience.

Yours sincerely,
Edward Jason

Notifying Applicant of Placing Letter on File:

Dear Mr. Harper:

We thank you for your letter of April 10 applying for a position here. Your education, experience and other qualifications are such as we would look for were there an opening. We regret that there is none at present.

We are placing your letter on file, and when an opening develops, we shall be pleased to get in touch with you.

Sincerely yours,
Henry E. Vail

Letter of Introduction:

Dear Harry:

I have a friend back from the army who will be a find for the house that has or will make an opening for him. Because I have as good a feeling about you as I have about him, I hope it will be your house. His name is Al Nelson, and he's a really keen promotion man.

Al can step back into his old job, but the prospects there are limited and he's looking for something better. I am confident he'd like it with you if you have a place for him. I think you ought to see him for future reference even if you can't offer him anything immediately. I've taken the liberty of telling Al that you'll get in touch with him. His address and some other information about him are on the enclosed slip.

I'll be on the coast for about a month. When I get back I'll look in on you.

As ever,
Murray

Acknowledging an Introduction:

Dear Mr. Thomas:

I thank you for your letter enclosing Mr. Sansom's introduction. Anyone Mr. Sansom advises us to meet is welcome here. Will eleven-thirty next Thursday be convenient for you?

Sincerely yours,
Albert Ehrhardt

Dear Mr. Sansom:

I thank you for bringing Mr. Thomas to our attention. We have had an interview with him and our impressions confirmed your good opinion of him. Although we have nothing for him now, we will certainly get in touch with him if anything turns up. You may tell him so.

Yours sincerely,
Albert Ehrhardt

Answering Situations Wanted Ad:

Box 166, Chronicle
San Francisco, California

Dear Sir:

We have an opening for which your experience as described in your advertisement would seem to qualify you. Please phone the undersigned for an appointment.

Very truly yours,
James V. Tucker

Postcard Notification to Applicants Answering Ad:

Mr. Vincent Peace will see applicants for the position advertised last Sunday, on Wednesday morning at 10 o'clock. Please bring references.

MAN SEEKS JOB

In applying for a job, the "you" attitude is all important. Forget how urgently you may need the job or how much you would like a connection with a certain concern. Think instead of what the prospective employer needs and of how your qualifications meet that need. He is going to make his selection on the basis of **his** needs, not out of sympathy for you or interest in **your** future.

Every employer—we can ignore the exceptions—wants neat and presentable employes. Let your letter, in its appearance, reflect you as such. Use good (but not fancy) stationery; fold it carefully. Retype or rewrite if you have had to cross out a word or have left a smudge. If you type, make sure that the ribbon is not too dim and that the type is clean.

Every employer—without exceptions— wants efficient employes. Your letter should leave an impression of an efficient person; that is, it should be direct, clear, uncluttered.

Generally speaking, efficient people are not stiff, avoid over-formality. But neither are efficient people, generally, Bohemians. So avoid over-familiarity, facetiousness, the "unbuttoned" approach. The letter that sounds dignified, sincere, and friendly will be the best representative of the writer.

There is a special reason for being brief and concise in application letters. In most cases your letter will be one of scores or even hundreds. At such a time the recipient will be particularly disinclined to read a long letter; and he will be particularly impressed by the ability of the writer to communicate a lot in a few words.

So make the letter as short as you can without omitting essential matter. Enclose a résumé, data sheet or a personal record sheet—all three terms are used—giving details about your age, education, experience, etc. Get them down in such a way that the recipient can find the item he is interested in at a glance.

If you are applying for a job, not because you are unemployed but because you seek a change, don't complain about your present boss. Your prospective employer is a boss, too, and he is more likely to identify himself with your boss than with you. Better say that you are applying to him because you are seeking a connection with a larger firm that offers better prospects. That will be pleasantly flattering. Besides, people esteem ambition and generally suspect a complainer. You may be fully justified in your complaints, but people won't be convinced merely by your saying so.

STRUCTURE OF THE APPLICATION LETTER

In general, application letters should be short and concise. That does not altogether rule out long letters, but they have to be very startling and able to sustain interest with unusual skill to offset the handicap of length. It is becoming general practice, in order to leave the application letter itself as direct and concise as possible, to omit details which can be listed in a tabular form on a data or personal record sheet enclosed with the application letter.

Application letters follow this general pattern:

The opening: Its aim is to gain the reader's attention. But, however that is done, whether by a sober appeal to the reader's self-interest or by a stunt, it must be directly related to the matter in hand. Clever applicants may outsmart themselves by a witty but long-winded opening. They are likely to annoy rather than amuse a busy executive with considerable mail on his desk. You will have no difficulty getting his attention by a clear, factual statement of the services that your qualifications enable you to render him.

Mentioning the name of a person in his organization, or otherwise favorably known to him, always makes a good opening. And a challenging question, provided it has a clear relevance to the work you are applying for, can also make a good opening.

Second paragraph: Expand on the qualifications referred to in the opening. Make them sound as useful as possible in the kind of position you are applying for.

Third paragraph: Try to make this a clincher by speaking of your references, or samples of your work that you are enclosing or offering to show him in an interview.

Closing: Avoid a neutral close. Suggest action by a direct bid for an interview at his convenience. Enclosing a stamped, addressed postcard, already typed up, on which he need only fill in the hour and date of the interview, is often helpful.

THE DATA OR PERSONAL RECORD SHEET

As we have noted above, in order to keep the application letter itself as concise and uncluttered as possible, detailed information is now generally furnished on an enclosed data or personal record sheet. Here is entered the age, education and experience of the applicant, his army record, his references, his sports and special interests, etc. A college graduate should include the courses he took which may be of value in the position he is seeking, and items about his scholastic record, his participation in student activities (sports, student organizations, college paper, glee club, etc.) and summer vacation or after-class jobs, etc. Veterans should include

any training or foreign languages which might be useful in the position applied for.

Sample Openings:

My last six years have been spent in the Credit Department of the .... Company. This and other experience and training I have had qualifies me, I feel, for the position of Credit Manager you advertised in this morning's *Record*.

* * *

My major in business college was Personnel Management. In my Psychology courses I concentrated on problems related to that. I therefore feel qualified for the opening in your Personnel Department offered to recent college graduates in your advertisement in this morning's *Herald*.

* * *

In business college, where I majored in Merchandising, I combined theory with practice by taking sales jobs, inside and outside. . . .

* * *

Every summer in the course of my studies in construction engineering I worked in various capacities at dams, roads and building construction. Consequently, in addition to formal university preparation I can offer an unusual background of practical experience in many forms of construction work.

* * *

Mr. .... of your Public Relations Department, for whom I did some manuscript typing, has told me that there might be an opening in your secretarial pool, and suggested that I write to you.

* * *

This is written at Mr. Edward Canby's suggestion. I translated an article for him from a French electronics journal. When I told him that I should like to give up free-lance translating for a permanent desk position he thought you might have a place for me in your Foreign Correspondence Department, since you carry on an extensive business in Latin America. I have a good command of Spanish and Portuguese, and French and German besides.

* * *

Do your sales letters draw a minimum of five per cent returns? Those I wrote for two mail-order concerns (see attached data sheet) never fell below five per cent and drew as high as seven and ten per cent in two campaigns.

* * *

Are you a rapid dictator? I can take dictation at the rate of 120 words a minute. . . .

* * *

Need a pinch hitter? I have done selling, promotion letters, collection letters; I have managed personnel, adjusted complaints, and expedited rush orders. I know that I can fill in in these and other capacities, averting delays, bottlenecks and embarrassments caused by illness, vacations and other absences.

* * *

An Oklahoman announced to his neighbor that he was moving to Texas. He was asked, "Ain't Oklahoma as good as Texas?" "Sure," he replied, "but there's more of it in Texas."

I feel pretty much the same about my application for a position with your firm. I have no complaint about my present position. I like my work and I like the people there. But I would like to move on to where prospects are a little wider. . . .

OPENINGS TO AVOID

"In answer to your advertisement in this morning's *Journal* I wish to apply for the position," or "I should like to be considered as an applicant for the position you advertised in this morning's *Dispatch*."

Such an opening says nothing useful to the prospective employer. The letter itself is sufficient evidence that its writer is applying for the position advertised.

"I hope you will find the enclosed information about my qualifications satisfactory." This is weak. If you have the necessary qualifications, you should feel confidence—not mere hope. And you should express it—not merely by using words "I am confident that I have the necessary qualifications," which imply hope as well as confidence—the whole *approach* should indicate confidence.

But don't overstep the bounds of confidence into what will impress the reader as conceit. An opening like, "You can file the rest of the applications in the waste basket. I'm the man you want!" is almost certain to draw from the reader a skeptical "Oh yeah!" If he reads the letter through it will be only to confirm his suspicion that the writer is an idle boaster.

Another type of opening to avoid is, "Leafing through the *Times* this morning I happened to see your ad for an editorial assistant."

This is unconvincing and frivolous. People seriously interested in a position do not leaf through a paper. They study the want ads.

Another bad opening: "In the recent recession you had to reduce your staff. Now that business is improving you are on the lookout for wide-awake, capable men."

Tactless and obtrusive. What the applicant says may be true but the prospective employer doesn't have to have it spelled out for him. The applicant will leave an unfavorable impression of a pushing rather than a forceful personality.

Examples of Good Closings:

May I have a few minutes of your time to show you samples of my sales letters. I can be reached by phone at . . .

* * *

I shall be glad to answer any further questions that may occur to you. I can be available at any time you find convenient. Just let me know when, by card to the above address, or by phone (telephone number).

* * *

I shall appreciate the opportunity to tell you the rest in an interview. I enclose an addressed

```
PHOTOGRAPH               NAME      Ernest S. Faulkner
                         ADDRESS   498 Oak Street, Minneapolis 17,
                                     Minnesota
                         AGE       26 years, 6 months
                         HEIGHT    5'9"  WT. 165 lbs.
                         MARITAL STATUS   Single

EDUCATION

  B.S.  Antioch College                    June, 1952
  M.A.  University of Minnesota            June, 1954

        MAJOR    Advertising
        MINOR    Selling

CLUBS AND ORGANIZATIONS

        Advertising Club              University of Minnesota
        Publicity Club                University of Minnesota
        Personal Management Club      University of Minnesota
        Editorial Staff, Yearbook     Antioch College, 1951-1952
        Journalism Coub               Antioch College, 1949-1952

EXPERIENCE

        Assistant copywriter, Elite Advertising Agency
                                1953-1954

        Salesman, Midwest Publishing Company, 1954-1955

REFERENCES

        Allen S. Brown, Chairman, Department of Business
                        Administration, University of Minnesota

        George F. McCormack, Professor, Department of Busi-
                        ness Administration, University of Minnesota

        Sinclair L. Salinger, President, Elite Advertising Agency

        James R. Barrett, Vice-President, Midwest Publishing
                                                   Company

OTHER INFORMATION

        Personnel Work, U.S. Army, 1946-1948
        Editor, College Yearbook
        Business Manager, Campus Newspaper
        Master's thesis:  The Psychology of Advertising
```

Fig. 36. The "personal data" (résumé) sheet may be varied in any number of ways, according to the requirements of situation and sender; but this is, in its major features, a standard form. The material is organized into logical progressions and sequences; and the data are composed in such a way that the essential features may be assimilated almost instantaneously. If the occasion seems to warrant, specific college courses having bearing on the position being applied for may be added; as may any other information which is immediately relevant.

card to let me know when it may be convenient for you to see me.

* * *

I have given here the essential facts about my experience and other qualifications; but there are probably some details you would like to have clarified. May I do so in a personal interview? My address and telephone number are given at the top of the enclosed data sheet.

* * *

Please use the enclosed, addressed postcard to let me know when I may come in for an interview or whom I may call to make an appointment.

Out-of-town Applicants:

My Christmas holidays will be from December 22 to January 3. I shall be in New York at that time and would like to call at your office. Could you please let me know on the enclosed, addressed postcard whom I may phone for an appointment after I arrive in the city?

* * *

I shall be in New Haven on June 5 and 6. Could you give me a few minutes on one of these days to show you some samples of my work? I enclose an addressed card for your convenience.

* * *

I understand that a representative of your company will attend the Convention here during the week of April 5. I shall be grateful for an opportunity to talk to him while he is in town. He can reach me at the above address or by phone at . . .

SAMPLE DATA OR PERSONAL RECORD SHEET FOR STUDENT OR RECENT GRADUATE APPLICATIONS

In such cases the data sheet should follow the same pattern but should describe major courses taken during studies and other courses that might be regarded as supplementary preparation for the position applied for. Details of the applicant's scholastic record, details of jobs held while in school, student activities, etc., might also be included. If a G.I. student, details of army experience should be included with mention of special training or foreign languages acquired while in the military service.

FOLLOW-UP LETTERS

If you are writing to a list of concerns, do not be deterred by lack of answers. Write a second and even a third letter to those that have not replied. Your persistence may impress some of them even if your first letter did not. In these follow-up letters try a new approach but link it up with your first letter.

If you have not yet found a position or consider the one you have taken as only a stop-gap, write again to concerns that have answered your letters. Their replies indicate some interest, and your letter may reach them at a moment when they have an opening for you.

In writing follow-up letters of this type, mention why you are still interested in becoming associated with the firm to which you are writing; some employers may feel there is something wrong with an applicant who has not found a job after a lapse of time.

LETTERS ASKING FOR REFERENCES

The tone of all letters depends on the subject and the nature of the relationship between the writer and the recipient. The three letters below represent respectively, informal, semiformal, and formal tones.

Dear Pete:

As you may have heard, that big, bad leviathan, General Publishing, has now swallowed up my firm. They're keeping about forty per cent of the staff, but on a seniority basis, which leaves me out in the cold.

So I'm job-hunting again, and I hope my letters are so good you'll be bothered by dozens of prospective employers checking on my references. I'm dating our connection as before, and describing it the same way—as your able assistant on the copy desk in the years of our Lord, 1942 to 45.

Yrs,
Joe

Dear Uncle Nat:

There's a possibility of my placing myself in a good position in Detroit. It would help if I could add a local reference to the New York references I am enclosing with my application.

Since you have had little opportunity to know me at such a distance, I shall understand it if you'd rather I didn't use you as a reference. But if what you've heard about me is favorable enough to make you willing to have me refer prospective employers to you, I should be very glad.

Should I land the job, one of the things I would look forward to would be to really get to know you and the other Detroit members of our clan.

Best regards to you and yours from the family here.

Yours,
Edward Dietz

Dear Mr. Holcomb:

I enjoyed my vacation thoroughly, and in one respect I think I made particularly good use of it. I have thought a good deal about my prospects and decided that I would be happier and could look forward to a better future as a credit man than if I were to continue in book-keeping. I am therefore applying to a number of concerns for a position in their credit departments.

While I was with you, as you will recall, I was frequently asked to sit in at conferences on credit problems, and when Mr. Ferris was away on several occasions, you called on me to carry on for him. I believe you felt that I made a competent substitute.

May I mention this and refer to you in other respects in my applications? Your help will be appreciated.

Sincerely yours,
Howard Fenton

Answers to Reference Requests:

Dear Miss Everitt:

I was sorry to hear that you are temporarily out of work. I'm sure it won't be for long.

Of course I was entirely satisfied with your work, and I will be happy to say so to anybody you refer to me. It will give me real pleasure to give you the testimonial of "good character" you deserve.

I suggest that you give whomever you refer to me my telephone number here. One can put so much more warmth into a conversation than in a letter.

With my best wishes for an early and fine placement, I am,

Cordially yours,
Alan Kennelly

Dear Mr. Gates:

Sorry. The answer is no.

I am surprised at your even making such a request. True, I had no complaint about your work, but frankly, I found you a real personality problem. Since we had to part company on that account, I can't see how you expect me to omit that from any characterization of our association. I would expect to be told the whole truth if I checked an applicant's references, and I can do no less if someone relies on me.

Please don't use my name. I suggest you turn to people from whom you can expect a more favorable response.

Very truly yours,
Mark Wilson

Sample Application Letters:

Dear Sir:

I believe I am the young woman your advertisement in this morning's *Times* was addressed to.

My preparation for secretarial work was unusually thorough. It was my major subject at high school, and I subsequently completed my training at Sinclair Business College.

I have been working with a small organization, but I think that has had real advantages for me and my future employers. Here I have been called upon to do a considerable amount of work other than what is narrowly considered secretarial. It has given me a rounded knowledge of business matters. I have been called on to handle bookkeeping, correspondence, checking and interviewing.

My employer, Mr. Walter Blum, of . . . has been good enough to tell me that I have the ability to handle a bigger job than he is in a position to provide or match in salary. He has given me permission to use his name as a reference.

I can also refer you to Mr. Harrison Sinclair, of Sinclair Business College, (address). I was one of the few whom Mr. Sinclair permitted to refer to him because of my good training record.

Mr. Blum is also permitting me to go out to interviews. I could stop in at your office at any time convenient to you. I can be reached here by telephone or postcard.

Sincerely yours,
Beverly Damon

Gentlemen:

Here are the facts which qualify me, I believe, for the receptionist's position advertised in this morning's *Sun*.

Training: After graduating from high school, I received a complete business training at the Holland Business Institute.

Experience: Two years as receptionist at Black Magazines, Inc. (1950–1952); one year (1952–1953), receptionist at Continental Products Co.

Age: 24.

Appearance: In both previous positions I was chosen in response to ads specifying "attractive appearance." I have natural blonde hair, a fair complexion, blue eyes and regular features. My height is five feet six inches.

Reason for seeking position: I resigned from Continental Products Co. to take advantage of an offer to travel abroad as companion to a relative. I returned to this country a week ago.

Additional Qualifications: I can type, take dictation, and do simple bookkeeping.

References: Mr. George Watkins of Black Magazines, Inc., (address) and Mr. Samuel Fried of Continental Products Co., (address).

Interviews: I am available at your convenience for a personal interview. I enclose an addressed postcard for notification of the time desired. I can also be reached by phone at . . .

Sincerely yours,
Henrietta Gorrell

Dear Mr. Spencer:

Professor Harkness of the Department of Chemisty of . . . University has suggested that I write to you. He has asked me to inform you that he will be glad to give you an opinion of my training, capacity, and prospects in industrial chemistry, the field I have chosen for my life's work. He has drawn such an interesting picture of the research being carried on in your laboratories that I can think of no better place to begin my work in. I shall receive my degree in industrial chemistry at the end of the month.

On a separate sheet I enclose personal data and details of my education, army service, student activities, and summer vacation and after-school employment.

I also enclose a paper on Colloidal Sulphur as an indication of my interests and research procedures.

Sincerely yours,
Wilfred Bent

Dear Mrs. Crane:

I have heard such fine things about your summer camp at Rockville that I should like very much to be associated with it. I assume that you will soon be assembling your staff for next season; please put me on your list for consideration when you choose your counsellors.

Although my formal experience consists of only one season as a counsellor at Camp Atkins, I think I can say that my actual experience goes back further. I began going to camp at the age of five and have spent my summers in camps ever since. On the enclosed personal record sheet I list all the camps I attended and their directors to whom you may refer. In two of them I was asked to serve as a junior counsellor in the course of the session.

I have led every type of group activity—swimming, games, crafts, dramatics, dancing, journalism. I have done particularly well in group singing. I play the guitar, sing in a chorus during the winter, and have a large repertory of camp songs, folk songs, rounds, and square-dance calls.

I have been invited to return to Camp Atkins but I would prefer a camp with more diversified groups of children and more diversified activities. That is the reason I hope to find a place at Rockville Camp.

I am making social work my career and have been accepted by the New York School of Social Work. I feel that my training and interests would help make me an asset to you.

I can be reached for an appointment after six P.M. at . . .

> Sincerely yours,
> Alison Carter

Dear Mr. Jonas:

This is being written from a sickbed. I've been hit by the current virus epidemic. I am writing this note, even though I should be taking it easy, because the position you advertise seems to be exactly what I have been looking for, and my qualifications fit every requirement you specify.

Since these data are supplied on the accompanying data sheet, I shall not go into details here about my experience, education, references, etc. I should like to explain here, however, why I wish to leave my present position as assistant to the Manager of the Direct-Sales department of a large firm similar to yours.

The head of our department is slated to become a member of the firm and will continue supervising direct-sales. Consequently, though I am given considerable freedom and range here, there is no prospect in the foreseeable future of my moving up from the post of assistant.

I feel that I have outgrown such a role. And as one whose sales letters have consistently drawn five per cent returns or better, I think I am justified in feeling so.

In becoming Direct-Sales manager for another firm I would be taking the step up that I cannot take here; and that firm, I believe, would be getting an experienced man of proven competence, a man who has demonstrated the capacity to create campaigns that get returns.

I regret that I must stay indoors for the next two days. I shall be available after that for an interview which can be arranged via the enclosed addressed card or by phone here at . . .

> Yours sincerely,
> Joseph A. Pell

Dear Mr. Cruze:

During the past six years I have been an advertising free-lance doing copy of all sorts, planning entire campaigns, pinch-hitting for vacationers and staff men who had run temporarily dry, analyzing campaigns that seemed perfectly planned yet lacked a vital spark; preparing special promotion pieces; writing captions and publicity handouts; and even ghosting banquet speeches.

Up to recently it has been fun. By now, frankly, the edge has worn off, and I'm finding it more legwork than I care for.

I do not wish to give the impression, which would be a mistaken one, that I look to a desk job as a sort of retirement. I remain the sort of person who took to free-lancing for its liveliness; you'll find nothing static or "easy-chairish" about me. I feel that I can bring to an association with your organization the gains of these strenuous six years—diversity of experience, quick improvisation when it is needed, and the ability to stand a "stretchout" when that is needed.

Since I am still free-lancing for the time being, I am not readily accessible by phone. I am therefore enclosing an addressed postcard for your convenience. Just a pencil notation of the time you wish to set for the interview and your signature will be enough.

> Sincerely yours,
> Ralph Taylor

Follow-up Letter:

Dear Mr. Paterson:

Am I still in the running?

I was surprised and disappointed not to hear from you. You found my approach and qualifications satisfactory enough to grant me an interview. At the end of that interview you told me that I had made a favorable impression and would be seriously considered for the position. I hope, therefore, since I have not heard from you to the contrary, that I am still in the running.

It may sound impatient for me to be writing again. But I have a reason for sending this letter. I have been offered a position by Clark Brothers, where I was interviewed the same day that I called on you. I am writing you because I would prefer being associated with you. I am to let them know at Clark Brothers by Wednesday. Could I hear from you before then how I stand with you? I enclose an addressed card for your convenience; or you may reach me by phone at . . .

Sincerely yours,

John Hayden

CHAPTER EIGHT

COMPLAINTS AND ADJUSTMENTS

There is, of course, nothing perfect in this world. Mistakes are bound to be made. Every sensible person realizes that.

If you are inconvenienced by a mistake made by a firm you deal with, you have a right to complain and ask for a reasonable adjustment; but the right does not extend to indulgence in bad temper. There is no right to abuse others. Remember that whenever you made an error, there was usually a reason for it. Assume as much for the other person. Don't attribute his error to ill intention or mere negligence.

Similarly, in acknowledging complaints, don't give way to irritation. Bear in mind the irritation inevitably caused by a mistake. On the other hand don't go to the opposite extreme and make rash commitments that it will never happen again. You never can tell when rush orders will multiply pressures that may impair your normal operation; when they will produce temporary strain and confusion; when illnesses may compel resort to untrained substitutes.

In writing or answering complaints try to bear in mind that indispensable "you" attitude. Try to see the matter from the other fellow's side in addition to your own.

THE COMPLAINT LETTER

The good complaint letter is **clear, concise, courteous,** and **reasonable** in its proposals for adjustment.

It is of the highest importance to make **clear** what is wrong and how you want it adjusted.

Make sure of your facts and get them all down accurately. Be precise about dates, quantities, trade names or numbers of models, sizes, shapes, methods of shipment, types of containers, etc.; be specific in setting forth the nature of the loss or inconvenience you have suffered and the adjustment you consider ought to be made. If you have all this down clearly, you make it simple for the other party to verify your claims and to make a prompt adjustment.

It is also important to be **courteous,** not to prove how civil you can be, but because courtesy is helpful and rewarding in many ways. Courtesy will help you restrain your anger and therefore make you better able to write the clear, accurate and convincing letter that is most likely to result in an early and satisfactory adjustment. A courteous tone will put the reader of the letter in a receptive and compliant mood. If you impress him as a reasonable customer, the sort he wants to keep on his books, he will be more likely to make a liberal adjustment in order to make sure of keeping you.

Two mistakes are to be avoided in a conscious resort to the courteous approach. Some people use a mask of politeness in order the more subtly to get in their digs. Examine your letter to make sure that under the polite expressions no barb of sarcasm is hidden. Such hidden barbs are particularly resented.

The other danger is that of weakness. It is no discourtesy to let it be known that you have suffered loss or inconvenience; it is no discourtesy to ask for what is due you. The "you" attitude is helpful if it serves to strike a balance; it can be harmful if it misleads you into seeing things the other man's way—all the way. So be **firm** as well as courteous.

It is important to be **concise** in order to make the presentation as clear as possible. Go over your letter to make sure that no irrelevancies, or superfluous words, or resentful tones have crept in.

And, finally, it is important to be **reasonable** in demands for an adjustment. Unfair demands may arouse suspicion of your claims, prolong investigation, and delay adjustment. Most firms want to be fair, if only to maintain a good reputation, and they will react favorably to a reasonable approach.

In closings, indicate that you expect a reasonable attitude on the part of the firm. Use such closings as "I am sure you will give this matter your prompt attention," or "I am sure you won't disappoint me in meeting this reasonable request," etc.

Examples of Complaint Letters:

Gentlemen:

Delivery on our order No. 1422, given to you September 14, was promised two days ago. It has not yet arrived. These goods were ordered for the pre-holiday sales period now in full swing. Every day's delay means loss and inconvenience for us.

If this shipment is *en route*, please telephone us and we will see what we can do at this end to expedite delivery to our premises. If the order has not yet been shipped, we will expect you to ship it *rush*. If the order has been held up because you are unable to ship certain items immediately, please telephone us and we will instruct you as to what items we need immediately, and what items we can wait for, and what items we may have to cancel.

In any event we shall expect a call from you on Monday. If you do not get in touch with us before the end of the day on Monday, please cancel the entire order. We shall have to call in goods available at the local wholesalers.

Yours sincerely,
Melvin Hooper

Gentlemen:

On May 4, at your store, I was given a demonstration of the . . . No. . . . television set. I was satisfied with the performance of the instrument and placed an order for it. I certainly did not expect to get the demonstration model, which works fine but is clearly shopworn. As a matter of fact I recognized it from a cigarette char on the top left hand corner which I had noticed during the demonstration.

I expected and must insist on having a new set. Please have one delivered here as soon as possible and instruct the deliveryman to pick up this shopworn model at the same time.

Sincerely yours,
Wallace Boyd

Gentlemen:

We regret to have to call your attention again to faulty deliveries—of wrong goods and goods received in poor condition.

Against our order marked No. 1728, sent you on September 4, we received 2 gross instead of 12 gross of ocean pearl No. 14. And instead of style No. 22 with 4 holes, we received No. 20 with two holes, which we cannot use. Furthermore, one package was so badly wrapped that four boxes in it were broken and part of the contents spilled, requiring tedious time-wasting labor to assort the goods.

If this were the first instance, we would merely ask you to correct the shipment and let it go at that. Mistakes can occur in the best conducted organization. But this is the fourth mishandled order and we cannot afford the delays, the inconvenience, and the extra labor this imposes on us. We have no complaint about the goods; but unless you render efficient service on replacement order, and in the future, we will be obliged to do business elsewhere.

Sincerely yours,
Clifford Scaife

Gentlemen:

On May 29, I ordered fifty dozen of your Perfection Model men's shirts in assorted sizes. We intended these for a one-day special in our series of June sales. In acknowledging this order you assured us of delivery in ample time to conduct the sale, which we scheduled for June 23. Relying on your assurance we had leaflet stuffers and display cards printed and sent out a large neighborhood mailing.

We did not receive the goods until June 25, two days after the advertised sale. You can imagine our distress and the inconvenience and confusion caused by the delay. We had to throw almost our entire regular shirt stock on the sales counters, regardless of costs; we had to hold our help overtime and call in extra help to get the goods ready and properly displayed.

Now I do not expect you to meet intangible losses such as several nights' sleep, possible future ulcers that the worry we suffered may kick up in my partner and myself, and lost good will on the part of customers who couldn't get the sizes they required. Nor do I insist that it is your fault; the trucking service you use may be at fault, in which case you can demand satisfaction from them. Up to now we have had the right goods at the right time on every order we placed with you; so we are giving you all the benefit of the doubt.

However, we expect you to make good the tangible losses we suffered. We can replace a good deal of the stock we had to put on sale, from the order as finally received. But other replacements will represent a considerable loss. Our bookkeeping calculations show that an 18% discount from your bill will cover our actual loss, and we propose this as the adjustment. We feel sure you will agree this is a fair settlement, and shall appreciate your sending us a credit for $ . . .

Sincerely yours,
Eugene A. Voight

Gentlemen:

I am sure that when your representative, Mr. Earl Hollander, reported back on his call on me he informed you that I was to get ninety days' term on the orders I placed with your or-

ganization. Your credit investigation, which you informed me was entirely satisfactory, was undertaken after I had made it clear that I wish to do business on those terms. My first order, numbered 1341 and dated October 2, specified ninety day terms.

Therefore I cannot understand your form letter of December 12, which I take to be the first of your series in cases of deferred payment on orders taken on thirty days' credit terms.

Please straighten this out at once with your credit department. I take pride in my credit standing and it is a distinct annoyance to get dunning letters two months before bills are due, according to the terms of our agreement.

Sincerely yours,
Horace Pierce

SERIES OF COMPLAINT LETTERS

Some business houses follow a poor policy in dealing with complaint letters. They are negligent and dilatory, and customers are put to the trouble of writing several letters before their complaints are attended to. Such houses learn, sooner or later, from bitter experience, to adopt a different policy.

If follow-up letters become necessary, these should retain a courteous tone. They should be increasingly forceful in expression but should never resort to abusive terms.

Assuming that the first unanswered letter has given all the facts, here are two follow-up letters that may be written:

Gentlemen:

On September 6, I returned to you twenty-five copies of *The Winter Story* which you sent me by mistake instead of the book, *The Story of Jane*, by Alice Winter. Although three weeks have elapsed, I have not yet received the books I originally ordered. There is a good demand for Miss Winter's book, and the delay has been costing me sales. I have filled customer's orders from a nearby dealer's stock, but at some inconvenience to my customers and myself. I must ask for immediate delivery or an explanation, so that I may know how to maintain stock on this title.

Sincerely yours,
(Mrs.) Millicent Nixon

Gentlemen:

I have received from you no acknowledgement of receipt of the twenty-five copies of *The Winter Story* that I returned to you on September 6; these had been mistakenly delivered to me instead of *The Story of Jane* by Alice Winter, that I ordered. Nor have I received the books I actually ordered, which is a serious matter, since every day's delay on this wanted book is costing me sales and good will.

I am amazed that I have not been extended even the courtesy of a reply to my two letters. I have been obliged to keep my customers waiting—some, of course, won't wait—while I fill orders piecemeal from other dealers' stocks.

I don't know how you wish to conduct your business, but I must know whether and when you can replace the books I returned. If not, I should like a prompt reply. If I do not receive it within the next five days, please close my account with you and instruct Mr. Evans that he needn't call on us on his next trip.

Sincerely yours,
(Mrs.) Millicent Nixon

ADJUSTMENT LETTERS

It is, unfortunately, almost an instinctive reaction to resent complaints as criticisms. Psychologists attribute such reactions to hidden and unrelated guilt feelings that stir up more emotion than the situation calls for. Whatever this response may be caused by, it complicates the matter. So guard against "over-reacting," as the psychologists call it, when a complaint letter arrives.

One important thing to remember is what was emphasized at the beginning of the chapter. We live in an imperfect world and it is foolish to expect perfection from human beings or any

of the organizations they run. Mistakes are bound to occur; so it is equally unrealistic, when a mistake is pointed out, to think that it can't be true, or to feel guilty or tragic over it.

One of the best ways to deal with mistakes is to avoid them. Here is some preventive medicine against mistakes. This does not mean that mistakes can be eliminated entirely, but you can reduce them to a minimum by such measures.

MISTAKE-PREVENTION MEASURES

Inspection: Have every shipment of goods inspected before it goes out. This will prevent wrong or imperfect goods going out and constitutes your best insurance against complaints about poor shipments.

Check-up: Most customers have a good idea of the kind of merchandise they can use or sell, and specify their preferences as to color, size, shape, decorative details, packaging, etc. Check up on all orders to see that such specifications have been followed.

Promptness: Begin shipments on the day the order is received, or as soon as possible. If delay is unavoidable, notify the customer immediately. That will be your best insurance against cancellations or complaints over delays. If deliveries are made before the promised date, it gives an impression of efficiency on your part and builds customer good-will.

Instructions: On any goods that may involve difficulties in handling, assembly, demonstration, or display, enclose clear instructions, in the shipments, for their handling; don't hesitate to give repeated warnings in these instructions, against procedures that may cause damage or deterioration. For example, give explicit warnings against excessive pulls or pressures at sensitive points, against neglect of oiling of frictional parts, against exposure to dampness or wrong temperature. A manufacturer of vacuum-cleaners found that it paid to give a personal demonstration, at the purchaser's home, with every machine sold.

Packing: Goods get pretty rough treatment in transit. Careful wrapping and crating, with liberal use of corrugated paper and other shock-absorbent materials, are your best assurance that goods will arrive in good condition.

Misrepresentation: Be sure that your advertising, and your sales-talk in general, sticks to the facts. Exaggerated claims lose more sales in the long run than they gain in the immediate transaction.

Over-selling: Warn salesmen against over-selling. Reorders are better and more profitable, in the long run, than big initial orders that are followed by returns of unsold goods. Not only is there the loss in shopworn and over-handled goods, but also the intangible but serious loss in customer good-will.

Accounting: Many complaints arise of erroneous billing or delays in billing, slow processing of orders or remittances, or careless recording of orders and payments. Check up on your accounting department now and then, to make sure that things are in order there.

Let us repeat that such measures will not entirely eliminate error. You must anticipate that some errors will occur despite precautions to avoid them, and, therefore, that you will have complaints to deal with. If you are wise you will not look at such complaints as nuisances; you will make use of them as danger signals showing you where some flaw or strain may have developed in your organization.

In handling a customer's complaint make a careful investigation to determine whether the fault is yours, his, or a third party's—railway, truck service, etc. In borderline cases most firms give the customer the benefit of the doubt, especially where the customer has a good record of reliability and above-board dealing,

or where it is desired to keep him on the books for any other reason.

Most people are fair-minded and reasonable. Assume that about the complaining customer, all the way, unless your investigation definitely indicates the contrary.

If your investigation discloses an error by someone in your organization, admit it. A ready admission usually disarms the complaining customer and predisposes him to be reasonable in his demands for adjustment.

A FEW DON'TS

Don't take a flippant or sarcastic attitude. You may think you are subtly avoiding outright accusation, but you are really implying that the complaint is petty or unjustified, and the customer will almost certainly take offense.

Don't use terms like "you claim" or "you state" or "you assert." These imply falsity and are bound to irritate.

Don't use a combative tone. Settling a complaint is not to be thought of as engaging in a controversy, rather, it is a mutual undertaking to rectify a situation that is distressing to both.

Don't adopt an apologetic tone. In admitting that the complaint is justified avoid expressions injurious to your firm's reputation. Avoid terms like "failure," "breakdown," "poor results," etc., which imply faulty organization, inferior goods or inefficient operations It is not necessary to admit more than that an error, you regret, has occurred.

Don't use scapegoats. It may seem convenient to put the blame on a packer or a file clerk. But you owe your employees the same loyalty you expect from them. And blaming them will simply leave the impression that you have an inefficient staff. It will injure your reputation. As we said before, it is not necessary to do more than admit and regret the error. Situations may, of course, arise where it becomes necessary to put the blame specifically on an employee, but each such case should be carefully judged.

Don't write more than is necessary to make your point.

ADJUSTMENT POLICIES

In making adjustments three policies may be followed. One is the "customer-is-always-right" policy. Firms that have such a policy grant customers' claims as a matter of course. Such firms are usually those dealing in very expensive merchandise with an élite clientele not likely to indulge in petty "chiseling."

Opposed to this is the *caveat emptor* policy. *Caveat emptor* is a Latin phrase meaning "Let the buyer beware." It is a legally permissible policy and the law will not indemnify a buyer who has failed to investigate the seller's claims and the merchandise before acceptance. But the *caveat emptor* policy is seldom used by reputable concerns today. They would not stay established very long if they did.

The most accepted policy is to investigate each complaint and to grant the adjustment the investigation calls for.

ESSENTIALS OF THE ADJUSTMENT LETTERS

The opening should express regret over the loss or inconvenience suffered by the customer. This should be followed by a clear explanation of the cause of the difficulty, so far as your investigation enables you to determine it. Next might come a clear statement of the adjustment you propose. The closing should attempt to regain or reinforce the customer's good-will.

It is not always possible to satisfy the customer. Although most people are honest and reasonable, there are always some who are not. Sometimes ordinarily upright citizens are tempted to take undue advantages of a mistake. And sometimes ordinarily reasonable people may be under a temporary emotional strain that causes them to "over-react" to inconveniences and to make unreasonable claims.

Even in such cases your tone should be calm. It should make clear that you don't like to be taken advantage of, that you are ready to co-operate with all your accounts, and that it is only reasonable to expect similar treatment from them. In that spirit express your position firmly and fairly.

THE CORRESPONDENT

The foregoing should make it obvious that the correspondent who handles complaint letters must be a tactful and responsible person. Yet many firms make the mistake of treating complaints or inquiries in a hit-or-miss fashion. They hand over complaint correspondence to anybody who happens to have time on his hands. This erroneous procedure makes impossible any consistent or reliable policy for which continuity and responsibility are essential.

It is a mistake to disregard the opportunities for promotion and building good will that the proper handling of complaints offers. Wise businessmen consider prompt handling of complaints by a high-status executive, and liberal adjustments when warranted, a form of public relations well worth the cost.

IN HANDLING COMPLAINTS

Avoid delay: Promptness is of the first consideration. The more time a customer is allowed to stew over his complaint the hotter he gets about it and the more unreasonable he becomes. Grievance over the delay is added to

THE KORFUND CO. INC.
49-15 THIRTY SECOND PLACE · LONG ISLAND CITY L.N.Y.

Vibration Control

NATURAL CORK, STEEL SPRINGS, RUBBER MOUNTINGS

Gentlemen:

We recently had the pleasure of filling your order for
Korfund Vibration Control Products.

Since you have no doubt installed them by this time, I am
writing to make sure that you are entirely satisfied with
their operation. We believe that the materials furnished
should provide excellent isolation for your equipment.
However, if you have experienced difficulty, please write
to us giving full particulars. We are anxious to make
every installation a successful one.

I will greatly appreciate a letter from you stating how
this installation is working, and if we can be of further
assistance on other vibration control problems, please
let us know.

Very truly yours,

THE KORFUND COMPANY, INC.

Donald H. Vance
Vice President

P. S. I hope you will pardon this form letter, but since
we attempt to follow up every major installation, I am
sure you'll understand that this is the only practical
means of giving this additional service to our customers.

SOLE DISTRIBUTORS OF ARMSTRONG STANDARD DENSITY VIBRACORK

Fig. 37. This may be characterized as a "customer relations" letter: it offers the firm's services should any adjustments be necessary, on its own initiative. This kind of special attention to customers results in valuable creation of good will, with all that asset's tangible and intangible benefits.

original grievance. And delay also gives him more time and more occasion to gripe about it to other businessmen, to the detriment of your reputation. If it is going to take extra time to investigate and work out the adjustment, tell him so at once; and keep him informed, step by step. Then he sees that his complaint is being acted upon, and that your firm is anxious to settle the matter as quickly as possible.

Avoid minimizing the complaint: A complaint may seem petty to you. But it isn't so to the customer, or he wouldn't have taken the trouble to write to you about it. Avoid any implication that you consider his grievance trifling or uncalled for. Try to give the matter the same importance he gives it.

Avoid grudging concessions: If you accede to the customer's demands, do it cheerfully. Beware of the grudging tone which, in effect, takes back again what has been given. If a customer's good will is important enough for you to grant a concession, then it is certainly important enough to do so without risking offense. A letter reading, "It seems to us that the damage was caused by dampness in your storeroom. Just the same we will replace the goods," is pretty sure to leave the customer resentful. A better letter would read: "We regret the inconvenience caused by the spoilage. A replacement shipment is on its way to you, and should reach you within the next four days. May we suggest that you store the goods in as dry a place as is available, to avoid possible similar spoilage in the future."

Avoid blaming the customer: Without going so far as "the customer-is-always-right" principle, it is a good rule to avoid blaming the customer. Not only should outright accusation be shunned but also any expressions that imply distrust. Telling a customer that a "shipment to replace the damaged goods will be made as soon as these goods are returned and examined"

is tantamount to saying "we don't trust you."

If you have a good reason for holding up such a shipment, give the reason. For example, explain to the customer that you will be better able to give him completely satisfactory service after you have inspected the rejected goods to determine what is the trouble.

TURNING COMPLAINTS INTO ASSETS

Good businessmen find ways to put to good service the complaints they receive. They use them to detect flaws in their goods or their operations. They also use the prompt handling of complaints to emphasize the efficiency of their services.

Indeed some firms actually seek to elicit complaints. They feel that dissatisfaction is less harmful when brought out in the open than when submerged in passive discontent. They send out letters designed to get discontented customers to air their complaints; and such letters usually more than pay their way in regained clients, increased business, and valuable testimonials.

Mail-order houses are continually combing their lists for names of customers who have stopped ordering goods. Letters asking them to voice complaints, if they have any, bring some complaints valuable for the weakness they spotlight, but also useful information of other kinds, and more than enough orders to pay for the mailings.

Makers of expensive or complicated equipment frequently ask customers whether they have any complaints and offer immediate servicing if they do. In that way they prevent more serious complaints, later, and so impress customers with their service that the latter are generally willing to supply the names of friends who might be prospects for the same equipment.

AT LEAST SYMPATHY

In the actual adjustment letter the correspondent should try to get on common ground with the customer by agreeing with him in some way—if nothing else, by expressing regret for the inconvenience his letter has reported. Leaving aside exceptional cases that require very special handling, this sympathetic attitude should extend to offering something to the customer even where his claims are rejected.

For example, a store that refused to exchange a suit with a stain, succeeded in appeasing the customer with a paragraph of advice on how to remove the stain from the wool, at the same time offering to clean the suit, if desired, free of charge. This evidence of the store's desire to be of some service helped to retain the customer's good-will.

THE DIPLOMATIC REJECTION

In the above paragraph an example was given of how a bit of helpful advice helped soothe a complaining customer whose claim was rejected. When not even that much can be done for the customer, remember that "a soft answer turneth away wrath." If one cannot satisfy the customer one can at least minimize his disappointment by an understanding approach.

Be impersonal in discussing the complaint itself but show sympathy for the loss or inconvenience described in the letter of complaint. Avoid anything that might be construed as an accusation of neglect, stupidity or dishonesty. Make your explanation of what happened at your end simple for him to follow. **Never let the refusal precede your explanation** because then the explanation may sound like an excuse. Always have the refusal follow the explanation and then the refusal will sound like a logical conclusion.

Never make the refusal an outright one. As noted above, try to make some concession, or offer some advice that will leave the customer with the feeling that he has not been entirely rejected. A washing-machine manufacturer will not exchange machines that have broken down from obvious mishandling, but the company always offers to repair a damaged part at cost. Usually the customer accepts, and this provides the opportunity to impart tactful instruction in the care of the machine while the repair is being made.

THE DIPLOMATIC AGREEMENT

If the complaint is justified, do not hesitate to acknowledge a mistake. Prompt and ungrudging acknowledgment of mistakes disarms the aggrieved customer and makes him more amenable to reasonable suggestions for adjustment.

But don't make the mistake, already warned against, of exaggerating the error and overplaying the customer's grievance. Never acknowledge a mistake in such a way as to disparage your organization's product or services. That mistakes do occur is explanation enough.

WHERE A THIRD PARTY IS AT FAULT

Where your investigation establishes that a third party is at fault—mishandling by a truckman or loss in transit—do not let the matter go with that explanation. Give all the service you can in an effort to rectify the fault. Notify the carrier, yourself, immediately. Ask that a tracer be sent out. Don't bother the customer with any of the chores of tracing unless he alone can take certain necessary steps.

Examples of Adjustment Letters:

Dear Mr. Struthers:

I thank you for your letter of April 12 about the good and bad points you have observed in your first hours of driving in your new automobile. Minor adjustments are usually necessary in a new machine, as you well know, and I am sure that we will satisfactorily take care of the "bad points."

From your description we think the brake bands may be out of alignment. The vibration in the radio dials probably comes from loose connections. Any time you can spare the car we will have these matters looked into and, if more than alignment and tightening is necessary, we will install new parts.

We are glad you reported this to us. We should rather have you know how good the car can be as the result of timely adjustments than risk more serious trouble later. We will regard it as a favor to be told of any way the car fails to give you the complete satisfaction you have every right to expect.

Sincerely yours,
Vincent Raferty

Dear Mrs. Barton:

This is to acknowledge receipt of the blouse that was scorched when ironed with the dial set at heat for cotton. The material is not all cotton, but a mixture of cotton and nylon. Our sales staff is instructed to make this clear to every purchaser. But sometimes a sales person assumes that the purchaser has heard the explanation just made to another customer and fails to repeat it. That was what may have happened in this instance.

We are sorry you suffered any disappointment or inconvenience as a result. We will make whatever adjustment you prefer—by sending a new blouse, which we shall ship out as soon as we receive your instructions, or a refund.

Sincerely yours,
Elaine Howell

Dear Miss Sarton:

We are sorry to receive your note cancelling membership in our book club. I think you might like to know some of the reasons for the increase in book costs we have been compelled to make. Perhaps, after you have considered them, you may wish to change your decision to resign from the club.

Production and service costs (paper, cloth,

printing, binding, postage and handling) have risen 112% since the year you joined the club. We did all we could to avoid passing on these heavy increases to our members. As a result of our efforts we limited the increases to members to 39% instead of 112%. We did this by reorganizing our operations and our arrangements with publishers and authors. Throughout, our aim has been to let as little of the burden as possible fall upon the members.

Consider other articles among your regular purchases. Are there many among them for which you are paying as little as 39% above the price you paid for them six years ago?

That isn't all. We have just entered into special arrangements with art-book publishers that will enable us to give our members extra values in book dividends. These values will enable members who purchase enough books to earn two or more dividends to pay *no more for their total book purchases than they did six years ago!*

So you see, we haven't joined in the "manhunt of the poor consumer," as you so graphically put it in your letter. We are working harder than ever to fulfill, even in these days of rising prices, one of the major aims with which we started in business—to give the bookbuyer the most for his budgeted book dollar that he can get.

The fact is, Miss Sarton, that to get the most for your dollar you need the club today as never before. I hope you will rejoin and take advantage of the special offer described in the enclosed folder.

Sincerely yours,
Averill Beaton

Dear Mr. Leslie:

We can understand your disappointment, during your Mexican vacation, over finding that you lacked fluency in speaking Spanish, though you had mastered our Home Spanish Course according to all the tests you reported.

Perhaps the explanation lies in this passage from your letter: "I am naturally shy and become tongue-tied when confronted with difficulties in self-expression. Imagine the embarrassment I suffered on finding myself practically inarticulate when I could not find the right word or the right construction."

Yes, we can imagine it, and sympathize with your difficulties. Yet, there is no doubt, from your reports in our records, that you had actually mastered the language as far as anyone can through a correspondence course. In fact, your tests show that you did considerably better than the average.

It would appear that the trouble is in lack of confidence in public speaking. Everything points to it, and also points to the remedy—some measures to build up your confidence in public speaking. Therefore I suggest your taking our course in public speaking. It will enable you to get the full value of your Spanish course by dealing with the difficulties that prevent you from speaking with confidence.

Because of your disappointment we should like to propose this special adjustment. We will let you take the public speaking course at a third off the regular fee. That will not only assure you a more pleasant vacation in Mexico the next time you go there, but will help you in countless other ways—in business and social relations, in making possible things that hesitation in public speaking has kept you from, in realizing innate capacities for leadership, and in developing other potentialities.

We think this adjustment will prove to be fair and valuable to you.

> Yours sincerely,
> Barrett Holmes

Dear Mr. Stechert:

A jar of our Hymettus Honey is on its way to you.

Your letter with the dollar enclosed never reached us. We have notified the Post Office at our end, and we suggest that you notify the Post Office at your end. Such loses are rare, but reporting them helps to keep them rare.

Meanwhile we hope this mishap will not deter you from expressing your enjoyment of the honey in the way our customers usually do —by regular re-orders.

> Sincerely yours,
> Gregory Toplos

Dear Mr. Chandler:

We were surprised by your letter of August 18, that you would like to return your unsold White Gas stoves. It was a relief to know that your action was not prompted by any shortcoming in the product, for we have put much effort and expense into its development.

The White Gas stove is useful not only for picnicking and outings. Therefore the potential sales season is not over by the middle of August. White Gas stoves have been designed also for emergency use, and emergencies may occur any time of the year. As a matter of fact, such emergencies are frequent in Long Island, where gales and heavy snowfalls knock down the power lines.

As you know, summer renters are staying longer; those who own their own cottages are coming out more fall and winter weekends; and many are settling down, in your area, as permanent suburbanites. In most cases the utility they use is electricity; and that utility is most vulnerable to hurricane, gale and snowfall damage.

It will interest you to know that Hollister's, in neighboring Port Jefferson, has just *re-ordered* White Gas stoves. They have been pushing the stoves to customers as emergency equipment against the expected September gales.

In view of the sales potential of the item, we feel your desire to return the stoves is not justified. We suggest that you take advantage of Hollister's experience and push the stoves to your own customers as emergency equipment. Let us know how you do. It will not surprise us if your next report takes the form of a re-order.

> Sincerely yours,
> Stephen Webb

Dear Mr. Parsons:

This is in confirmation of our wire today, "Duplicate shipment on way. Tracing first shipment."

On receiving your letter informing us that the goods had not reached you, we immediately checked our records. We found that your order had been made up the day it had been received and that it had been shipped the following morning via the . . . Railroad. We reported the delay to them but did not wait for the outcome of their investigation. We immediately made up a duplicate shipment which, as we wired you, is on its way to you. We sent it "Special—Rush" and it should reach you in time for your sales week.

I believe this is the first time anything of this type has happened and, as you can see, it was through no fault of ours. We want to thank you for letting us know so promptly so that the replacement shipment could be made in time.

Sincerely yours,
Claude Pilcher

The following is reprinted from an article by Charles A. Emley in *The Mailbag:*

George Hankins, a letter writer I know, has boosted his firm's sales several thousand dollars in the last two years by the simple process of turning complaints into orders.

Let's see how George does it. Perhaps we can do likewise.

A customer wrote George's firm a sizzling letter demanding an explanation as to why it had taken ten days to fill his last order whereas orders sent previously had been filled in three days. The delay, it developed, was due to the fact that at the time the order arrived the factory was oversold. True, someone should have so informed the customer. But, as often happens in the best regulated (?) offices, someone didn't.

Now, it is likely that the "average" letter writer would have undertaken to soothe the angry customer and let it go at that. George, however, scenting an order, went a step further and wrote the customer the following letter. The result was a $300 order.

Your letter of . . . , for which we thank you, came this morning.

Certain it is we're sorry that there was a delay in shipping the . . . you ordered on May 26. It really couldn't be helped. The demand for . . . has been so big lately that we've found it utterly impossible to fill all orders as promptly as formerly.

As the demand is increasing and as it will take some little time for us to increase our manufacturing facilities, we wonder if you'd like to co-operate with us by anticipating your needs.

If you can see your way clear to send your orders about two weeks before you need . . . it will help us lay out our plans so as to get the . . . to you by the time you need them.

Perhaps you'll find it convenient to mail us an order now to be filled in two weeks or so. We'd appreciate it if you would do this, for we certainly want to give you the kind of service that will please and satisfy you.

A customer wrote for a price on an item. George quoted. The customer came back with the information that a commission house in New York was selling the same article at a price lower than the one George had quoted. "Moreover," wrote the peeved customer, "I can buy the Jones brand, just as good as yours, for . . . a gross less than you charge for yours." He left-handedly accused George's firm of maintaining a two-price policy and wound up with this ominous threat. "You may ship the 25 gross at the price I specify on the attached order" (10% lower than the price George had quoted), "or cancel the order."

George lighted a cigar, wheeled around to his typewriter and wrote this letter which brought a courteous answer from the customer and instructions to ship the twenty-five gross at the price originally quoted:

As much as we appreciate your order of June 10, we cannot fill it at the special price you mention because our best price is the one quoted in our letter of June 2.

You realize, of course, Mr. . . . , that if we were to give you the benefit of a special price we would do an injustice to our many other customers. Moreover, you wouldn't have much confidence in us if we were to quote you a price, asserting it to be our best, and then, upon your insistence, give you a better price. You would look upon us as a two-price house and forever after regard our quotations with suspicion.

Obviously, we want you and all our other friends to think of us as a one-price house—as a house that puts out quality products and sells them at a price consistent with quality.

True, you may be able to buy the A brand at a lower price than we charge for ours. The A brand may be as good as ours. We don't know. We do know that you can buy (name of product) at a lower price than that charged for the A brand; but we doubt very much if you'd want to offer it to your customers.

The one thing you are sure of when you buy our . . . is that you're getting a strictly quality product, the kind that will satisfy the folks upon whom you and your customers are dependent for your progress. That's worth thinking about, isn't it?

Whichever of the New York commission houses is selling our . . . at the ridiculously low price you mention is not making any profit, for our rock bottom price to *everybody* is . . . You will agree, Mr. . . . , that no firm could long exist by making a practice of selling on such a narrow margin.

Anyway, you may rest assured that we are not giving this house, or any other, the benefit of a special discount.

So, all things considered, we're confident that you will instruct us to ship the . . . on your order of June 10, at the price we quoted in our letter of June 2.

Increases in the cost of material and labor made it necessary for George's firm to increase the prices on small quantities of one of its products. A letter explaining the why and the wherefore of the advance in prices and a new list were sent to each customer, or supposedly so. One morning shortly after the new prices had gone into effect the following letter came to George's desk:

We have received your invoice of August 5 and note that you charge us . . . for. . . . This is a mistake. The price should be. . . . Send us corrected invoice at once and tell your billing department not to make such mistakes, for they cause us a lot of trouble and extra work.

Evidently one of two things had happened: either the letter and price list had gone astray or someone had neglected to send them. So George wrote the customer this letter:

Thank you for your letter of August 9 in which you question the price of the . . . on our invoice of August 5.

That price is correct, Mr. Jones. Owing to recent increases in the costs of materials and labor it is necessary for us to charge a little more for our . . . in small quantities.

At the time the new prices went into effect we sent to each of our customers a letter explaining why the increase was necessary and a new price list. Evidently we may have neglected to send a letter and a list to you, or if we did send them they've gone astray. We're sorry.

You'll observe from the attached price list that there is an extra discount of 10% on shipments of 25 gross. Now if you'll send along an order for 13 more gross we will gladly combine it with your order of August 1, bringing the total up to 25 gross and give you the benefit of the extra 10%.

As . . . is a brisk seller with you, we're confident you'll welcome the opportunity to take advantage of this offer.

Here is the customer's answer:

We thank you very much for your courteous letter of. . . . You may ship us 13 additional gross at once and give us the benefit of the extra 10% discount on the entire 25 gross.

We assure you that we appreciate your kindness in telling us about the additional discount.

It isn't wise, of course, to try to turn all complaints into orders. It is better in some cases, depending on the nature of the complaint and how mad the customer is, simply to "pour oil on troubled waters." Nevertheless, hundreds of complaints that are adjusted in the old familiar way could be turned into orders with the aid of the right kind of letters.

George has given us a few hints on how to write this kind of a letter.

CHAPTER NINE

MISCELLANEOUS BUSINESS LETTERS

Inquiries and Replies; Orders and Acknowledgments; Introduction and Recommendation; Social Correspondence in Business, Inter-Office; Good Will; Payments by Mail.

ROUTINE LETTERS

In terms of quantity the largest part of business correspondence consists of routine letters —inquiries, replies to inquiries, orders and remittances, acknowledgments, bills, etc. In these letters the writer needs little art; the basic requirements are to be clear and accurate.

INQUIRY LETTERS

Inquiry letters and replies to inquiries should be concise, simple, and direct, except in cases that call for sensitivity, judgment, or tact. An inquiry about the price of an article need do no more than ask the price. But an inquiry about credit standing or about a job opportunity, and the answers to such inquiries, require care and tact. (See chapters on **Credit, Collection** and **Employment Letters.**) Similarly answers to inquiries in mail-order campaigns, where the objective is to produce sales, call for thought and skill. (See chapter on **Mail-Order Sales Letters.**)

In ordinary inquiries, however, the important thing, on the part of the inquirer, is to phrase his questions simply, precisely, and inclusively so that he can be told just what he wants to know, without extraneous matter; and also all that he wants to know so that he does not have to send further letters to fill out details. Similarly, the important thing on the part of the correspondent in answering such inquiries is to make the reply full and precise so that the inquirer does not have to come back to him to have matters cleared up or filled out.

If the information sought is adequately covered in a catalogue or booklet, enclose it in your reply and use the letter to refer to the paragraphs or pages dealing explicitly with the matter inquired about.

To facilitate quick comprehension both of the inquiry and the reply it is advisable to present them as separate items, allowing an individual paragraph for each.

If either the question or the answer is to be kept confidential, do not rely on the other person to guess it. Say so. Examples:

Gentlemen:

We are organizing a summer camp for boys and are in the market for 24 two-occupant portable tents for camping out. We are undecided whether to use conventional canvas tents, with which we are familiar, or your new nylon tents. Would you be good enough:

To send us whatever literature you have available on the construction of your nylon tents, accessory equipment, etc.

To inform us of their suitability to the summer climate of the Catskill Mountains, where the camp is located.

To furnish comparative weights and costs between canvas and nylon.

To give us an idea of the durability of your product with estimates of how many years of service may be expected in ordinary use.

We shall appreciate your referring us to customers who have had experience with your tents in conditions approximating those of the boys' camp in the Catskills.

> Sincerely yours,
> Arthur Ives

Gentlemen:

We are in the market for a line of work pants. We should like to know—

What fabrics you make up.

What colors.

Minimum orders accepted per size.

Terms (including discount for cash).

Please send us a swatch catalogue with your reply.

> Sincerely yours,
> Bruce Samuelson

Gentlemen:

My wife and I will be in New York for the Christmas week vacation. We are people of modest means—I am an associate professor at the University here. We should like good (not lavish) hotel accommodations in Manhattan, but a little out of the immediate railroad-terminal district. We would like to take in the theater (dramas, not musicals). We enjoy good cooking, preferably without noisy entertainment.

Would your bureau book reservations such as we describe and provide information about restaurants?

Could you send us a selected list of hotels that would come within our description, listing locations and price ranges for rooms for two?

Could you list the well-reviewed plays and the price range for seats in medium locations. Fortunately our vision and hearing are good.

If you can provide such services, we will send you, by return mail, our first and alternate choices of hotel and theater reservations and a check for whatever sum you may require for deposit.

> Sincerely yours,
> Howard Carver

ANSWERS TO INQUIRIES

Dear Mr. Alexander:

We thank you for your letter of August 16 about our line of women's belts.

We wish to call your attention to the perforated pages in the back of the enclosed catalogue containing information on terms and convenient order forms.

Ours is a quality line. It is used for accessories by manufacturers serving exclusive shops, and is stocked by the New York Fifth Avenue stores.

We hope to have the pleasure of serving you.

> Sincerely yours,
> A. S. Cantor

Dear Mr. Jones:

Because of the decline in demand we have discontinued manufacture of the "union suit" type of men's underwear.

As the enclosed catalogue illustrates, we carry a full line of the currently popular types of men's underwear in a wide range of styles, colors, and prices.

We will be happy to serve you.

> Sincerely yours,
> V. A. Miles

Dear Mr. Hector:

Since your letter does not make clear what your speech defect is, we are unable to furnish a specific answer.

Our public speaking course has been designed to help shy people who are not sure of themselves to speak readily and effectively in public. If your defect is among those associated with shyness, we are confident that the course will help you overcome it.

But if the defect is organic, that may require surgical treatment. If it is a long-standing problem, such as chronic stuttering, that may call for psychiatric treatment. We recommend that you try to determine the cause with the aid of a physician or professionally qualified person.

But common difficulties in speaking—such as inability to face an audience, lack of practice of organizing a speech, unfamiliarity with the techniques of preparing material, groping for words, difficulties over parliamentary rules, etc.,—can be overcome by our course of study.

If you do not find here the answer you require, please try us again with the questions put in more specific terms.

Sincerely yours,
Marc Rafferty

A final note: Though answers to inquiries need not be elaborate, they should avoid stuffy over-formality. For example, instead of "Acknowledging yours of the 20th requesting a copy of our booklet, *Paint It Yourself*, we wish to advise you that the booklet is being mailed to you forthwith," write something like: "We are pleased to send you our booklet, *Paint It Yourself*, which you requested on May 20. Its suggestions have been useful to people of good taste who must keep within a modest budget." Or, instead of "Yours of September 10 received and contents noted. Be advised that the matter has been put into the hands of our Sales Department from whom you should hear shortly," write something like, "Our Sales Department has your inquiry of September 10 and is assembling material which should be helpful in answering your questions."

ORDERS

Many firms use printed order forms. If for some reason a letter is needed to accompany or precede the order to add some specific instructions about the order, make the letter concise and unmistakably clear.

Where the letter itself constitutes the order, care should be taken to make it direct, clear, and accurate. To facilitate this it is advisable to arrange the items in tabular form, giving a separate line to each. Details of color, size, material, price, identifying mark or number, etc., should be precisely stated. Manner of shipment should be specified—whether by mail, express, freight, etc.

If the goods are needed by a certain date, if method of payment is, in any way, to differ from the customary procedure, if delivery is to be made to an address other than the regular mailing address, anything requiring specific instructions should be made clear, and should be given a separate paragraph to prevent its being misunderstood or ignored.

Where remittance is enclosed, attention should be drawn to it and its nature specified—whether it is by check, money-order, express-order, draft, cash, or stamps.

Even in letters transmitting orders for goods, ordinary courtesy and tact should be observed. In his book *"Effective Letters in Business,"* Robert L. Shurter gives an example of a tactless order letter that drew a deservedly caustic reply: The letter—"Gents. Please send me one of them gasoline engines you show on page 785 and if it's any good I'll send you a check for it."

The reply—"Dear Mr. . . . Please send us the check and if it's any good we'll send you the engine."

Variations from ordinary punctuation are frequently used in orders. To compress items into single lines or a minimum number of lines, customary punctuation may be omitted and every possible abbreviation used. Names of separate articles are capitalized and also words that help to distinguish them from other kinds of goods of the same order. Thus Red will be capitalized to distinguish it from other colors an article may be manufactured in; or Wool to distinguish a garment in that fabric from garments in other fabrics. The objectives are conciseness and clarity and any typographic or grammatical means that promote these ends is justified.

ORDER LETTERS—SOME EXAMPLES

Gentlemen:

Please rush to us to reach our stockroom next Thursday: 10 doz. Yo-yos, 50 checker sets, 50 anagram sets. This is for a special sales week which is going well. Our stock on these items is running out.

Our regular purchase order is being made out in the routine way and should reach you in a day or two; but please do not hold up delivery of this special order. A delay of even a few hours may mean lost sales.

Sincerely yours,
Kenneth Miller

Dear Mr. Bates:

The enclosed purchase order is in confirmation of the order we placed with you over the phone this morning. The order was phoned in to avoid delays. I must emphasize again that the shipment must reach us before October 4, when our sale will start.

Sincerely yours,
Seth Bellows

Gentlemen:

Please send us, for earliest possible delivery, the following goods selected from your latest catalogue. Charge my account.

3	doz.	Men's Nylon Hose, Black, asst. sizes @ $4.00	$ 12.00
3	doz.	Men's Nylon Hose, Blue, asst. sizes @ $4.00	12.00
3	doz.	Men's Nylon Hose, Brown, asst. sizes @ $4.00	12.00
1½	doz.	Men's Nylon Hose, Green, asst. sizes @ $4.00	6.00
4	doz.	Men's Cotton Hose, Black, Triangle Clocks @ $4.50	18.00
2	doz.	#61 Work Shirts, asst. sizes @ $9.00	18.00
2	doz.	Men's White Broadcloth Cotton Shirts, asst. sizes @ $16.00	32.00
			$110.00

Ship freight.

Sincerely yours,
Charles Bloom

ACKNOWLEDGMENTS

Dear Mr. Thayer:

Thank you for your order of October 5. As you instructed, it will be shipped freight, via the D & W. The order is being made up today and will be at the yards tomorrow. It should reach you well within the time you specified.

Sincerely yours,
J. H. Hudson

Dear Mr. Jones:

We have just telegraphed you the following: "Cannot ship your order May 10. Goods not available." The telegram was sent to minimize any inconvenience this may cause you. We can supply the cheaper grade, #43, on the date required. The earliest we can supply the #41 grade specified in your order would be June 11. If the #43 grade is all right, please wire collect and we will ship immediately.

Sincerely yours,
Adam Pierce

Dear Mr. Poynter:

Thank you for your order of August 14.

Unfortunately your letter did not specify which color or colors, and which weight or weights, you wish. In our Queen's Taste stationery line the colors are Rose, Fern, Mauve, Beige, Robin's Egg, Canary, Russet, Shell White, and Alpine Snow. The weights are Tissue, Regular and Baronial. Probably our catalogue was not at hand when you made out your order. We are enclosing another giving samples of each color and weight.

A prompt reply will be to our mutual advantage.

Yours sincerely,
Eric Hunter

Dear Mr. Magnes:

Thank you for your order for Clover Danish Blue Cheese. It is being shipped out to you today.

We enclose a catalogue of our other products. Please note that with orders of $10.00 or more, customers may receive, free, their choice of a jar of Lingonberry or Currant preserves.

Yours sincerely,
Einar Toksvig

FOLLOW-UPS ON ORDERS

Sometimes orders are poorly attended to and it is necessary, strange as it may seem, to jog the attention of the supplier. Here, again, as emphasized in the section on **Complaints and Adjustments,** an irritable tone is inadvisable, even where loss or inconvenience has been caused by the delay. A calm letter will get quicker and more favorable attention and will enhance the writer's status as a considerate customer whose patronage is worth retaining. It is seldom necessary to write more than one reminder; but when that becomes necessary, a sharper tone is not always politic, especially where the writer has reasons of his own for maintaining business relations with the inefficient firm. Examples:

Gentlemen:

Although our order #216 was acknowledged on June 2, and it is now near the end of the month, the air conditioners have not yet arrived. We have already undergone a hot spell, and soon July will be upon us. I cannot understand the delay or your leaving us without an explanation for your delay in delivery of such a seasonal article. Up to now your deliveries have been prompt; and expecting delivery any day, I did not write to you. There is no question now that I shall lose some sales and I expect you to make up for the lost time, not to speak of the lost business, by shipping the goods by express at your expense. Please wire what you plan to do in the matter.

Sincerely yours,
Edward Hines

Answers to follow-ups on orders should be prompt, and they should be tactful even where the tone of the complaining letter is disagreeable. Give the reason for the delay, assure the customer that care will be taken to avoid such delays in the future, and specify the date and the manner of the planned shipment.

Dear Mr. Osgood:

We regret the delay in shipping out your order #644, dated February 10.

You probably have read of the recent labor troubles in the lumber industry. These made it difficult for us to secure proper crating materials for the goods. Rather than risk damage in transit we held up the shipment until satisfactory crates were available. We have now managed to get some from another source of supply. Even though our shipping costs have risen, we feel the added expense, like the delay, is preferable to having the machinery arrive in poor condition.

Your order was shipped out today, express. We hope it reaches you in good time as, we are confident now, it will reach you in good order.

Sincerely yours,
Mark Lyons

LETTERS WITH ENCLOSURES

When remittances such as checks, etc., or when invoices or special notices are enclosed, the number of enclosures should be stated in the letter. This is customarily done in a separate line, at the left margin, under the signature.

Gentlemen:

The enclosed check for $146.00 is in settlement of our account to date. We also enclose your bill. Please receipt and return it.

Sincerely yours,
Joseph Evans

2 enclosures

Gentlemen:

Thank you for your order #324 for a dozen Pop-Up Toasters. They were shipped today. The invoice is enclosed. We also enclose the catalogue on waffle irons requested in your letter.

Sincerely yours,
Morton James

2 enclosures

LETTERS OF INTRODUCTION

Letters of introduction should not be given thoughtlessly. Avoid them unless you can feel that it would actually be in the interest of both parties to get acquainted. Good-natured people often do harm when they mean to do good, by writing letters of introduction indiscriminately. The tenth "promising" young chap sent to glean advice in the field of his ambition from a busy executive is likely to get a discouraging brushoff.

Therefore, the first consideration in writing a letter of introduction is whether to write it at all. Having decided that the letter should be written, you might well consider several other elements. Since the best way to present letters of introduction is in person, the envelope containing the introduction should be unsealed and should bear the name of the person to whom it is addressed and, in the lower left-hand corner, the line "Introducing Mr. . . ." This enables the recipient to welcome the caller by name and facilitates the relationship.

The letter should be brief and restrained. A long letter might impose an embarrassingly long wait on the caller while the letter is read. And extravagant statements about the caller, if they do not predispose the reader to skepticism, may evoke embarrassing comments of other sorts.

Sometimes there is a reason to mail the letter to the person addressed; for example, to allow him to appoint a time for the meeting. In that case a copy should be sent to the person being introduced so that he will be familiar with what has been said about him. Examples:

Dear Mr. Clements:

I hope you will have the time to see Mr. Wilbur, who was a student in my class this semester. You have several times expressed an interest in seeing "the cream of the crop" in each graduating class. It is because I can unreservedly place Mr. Wilbur in that category that I have suggested that he call on you.

Yours sincerely,

Roger Hessian

Dear Mr. Canning:

It gives me great pleasure to introduce to you Mr. Harvey Wright, who operates a large bottling plant in our city.

Mr. Wright is contemplating opening a branch in your city, and I could think of no one better for him to see than you for a quick survey of local conditions and prospects. My business association with Mr. Wright is now in its twelfth year and has led to a friendship which has enabled me to discover and appreciate his personal qualities.

I feel certain that any association this introduction may result in will be valued on both sides.

Yours sincerely,

Hiram Godkin

LETTERS OF RECOMMENDATION

There are two main types of recommendation—the general recommendation "to whom it may concern," and the individual recommendation addressed to a specific person. The latter obviously is preferable, since the writer's personal acquaintance with the person addressed generally means that the letter will be given more attention than might otherwise be the case.

The best kind of recommendation is the one that performs a mutual service to the recommended person and the one to whom he is sent. So far as possible, therefore, it is well to find out beforehand whether and how the person about whom you are writing can be of service to the individual you are addressing.

Vital to any letter of recommendation is truthfulness and restraint. False statements are almost inevitably found out. In time they create handicaps that outweigh any temporary advantage that they gain for the person recommended. And exaggerated claims usually predispose the reader to skepticism and suspicion, and thus are often more injurious than helpful. Examples:

To Whom It May Concern:

Mr. Clarence Loman has been on our sales staff for the past eight years and has compiled an excellent sales record. He is a friendly person by nature and has won the friendship as well as the business patronage of his customers. We have convincing evidence of that from the letters we have received in response to the announcement of his retirement from traveling.

For reasons of health he cannot continue traveling, but he can serve in an inside position. We regret there is nothing of this kind available in our organization. He would make a cracker-jack inside salesman and we can unreservedly recommend him to anyone in need of a person with real selling talents. It would take him no time to get a feeling of your stock and your methods; and to establish really friendly relations with customers. We are confident that he would be an asset to any firm that can use his services.

Very truly yours,
Martin Ullmann

Dear Mr. Carter:

I am taking the liberty of writing to you because I know that you sometimes give out manuscripts for first readings, and accepted manuscripts for preparations for the printer, to qualified young people, on a free-lance basis. I have heard that you do this, as a means of testing or training candidates for anticipated future openings on your editorial staff.

If that is the case, I feel that you will appreciate my sending Miss Ethel Willison to you. You have already become acquainted with her work and have even complimented her, without knowing it, when you complimented me on the excellent shape of the manuscript I turned in, and again, when I sent back corrected proofs. Miss Willison assisted me through all the stages of my book, and it is to her that I owe the smoothness and ease with which it went through all its stages.

Miss Willison has taken all the courses given here in preparation for a career in publishing and has applied what she learned, first on the college paper and, later, in helping other faculty members, as she has helped me, in preparing articles and books.

I am confident that she is just the kind of person you will look for when you are considering taking on a new editorial assistant. I take great pleasure in recommending her to you.

Sincerely yours,
David Proctor

SOCIAL CORRESPONDENCE IN BUSINESS

Though the phrase "strictly business" symbolizes freedom from emotional involvements in or out of business, the words connote an attitude or a goal, rather than the reality of business itself. It would be unnatural to expect that human beings, who spend most of their waking hours in business, would not form personal relationships of varying degrees of closeness in the course of their business. The truth is that most of the friendships men form in their mature years arise out of business contacts. And friendly qualities are recognized as assets in business.

This is so generally understood that trade associations of businessmen have the fostering of friendly cooperation as their major aim. Generally, too, a business relationship would hardly be accounted good or secure if it failed to develop some measure of personal regard between heads or representatives of the two firms.

Consequently, there are many occasions for letters that should not be "strictly business," although they are essential to the conduct of business. Examples are given in the following pages:

LETTERS OF CONGRATULATION

Dear Mr. Leonard:

What a pleasure it was to see the item in *The Times* business section this morning about your promotion to the position of Sales-Manager.

Actually I think I ought to write to the President of your concern, Mr. Tate, to congratulate him. He had the good sense to recognize a good man. From what I know about people in the field he couldn't have picked a better man. Congratulations on a well-deserved promotion.

Cordially yours,

Rodney Mackinder

Dear Mr. Slocum:

I don't know how others are reacting to the news in this morning's real-estate section, but I want to congratulate you on taking such a far-sighted and enterprising step. I have already heard some say that the site is too remote for such a development, but I put them with those who once thought Forty-second Street was too far outside the city. I think you have judged correctly that the site is directly in the path of the city's future growth.

Again, my congratulations and my best wishes for the success of a project which should serve the community as well as bring you well-deserved returns.

Admiringly yours,

Edmund Gates

LETTERS OF SYMPATHY AND CONDOLENCE

Dear Walter:

When your secretary called this morning to tell me that you wouldn't be able to keep our appointment because of your sudden illness, I was deeply disturbed. She told me that you were to spend some days in the hospital, under observation, to determine whether an operation will be necessary. I hope the tests indicate no such necessity and that you will be back in your office very soon and in condition to renew our postponed engagement.

Cordially yours,

Arthur Reinhardt

Dear Mrs. Rodd:

It was a hard blow to us, too, to hear of your husband's death. We missed him here, very much, two years ago, when he retired. During our association with him over the twelve years that he was with us, all of us developed the highest regard for his wonderful qualities. We can fully understand how deeply you must feel his loss. But it must be a consolation to you that his last years were serene. We and his other friends feel grateful to you for having contributed so much to making him so happy.

Sincerely yours,

Charles U. Clifford

Dear George:

I was very sorry to receive the sad news of your great loss. I know that nothing anyone may say at a time like this can assuage your deep grief, but I hope that you will soon find abiding comfort in the high regard everyone had for your father's accomplishments, and in the good health, happiness, and achievements of those dear to you. I hope you will have no more sorrow for many years to come.

Sincerely yours,

Frank

Dear Mr. Cass:

I have just learned of the emergency appendicitis operation you have had to undergo. I had Miss Hale phone the hospital immediately and was reassured to hear that there were no complications and that you are getting along nicely.

That's fine and we want to keep it so. Therefore, I want it understood that no matter how good your recovery is, you are not to come back to the office until the doctor, on his most conservative estimate, tells you you may. And don't think of the office. This is an order!

In the meanwhile, to help you pass the time, there will be a package of books soon at the hospital. The well-read Miss Hale did the choosing and I think she has a good idea of your taste.

With all best wishes,

Robert E. Griffin

ACCEPTING INVITATIONS

Dear Mr. Canby:

It will be a pleasure to see you when I visit New York next month. Thank you for suggesting it. Indeed one of the prospects that made the trip so pleasing to me was the opportunity it might give me to become acquainted with you personally.

Sincerely yours,
Elmer Robinson

Dear Sir:

I consider it a great honor to be asked to speak at the Credit Men's Luncheon next month. Thank you very much.

I hope the enclosed data are what you need for the newspaper release. And I will be on hand an hour before the start of the luncheon, as you suggest, to talk over the details of the program.

Yours very truly,
Leon Hart

DECLINING INVITATIONS

Dear Mr. Hopkins:

Unfortunately I will be out of town during the week of March 10 and will not be able, therefore, to be present at the reception celebrating the opening of your new store. Since I will not be there to offer my congratulations to you in person, permit me to do so here. And I wish to add my sincere best wishes for the success of the new store and the continued growth of your business.

Sincerely yours,
Anthony Asch

Dear Mr. Mann:

It is with deep regret that I must decline the great honor of organizing and heading the committee to arrange a reception for the Vice-President, who is to be one of the speakers at our coming convention. As you may have heard, Mr. Bixby, head of our Foreign Department, died suddenly last week. I have had to take over his duties temporarily, which for the present rules out any other activities for me. I will let you know as soon as I am free again for any service to the organization.

Sincerely yours,
Horace Seton

RESIGNATIONS

Dear Sir:

I have just been appointed Coordinator of Sales for our firm. This will mean extensive traveling in order to keep in continual contact with our stores throughout the country. It will, therefore, be impossible for me to continue to serve as secretary of the club. And, so, with deep regret, I must tender my resignation from that office.

It has been a pleasure to serve the club during the past four years, and I have enjoyed and profited from the association with its able officers and members. Needless to say, I will be on hand for every get-together my new duties will permit.

Sincerely yours,
Edwin Robbins

Dear Sir:

I have agreed to serve on the Mayor's Committee for Emergency Housing. Since it may prejudice the value of the work I can do for the committee, if I continue as a member of the firm, I am submitting my resignation to take effect immediately.

This is a step I take not without regret, for the years I have been privileged to spend with the firm have been happy ones. But I feel that the opportunity afforded me by the Mayor to serve the community in so important a sphere of activity is one that I cannot pass up.

Sincerely yours,
Alan W. Furness

INTER-OFFICE CORRESPONDENCE

In concerns of any size a good many memos pass between departments, between the management and the staff, between individuals in different departments, etc. Thus the Stock Department may inform the Sales Department of the arrival of certain needed goods; or the management will send memoranda to department heads about certain changes of policy; or it may send a memo to the entire staff about price changes, the announcement of a special holiday, etc.; or a salesman may send a note to Shipping giving special instructions regarding the shipment of an order; or Promotion may send a memo to Sales and other departments concerned, reminding them of the start of a national advertising campaign so that they can prepare for the anticipated inquiries and orders.

Most firms provide printed forms and restrict inter-office correspondence to one subject only in order to encourage conciseness and clarity and to facilitate filing and reference. The printed forms also assure that the date, the department, the person, and the subject are clearly indicated. This makes salutations and signatures superfluous and they are omitted except in memoranda with a deliberately personal touch.

Although such notes are "stripped for action," the tone should nevertheless always be courteous. Inter-departmental feuds have often begun over tactless expression in such memoranda. And office morale has sometimes been damaged by an unintended curt note by management. Certain indispensable formalities of respect should be observed in inter-office correspondence as in other forms. Examples:

Form G-14
Inter-Office Memorandum

| One Subject Only |
| Made Simple Books, Inc. |

To:
Department:
Subject:

From:
Department:
Date:

* * *

To: Staffs
Department: Sales, Correspondence
Subject: New Price List

From: J. B. Wolcott
Department: Management
Date: April 10, 1954

On May 1, our new price-list goes into effect. Copies should be in the hands of all our salesmen before the end of the week and in the hands of our dealers by April 28. Copies can be obtained from Miss Andrews.

* * *

To: Staffs
Department: All departments
Subject: July 4 Holiday

From: G. E. Anderson
Department: Personnel
Date: July 1, 1954

Since July 4, this year, falls on a Sunday, the office will be closed Monday, July 5, to allow a full holiday weekend.

* * *

To: Mr. Taylor, Mr. Green, Mr. Johns, Mr. Maxfield
Department: Sales, Shipping, Personnel, Accounting
Subject: Advertising campaign

From: Edward Earnshaw
Department: Promotion
Date: February 10, 1954

This weekend our special advertising campaign on our new Infra-Red cooker opens with full pages in the magazine supplements of metropolitan newspapers. There will be page ads in leading national magazines, along with other promotion. Most of the advertising will carry keyed coupons. Your departments should be prepared for the special load of mail that will come in. Just a reminder.

* * *

To: E. Dirksen
Department: Shipping
Subject: Johnson Brothers order

From: J. Myers
Department: Sales
Date: January 11, 1954

Dear Ed:

When Billing sends down the Johnson Brothers' order, please put a note on it to double wrap the shipment. Old Mr. Johnson complains that our wrapping paper isn't thick enough. The trouble is in his storeroom, which is a filthy, damp place. So it'll be best to double wrap his stuff, or he'll come back at us with claims for spoilage. Hope it's not too much bother. Thanks.

Joe

CONTINENTAL TOOLING SERVICE, INC.

19 WEST FOURTH ST., DAYTON 2, OHIO

H. E. FOLKERTH, MGR.   •   TELEPHONE HE-9737

Formerly Continental Design Service

WE OUGHT TO GET TOGETHER

DOG-gone it!

I want to put in another PLUG for Continental Tooling
Service.

I'd like to do it in person. I'd like to tell you all
about Continental ... about the long, nine years on the
average, experience of our men ... about all the DIVER-
SIFIED work we've been doing ... about our efforts to
keep up to and a little ahead of date with our designs
... about the way we can work WITH your own tool department ... about the tools we've designed to cut down
production costs for dozens of companies ... about our
constant effort to see that every single tool we make
is ...

Cheap ... Simple ... Good.

But, as long as I'm doing it in a letter -- and a letter
that starts out with a dog and his unofficial headquarters
at that -- I'd better just say:

When it comes to tool design, we want you to consider us
as stable and dependable as a fire-plug and as eager and
enthusiastic as a pup ... we'd like to TELL you the whole
story. In short, DOG-gone it ...

We ought to get together,

H. E. Folkerth

Fig. 38. In offering the services of his firm to prospective customers,
the writer of this letter has employed a device more often associated
with the sales letter—using both pictorial illustration and a variety of
verbal references in the text of the letter which sustain the pictorial
idea. Again, we urge discretion and call attention to the possible dangers of such an approach: the "cuteness" of the idea, intended to attract and sustain attention and amusement, may instead offend and
revolt.

Other types of memo forms frequently used are:

From the Desk of Frank Gannon

To: —————————— Date: ——————

To: —————————— Date: ——————

From: ——————

It might be noted, in passing, that in large corporations or organizations, intra-company mail is frequently placed in heavy-stock envelopes that can be used over and over again. These envelopes have ruled lines on the outside, and the sender need merely place on the first free line the name and department of the person to whom the communication is addressed. That person in turn can use the same envelope by doing similarly the next time he wishes to dispatch a memo or some papers to another person in the organization.

GOOD-WILL LETTERS

It should be enough, of course, to service customers promptly and efficiently. Yet it is human for them to want to be appreciated as well and to be given personal attention. If thanking a customer for his order has been overlooked, write him a special note of appreciation for his business.

Letting customers feel that they are "in" on your operations is another way of building their good will. If you are expanding your business, or promoting a man on your staff with whom your customers may have had occasion to become acquainted, or if you are making any operational change of interest to them, let your customers know about it.

If you are making gifts—calendars, personal memo-pads, initialed pencils, etc.,—to new customers, don't leave the old customers out. Give it to them, also.

There are also occasions and circumstances that might be used for the promotion of good will by drawing attention to them. We have already mentioned letters of congratulation and letters of sympathy and condolence. Watch significant dates in the lives or careers of customers, when it is possible or advisable—anniversaries of the concern, birthdays of the officers, marriages in their families, and send congratulations and appropriate gifts. Send Christmas greetings to all customers, and mail them well in advance of the rush period, so that they don't come so late as to seem like afterthoughts.

Unusual occurrences may be made the occasion for a good-will note. Thus when Lever Brothers were constructing their striking New York building, they sent letters to all in the neighborhood within range of the sounds of construction, private families in nearby residential blocks as well as business neighbors, apologizing for the noise. They gave assurance that everything was being done to finish the building as soon as possible and that all avoidable construction sounds were being eliminated.

During the recent period of rapid and successive price boosts some firms notified their customers that they were not raising their prices though raw-material costs had risen; and others explained what they were doing to absorb part of the necessary price advances in operational economies.

Good will within an organization is as important as the good will of outside customers and neighbors. Well run concerns make use of their inter-office correspondence to keep up office morale through informational memoranda that make the staff feel they are part of what is happening: through announcements that will please the staff; and through personal notes of congratulation from management on

```
            IT HAPPENED IN ROME


Gentlemen:

I recently flew to Europe via XYZ and also used XYZ
services while in Europe.  The service of your per-
sonnel throughout was excellent.

Particularly, I am writing about the personnel in
your city ticket office on Via Marconi in Rome.
They were of great assistance to me, and went far
beyond their normal line of duty on my behalf.

I had a small handbag that needed to have the zipper
repaired.  The manner in which the personnel at your
Rome office took care of it was very highly appreciated.

                            Sincerely yours,

                            Robert Stevens
```

```
            XYZ PRESIDENT REPLIES


Dear Mr. Stevens:

Thanks very much for your letter which was forwarded
to my New York Office.  I certainly appreciate your
nice comments about our services, and especially
those for our personnel in Rome.

In training our personnel, courtesy and efficiency
are repeatedly stressed, and nothing pleases me more
than to learn when our people have excelled in per-
formance of their duties.  I'm sure our personnel in
Rome will be happy to know of your praise, and I am
passing along your nice comments -- adding my personal
thanks for the fine job.

Your selection of XYZ and your interest in writing are
greatly valued.  We shall anticipate the opportunity
of extending our services often, and I hope you will
continue to receive fine treatment all along the XYZ
way whenever we are privileged to serve you.

                            Sincerely,

                            Howard W. London, President
```

Fig. 39. A courtesy letter from a pleased and satisfied customer; and a letter in kind from the firm, inviting the customer to make future use of the firm's services. Although not part of "routine" business letter writing, the value of such letters cannot be exaggerated. Indeed, such letters *should* be regarded as a "routine" element in the conduct of business.

pleasant occasions, such as the birth of children, the graduation of sons, etc.; and condolences in bereavements. Examples:

Dear Mr. Smythe:

The enclosed is the latest issue of our house organ, *Cuttings*. I am sure you will be interested in the piece on page twelve, on the old Smythe Tool Works which, I believe, were founded by your great-grandfather.

Would you like to get *Cuttings* regularly? I'd have it sent without asking if it weren't for my own experience. I groan at the amount of unsolicited mail I get from people who send it with the best of intentions; there aren't enough hours in the day to read everything that comes through the mail. So for that reason I have made it a policy to send *Cuttings* only if customers let us know that they want it. Incidentally, I shall be happy to send you as many copies of this issue as you may require.

Sincerely yours,

Gabriel Harcourt

Dear Mr. Connor:

It occurred to me, recently, that it was just about ten years ago that I entered your first order with our company in my order book. I was not then sales manager, of course—that came as the result of the good orders you and other friendly customers favored me with.

To make sure, I had my secretary look it up, and it turned out, sure enough, that our business connections did begin ten years ago, this month! That first order, incidentally, was for an assortment of our fans. Your latest order is for air conditioners! Time does move.

If we could get together today, we'd be celebrating the glad occasion properly at Ludlow's or Keen's. But since that's not possible, here's the next best thing. Please join me in a glass of champagne of a kind I've found particularly palatable. A case of it should be in your office this morning if American Express is on its toes.

Your health and best wishes for ten more good years of business together.

Cordially,

Ed Schacht

Dear Mr. Alter:

We prepared a map for use by our office staff of the new city postal zones. It proved to be such a convenience that we decided to print up copies for our customers. Here's your copy and we hope you'll find it useful.

Sincerely yours,

Conrad Dietrichstein

Dear Mr. Freud:

As a customer of the Hooker Hat Company you will be interested to know that we have just completed negotiations which bring this fine firm into our organization. It was our desire to fill out our line of men's furnishings with a quality hat line, and Hooker was our choice.

We were glad, of course, that with so fine a product we could make the acquaintance of new customers appreciative of fine quality apparel for men.

We want to assure you that you will continue to receive the efficient service you have become accustomed to from the Hooker staff (which is being preserved intact), plus, we venture to add, special services made possible by the facilities of our larger organization.

On his next call your Hooker salesman will have our other lines of quality goods to offer you. We are mailing you our catalogue so that you may become acquainted with them. Any orders you wish to place from the catalogue will be credited to the salesman's account, and you will be billed on the same terms as in your account with Hooker.

Please let us know if there is any way that we can be of service to you. I look forward to the continuance of what I hope will be a pleasant and profitable relationship for us both.

Sincerely yours,

A. E. Handley

Dear Mr. Gates:

Thank you for your order number 112, which arrived this morning. It will be shipped today; the invoice is enclosed.

The same company is making a new line of waffle irons, and the introductory offer is so attractive we decided to call it to the attention of all our customers. We have tested the device and found it sturdy and efficient. We are enclosing a circular giving the details. Perhaps you'll want to take advantage of this offer.

Sincerely yours,

Morton James

2 enclosures

Dear Mr. Magnus:

Thank you for your order of Clover Danish Blue Cheese. It is being shipped to you today.

I think you will be interested in seeing a copy of a periodical we issue, *Good Cheer*, which contains recipes and notes about new European delicacies being introduced to American lovers of good foods. If you would like to receive it regularly, we shall be glad to put you on our mailing list.

Sincerely yours,

1 enclosure

REQUESTS FOR CHARITY

Although the solicitation of contributions for charity is a highly specialized, professional activity these days, businessmen frequently have occasion to sell theater tickets or to ask for donations for a pet organization. In such cases make your letter brief; leave the "selling" to the professional fund-raiser. You will get a check because the person you are writing to knows you, and values your friendship or patronage. Some examples:

Dear Mr. Adams:

I am taking the liberty of sending you the enclosed advertising blank in behalf of the United Orphans League. I am very much interested in the organization and know of its good work and great need. I shall appreciate your check to the best of your ability. With many thanks and good wishes, I am,

Sincerely yours,

Sam Laury

Dear Ben:

Enclosed are a couple of tickets for "Ah, Take the Cash." The seats are not so good, and I don't know anything about the show, but the cause is good. So I'd appreciate your taking the tickets and letting me have your check for $20 made out to the Community Chest. I hope you will enjoy the show and have the double satisfaction of knowing you've aided a worthy cause.

Sincerely yours,

Norman Rich

Although it is desirable to keep letters of this type short, they can vary in tone, length, and appeal if in the judgment of the writer, the nature of his relationship with the person to whom he is writing requires more than the semi-formal approach illustrated above.

EXAMPLE OF AN ACCEPTANCE LETTER

Dear Mr. Bingham:

I am happy to send you the enclosed check for the theater tickets you sent me. I know the cause is a good one, and I hope the project is a success. Keep up the good work.

Sincerely yours,

David K. Nelson

PAYMENTS BY MAIL

In payments by mail the remittance should be such as can be convertible into cash without expense and with a minimum of trouble to the recipient. The sender should secure evidence, wherever possible, that the money was sent and that it was received.

Remittances may be made by check (personal or certified), money order (postal or express), bank drafts, stamps, or currency. (If currency has to be mailed, it is advisable to send it in a registered letter, particularly if the sum is large; in such case the sender gets a receipt that the envelope has been delivered. In no way does this serve as a receipt for the contents.)

CURRENCY AND STAMPS

Currency or stamps are used when the remittance is under a dollar. Mail order advertisers urge this because readers are more apt to respond, when such remittances are called for.

In mail order letters, coin cards are often enclosed to facilitate payment by that means. These cards are made of cardboard from which holes, the sizes of the required coins, have been cut. A paper flap is attached to fold over the coins and keep them in place.

Home made cards to fill the same purpose are easy to prepare. If the coins do not fit into the holes exactly, they can be held in place by scotch tape or rubber bands.

When the remittance is in stamps, insert them into a small envelope or fold them into waxed paper, which will prevent the gummed surfaces from sticking.

POSTAL MONEY ORDER

A safe, cheap, and convenient method for transmitting money is available at any post office. By this method the sender is assured that the money reaches the person for whom it is intended, though neither sender nor recipient is identified on the receipt.

EXPRESS MONEY ORDERS

Postal money orders may not exceed $100 per individual order. In larger amounts the rates are higher than those of the express companies. Express money orders have one big advantage over postal money orders. The form includes the name of the sender and must be endorsed by the recipient. The completed form is kept on file at the express company; thus there is a record of the complete transaction.

CHECKS

Checks are probably the most convenient form of payment. Most banks provide two types of checking service—**regular,** which generally requires maintaining a stipulated average balance during the month; and **special,** which permits the writing of checks at a set fee, usually ten cents, per check. After endorsement and clearance, the check is returned to the maker and serves as a receipt and permanent record. For a small fee banks also furnish **cashier's checks** in exchange for cash, and can be made out to anyone indicated by the purchaser; a receipt is given.

CERTIFIED CHECKS

Certified checks are used when it is necessary to assure the recipient that the check is good. A certified check is an ordinary check on whose face there is stamped or written certification by the cashier of the bank on which it is drawn. This indicates that the bank has deducted the amount of the check from the drawer's account and has assumed responsibility for payment.

BANK DRAFTS

A bank draft is a written order for money from one bank to another. It is a convenient way of paying a bill incurred in another community, is more convenient than a check, since the recipient receives cash immediately and does not have to wait until a check is cleared.

Suppose a man in New York wishes to buy

certain goods in Boston. He asks his New York bank for a draft for the necessary sum. He is charged a small sum for this service, usually twenty cents per $100. Endorsing the draft by writing on the back of it, "Pay to the order of (name of Boston firm)" and signing his name underneath, he sends the draft on to Boston.

Figure 40

FORM OF CHECK

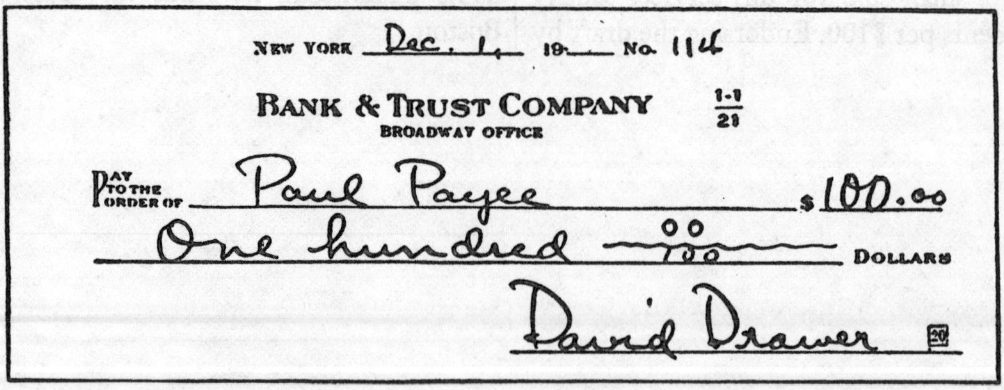

NEW YORK _Dec. 1,_ 19__ No. _114_

BANK & TRUST COMPANY $\frac{1\text{-}1}{21}$
BROADWAY OFFICE

PAY TO THE ORDER OF _Paul Payee_ $_100.00_

One hundred ——— $\frac{00}{100}$ ——— DOLLARS

David Drawer

A check is really a bill of exchange which is always drawn on a bank and always payable on demand.

Figure 41

FORM OF BILL OF EXCHANGE

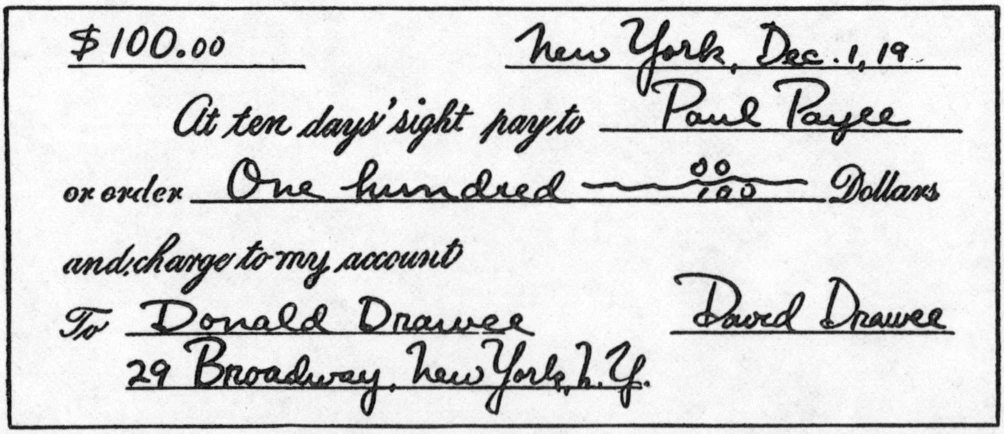

_$100.00_   _New York, Dec. 1, 19_

At ten days' sight pay to _Paul Payee_

or order _One hundred_ ——— $\frac{00}{100}$ ——— _Dollars_

and charge to my account

_To_ _Donald Drawee_   _David Drawee_
29 Broadway, New York, N.Y.

A bill of exchange or draft, often used for collection of debts owed to the drawer by the drawee, is an order addressed by one person to another, requiring the addressee (drawee) to pay on demand, or at a fixed or determinable future time, a certain sum of money, to the payee or to his order or to the bearer.

CHAPTER TEN

POST CARDS AND TELEGRAMS

POST CARDS

In general use the words **post card** and **postal card** are interchangeable. But the Post Office makes this distinction: A **postal card** is the one issued by the government, with the stamp imprinted; a **post card** is a private mailing card with a stamp affixed or metered on.

The advantages of the post card are that it makes possible brevity and economy. Where a message need not be elaborate or detailed, post cards serve particularly well. Economy in cost is not in the low postage alone. In correspondence, cost of dictation, typing, filing, and handling far exceed postage costs. Therefore, post cards, which reduce such costs to a minimum, are favored wherever other considerations, such as making an impression, do not count.

Business houses commonly use post cards in sending for catalogues or acknowledging requests for catalogues, in acknowledging mail orders for low-cost articles, in announcing sales or receipt of new stock, and in minor or routine procedures.

In post card correspondence, salutations, complimentary closings or even signatures may be dispensed with. The nature of the communication determines their use. Examples:

Gentlemen: Please send us three copies of your fall and winter catalogues. S. W. Wilson Co. (address)

Gentlemen: The catalogues you requested will not be ready for ten days. Copies will be mailed to you as soon as possible.

Dear Madam: We regret that the Neon lamp specified in your order is temporarily out of stock. We expect a new supply in a few days and will ship your order as soon as stock arrives. Yours sincerely, Lamplighter, Inc.

Dear Sir: Thank you for your order for the smoked turkey. It is being shipped today. Yours sincerely, Concord Turkey Farms.

Dear Madam: The new Flora Bailey sweaters, adapted to the new swing skirt style, and exclusive with us, will be in Wednesday morning. Come early to make sure you get your pick. The Madison Shop.

Dear Madam: One of our employees, bearing an identifying badge, will call next week to inspect your gas fixtures to see whether any adjustments will be necessary in the changeover to natural gas, explained in our letter to you last month.

TELEGRAMS

Next to direct communication by telephone or radio, the fastest means of sending a message is via a full-rate telegram. It is accepted any time, night or day, for immediate transmission.

Day letter-telegrams can be used for messages which can be deferred slightly in handling and still serve their purpose. They are cheaper and therefore more economical where messages must be long and don't require immediate transmission.

Night letter-telegrams are accepted up to 2 A.M. for delivery the following morning.

Sending money by telegraph is the quickest way to transmit money over distances. Bring money to the nearest Western Union office where, for a small fee, it will be telegraphed to its destination.

POINTERS ON TELEGRAPHING

Don't try to economize on words in the address. Since no charge is made for words in the address that will facilitate delivery, include whatever will be helpful—apartment number, hotel room number, office number, etc. In domestic telegrams you may include the name of the company; alternative recipients (e.g., Robert Smith or John Jones); the words "**Attention of,**" if written under the name of a company; the words "**care of,**" or a telephone number if the message may be phoned in.

If the word "**personal**" is used, it will refer only to the contents of the message. To ensure delivery to the addressee alone, add the words "**Personal Delivery Only**" to the addressee's name.

The common practice is not to use **Mr.** before a man's name, but abbreviated titles like **Dr.** or **Prof.** are permissible. **Mrs.** or **Miss** may be used in addressing women.

If it is prearranged for the addressee to call for the telegram, use the line "**will call**" under his name in the address.

If the message is being sent to a hotel or other public place, the words "**hold for arrival**" may be included. In addition, a time for delivery may be specified, such as "**deliver at 10 A.M.,**" and may be included in the address without charge.

In the signature, an identifying title, such as "**Cora Weil, Secretary,**" may be added without charge.

TO SAVE WORDS

It is wise to write out a message first, using all the words that seem useful; then, words that can be spared may be cut in order to bring the message down to the 15-word minimum. Here is an example of a message as first set down and then cut:

> Called away on urgent business. Will not be able to see you Wednesday. Will be back following week and will be available any time any day. Fix date with my secretary.

> Called away urgent business. Cancel Wednesday. Available any time next week. Fix date my secretary.

Initials in the text of a telegram are counted as separate words if spaced out as in A. B. Jones; but if written together as ABC Jones, the three initials count as one word.

Numbers containing up to five characters count as one word. Each space, decimal point, etc., counts as a character. Thus four numerals and a decimal point, e.g., 25.22 count as one word, while 253.22 counts as two words.

In fractions the dividing bar counts as a character. Thus 14½ counts as one word, but 141½ as two words.

Signs such as $, %, #, &, ' for feet or minutes, and " for inches or seconds, count as characters; but not @, ¢, and *, because these are not on the teleprinter used in sending telegrams. The latter group, therefore, has to be spelled out.

Abbreviations up to 5 letters, with or without periods, but **without spacing,** count as one word, cod, or c.o.d. but not c. o. d.; NY or N.Y., but not N. Y., etc.

Coined words in which several words are packed into one, and which have become common also count as one word. For example, **retel** (re your telegram); **urtel** (your telegram); **artel** (our telegram); **mytel** (my telegram); etc.

Code words may be sent in domestic telegrams. In code messages five letters count as a word. They should be typed out, all in capitals.

WESTERN UNION

1207   10-51

W. P. MARSHALL, PRESIDENT

DOMESTIC SERVICE

Check the class of service desired;
otherwise this message will be
sent as a full rate telegram

FULL RATE TELEGRAM
DAY LETTER
NIGHT LETTER

INTERNATIONAL SERVICE

Check the class of service desired;
otherwise the message will be
sent at the full rate

FULL RATE
LETTER TELEGRAM
SHIP RADIOGRAM

NO. W.DS.—CL. OF SVC.   PD. OR COLL.   CASH NO.   CHARGE TO THE ACCOUNT OF   TIME FILED

George R. Burnett

Send the following message, subject to the terms on back hereof, which are hereby agreed to

To _____ Henry Compton Green _____ April 15   1955

Street and No. _____ 127 Main Street
Care of or
Apt. No. _____ Place Wilmington, Delaware

Temporarily out stock you ordered. Would you
accept pastels instead?

Sender's name and address (For reference)
George R. Burnett
1819 Madison Avenue
New York, New York

Sender's telephone number

SU 7-2683

Fig. 42. The principle of a good telegram is to compose it so that, without slightest sacrifice of clarity, all unnecessary words are eliminated.

72 (Rev. 3-50)

WESTERN UNION
TELEGRAPHIC
MONEY ORDER

W. P. MARSHALL, PRESIDENT

THE FASTEST
AND SAFEST
WAY TO SEND
OR RECEIVE
MONEY

A MESSAGE
WITH YOUR
MONEY ORDER
IS ALWAYS
WELCOME

Send the following Money Order subject to conditions below and on back hereof, which are hereby agreed to:

CHECK   TIME FILED

SENDING DATA   OFFICE   DATE _____ 19___

ACCTG INFM.

$ AMT.
$ CHGS.
E TOLLS
TAX
TOTAL

MOD

AMOUNT ☞   Eight Hundred and Fifty _____ DOLLARS AND 00 CENTS

PROOF AMOUNT DOLLARS   FIGURES

PAY TO   Sidney J. Porter

PLEASE PRINT. IF WOMAN, GIVE MRS. OR MISS

STREET ADDRESS   Pacific Hotel, State Street

DESTINATION AND SENDER   Seattle, Washington _____ Aubrey L. Nell

DESTINATION   NAME OF SENDER

WRITE YOUR MESSAGE HERE ONLY   Approve request purchase shipment Lot Number 1728;

A FEW CENTS PER WORD   but only blue and brown colors. Notify us immediately

WILL BE DELIVERED WITH MONEY ORDER   upon conclusion of transaction.

● Unless signed below the Telegraph Company is directed to pay this money order at my risk to such person as its paying agent believes to be the above named payee, personal identification being waived.

Aubrey Lloyd Nell

SENDER'S FULL NAME

111-15 Fifth Ave., New York, N.Y. MU 3-7650

SENDER'S ADDRESS   TELEPHONE NUMBER

Information for test question: _____

Fig. 43. The swiftest and most effective method of transmitting money. In the message section, apply the same principles which hold for the telegram.

PUNCTUATION AND FORM

The comma, period, colon, question mark, parentheses, dash, hyphen, quotation marks, and apostrophe, but not the exclamation point (which is not on the teleprinter), are not charged for in telegrams. In cables, however, such punctuation is charged for.

Double space all telegrams no matter how long. Except for code words use ordinary type, not all capitals. Telegrams are received in all caps because the teleprinter keys are in caps.

The communications agencies furnish regular forms for dispatches, but any plain paper, preferably white or yellow, may be used. Telegram blanks need not be used for the extra sheets if the message runs beyond one page.

PHONETIC CODE

In telephoning a message, words or names difficult to transmit should be spelled out. Correct spelling can be facilitated by supplying key words, familiar and easy to pronounce and hear, and that begin with the letter for which the key word is being used. The following phonetic code is used in telegraph offices:

A for Adams	J for John	S for Sugar
B for Boston	K for King	T for Thomas
C for Chicago	L for Lincoln	U for Union
D for Denver	M for Mary	V for Victor
E for Edward	N for New York	W for William
F for Frank	O for Ocean	X for X-ray
G for George	P for Peter	Y for Young
H for Henry	Q for Queen	Z for Zero
I for Ida	R for Robert	

TELEGRAMS IN BUSINESS

Telegrams are often used to inform about delays or problems in delivery:

Shipment, order 211, due yesterday, unreceived. Will return if not delivered before end week.

Sales departments may use telegrams to stimulate business:

New spring models in showroom Thursday. Come morning to make sure your pick.

Night letter telegrams are often used by collection departments to emphasize urgency. Profane or abusive language or threats must be avoided:

No reply to our letters. This is notice account must be settled before end of week. Urge immediate remittance to avoid trouble and legal costs. Will place with attorney if settlement is not made this week.

Telegrams constitute a regular form of business correspondence, and should be treated as such. Make carbon copies of all messages dispatched and file them. While economy of expression reduces the transmission cost of a message, the saving should not be made at the expense of effectiveness or completeness. Watch the tone of the language used.

Cable messages are generally followed up with an air mail letter to the addressee repeating and amplifying the cable dispatch.

SUMMARY OF SPELLING RULES

	RULE	EXAMPLES	EXCEPTIONS

IE and EI	I before E, except after C.	achieve, but ceiling	1. Use EI when:
			  a. Sounded as $\bar{a}$: neighbor, weigh
			  b. Sounded as $\breve{\imath}$: counterfeit
			  c. Sounded as i: height
			2. Use IE for almost all other sounds: friend, lieutenant.
			3. If i and e do not form a digraph, rules do not apply: fiery, deity.

Final Silent E	1. **Drop** before suffix beginning with a vowel. 2. **Retain** before suffix beginning with a consonant.	grieve—grievance absolute—absolutely	1. Retain e after soft c and soft g before suffixes beginning with a or o: peaceable, manageable.
Final Y	1. **Change** final y to i if y is preceded by a consonant and followed by any suffix except one beginning with i. 2. **Retain** final y if it is preceded by a vowel.	beauty—beautiful BUT carry—carrying boy—boys; valley—valleys	dry—dryness; sly—slyness. day—daily; pay—paid

Final Consonants	**Double** final consonants when:
	1. Preceded by a single vowel.
	2. Followed by a suffix beginning with a vowel.
	3. The consonant terminates a monosyllabic word.
	4. The consonant terminates a polysyllabic word accented on the last syllable.
		1. drop—dropped;
		  beg—beggar
		2. quit—quitting;
		  swim—swimmer
		3. hit—hitter;
		  run—running
		4. omit—omitted;
		  transfer—transferred
			Final consonant is not doubled if:
			1. Accent shifts to preceding syllable when suffix is added: confer'—confer'ring BUT con'ference.
			2. Final consonant is already doubled: start—started.
			3. Final consonant is preceded by two vowels: beat—beating; boil—boiling.

k added to words ending in c	**Add** k to words ending in c before a suffix beginning with e, i, y.	frolic—frolicking—frolicked; picnic—picnicking—picnicked	
-cede -ceed -sede	Except for supersede, exceed, proceed, succeed, all words having this sound end in -cede.	accede, precede, recede, concede	

Plurals	1. Regular noun plurals add -s to the singular.
	2. Irregular plurals:
	  a. Add -es if noun ends in o preceded by consonant.
	  b. Change y to i and add -es if noun ends in y preceded by consonant.
	  c. Add -s if noun ends in y preceded by vowel.
		boy—boys;
		book—books
		
		a. echo—echoes;
		  Negro—Negroes
		b. sky—skies;
		  enemy—enemies
		
		c. play—plays;
		  day—days
			a. piano—pianos; zero—zeros; solo—solos.

SUMMARY OF SPELLING RULES (*continued*)

	RULE	EXAMPLES	EXCEPTIONS
Possessives	1. Don't confuse contractions with possessive pronouns.	*Contraction* *Possessive* 1. *Pronoun* it's (it is) its they're their (they are)	
	2. Use no apostrophes with possessive or relative pronouns.	2. *his, hers, ours, yours, theirs, whose*	
	3. If singular or plural noun does **not** end in *s*, add **apostrophe** and *s*.	3. prince—prince's (Sing.), princes' (Plur.); soldier —soldier's (Sing.), soldiers' (Plur.)	
	4. If singular or plural noun **does** end in *s*, add apostrophe.	4. hostess—hostess' (Sing.), hostesses' (Plur.); Jones—Jones' (Sing.), Joneses' (Plur.)	

SPELLING LISTS. List of Words Most Frequently Misspelled by High School Seniors.

The list of words below* contains 149 words most frequently misspelled by high school seniors. These words and word-groups (those which are variants of the same word, as *acquaint* and *acquaintance*), were compiled by Dean Thomas Clark Pollock of New York University from 14,651 examples of misspelling submitted by 297 teachers in the United States, Canada and Hawaii. Each of the words represented was misspelled twenty times or more, and yet these words, comprising fewer than three per cent of the original list of 3,811 words, account for thirty per cent of the total misspellings.

NOTE: The trouble spots in each word are italicized. Numbers beside the words indicate how frequently each word was misspelled.

the*i*r	179	a*ll* right	91	*i*ts	52
rec*ei*ve	163	separate	91	i*t's*	22
too	152	unti*l*	88		
		privi*l*ege	82	*occu*r	9
writer	11	defin*i*te	78	*occu*rred	52
writing	81	the*r*e	78	*occu*rrence	10
written	13	bel*ie*ve	77	*occu*rring	2

*The list compiled by Dr. Pollock appears in the *Teachers Service Bulletin in English* (Macmillan, November, 1952).

describe	28	*study*	1	prob*a*bly	33
description	38	stud*i*ed	3	speech	33
		stud*i*es	3	arg*u*ment	32
tragedy	64	stud*y*ing	34	*image*	3
decide	48	conven*i*ence	5	*imag*ine	7
*decis*ion	15	conven*i*ent	33	*imag*inary	5
		difference	15	*imag*ination	17
occasion	54	*different*	23	qu*i*et	32
*occasion*ally	8			the*n*	32
		tha*n*	38		
succeed	25	*athletic*	37	pre*j*udice	30
success	22	*to*	37	sens*e*	30
*success*ful	12	*business*	36	sim*i*lar	30
interest	56	equip*p*ed	21	*your*	2
beginning	55	equip*p*ment	14	*you're*	28
immediate	3	*principal*	18	ap*p*earance	29
immediately	51	*principle*	18	cons*cious*	29
				pleas*a*nt	29
coming	53	*prophecy*	35	*stop*	1
embarrass	48	*prophesy*	35	stop*p*ed	24
grammar	47	*benefit*	16	stop*p*ing	4
		beneficial	5		
humor	2	*benefited*	11	surprise	29
humorous	45	*benefiting*	1	*excite*	1
exist	3	*develop*	34	*excited*	7
existence	43	*environ*ment	34	*excitement*	13
		recommend	34	*exciting*	7
lose	28	*fascinate*	33	experience	28
losing	15	finally	33	govern*m*ent	27
				laboratory	27
disappoint	42	*necessary*	24	tr*i*ed	27
rhythm	41	*necessity*	9		

acquaint	17	foreign	14	familiar	21	maintenance	referred
acquaintance	9	foreigners	9	escape	21	marriage	relieve
				meant	21	mischievous	rhythm
affect	26	performance	23	where	21	noticeable	schedule
accept	25	together	23	chief	20	occasion	seize
accommodate	25	descend	13			occurred	separate
excellent	25	descendant	9	hero	10	occurrence	shining
opportunity	25	during	22	heroes	9	o'clock	stationery
marry	4	forty	22	heroine	1	omitted	strength
marries	6	woman	22			parallel	succeed
marriage	15	certain	21	lonely	20		
				opinion	20	perhaps	superintendent
character	24	commit	4	parliament	20	principal	supersede
complete	24	committed	12	possess	20	principles	tragedy
friend	24	committing	5	professor	20	privilege	tries
				restaurant	20	proceed	truly
truly	24	criticism	21	villain	20	pronunciation	villain
accidentally	23	disappear	21			quiet	Wednesday
doesn't	23	exaggerate	21			quite	weird
						received	whether
						recommend	woman

List of 100 Words Most Frequently Misspelled by College Freshmen.

absence	conscientious	forth
accidentally	conscious	forty
across	coolly	fourth
aggravate	council	friend
all right	counsel	government
amateur	criticism	grammar
argument	deceive	grievance
around	definite	hadn't
athletic	desert	height
believed	dessert	indispensable
benefited	dining	interested
business	disappointed	its
busy	doesn't	it's
capital	don't	knowledge
cemetery	effect	laboratory
choose	eighth	latter
chosen	embarrassed	literature
coming	environment	loose
committee	exercise	lose
competition	February	losing

List of Words Frequently Misspelled on Civil Service Examinations.

accident	municipal	society
all right	principal	simplified
auxiliary	principle	technicality
athletic	promotional	tendency
buoyant	president	their
catalogue		thousandth
career	precede	transferred
comptroller	proceed	transient
criticise	promissory	truly
dividend	recommend	villain
	personnel	
embarrass	purchasable	Wednesday
expedient	responsibility	writ
government	received	whether
inveigle	regrettable	yield
monetary	supersede	

PUNCTUATION

The general trend to simplicity and informality in modern letter-writing applies to punctuation also. Letter-writers, today, use only about half the punctuation regarded as correct half a century ago. The Government Printing Office Style Manual declares, "The general principles covering the use of punctuation are (1) that if it does not clarify the text, it should be omitted; and (2) that in the choice and placing of punctuation marks, the sole aim should be to bring out more clearly the author's thought."

The following material was adapted from *English Made Simple* by Arthur Waldhorn and Arthur Zeiger (Made Simple Books, Inc., New York, 1954), with the examples in business English.

END PUNCTUATION

End marks of punctuation point out that a sentence has come to a full stop. (The end or sentence marks of punctuation are sometimes called full stops.)

THE PERIOD

Use the period to mark the end of a declarative sentence, or of an imperative sentence that issues its command mildly rather than forcefully.

Thank you for your order of May 10.
File complaints with Mr. Conrad.

THE QUESTION MARK

Use the question mark (interrogation point) to mark the end of interrogative sentence (sentence asking a question).

What colors does your Candlelight hosiery line come in?

Where a sentence consists of one or more successive or related questions several question marks may be used inside the sentence:

When were the goods shipped, and where? this week or last week? to our Newark or our Jersey City store?

Question marks may be used to indicate uncertainty:

We can take an example from this old firm, established in 1890 (?), which uses completely up-to-date methods.

WHEN NOT TO USE QUESTION MARKS

When the query is indirect:

We should like to know why you found the goods unsatisfactory.

In courtesy questions such as: "May we hear from you." In this case, while the trend is to drop the question mark, the former style of using it is still general enough to make the use of the question mark optional.

THE EXCLAMATION POINT

Exclamation points are used:
After exclamations, whether full sentences, clauses or phrases:

We decidedly cannot permit such delays in payment!
It is now ten days past the promised delivery date—a delay which cannot be tolerated!
Please ship our order without further delay!

The exclamation point may also be used to mark a vigorous interjection or emotion in addressing somebody by name or title:

What a question!
Mr. President! How can you write to stockholders in such terms!

159

WHEN NOT TO USE EXCLAMATION POINTS

When they do not serve a really essential purpose. Overuse of exclamation points results in what is called the "schoolgirl style." Mild exclamations do not call for exclamation points. A congratulatory business report which concludes,

"It was a high production figure to set, but we accomplished it,"

is better without than with the exclamation mark unless a special emphasis is intended.

THE COMMA

The comma serves to separate elements of a sentence; it is the most frequent but the least emphatic of punctuation marks used inside a sentence.

USES OF THE COMMA

To separate two independent clauses joined by a coordinating conjunction (**and, but, or, nor, for, either—or, neither—nor**), except when the clauses are short and closely related.

Delayed deliveries mean lost sales and lost sales mean lost customers.

It may be a temporary convenience for you to withhold payment, but the long term injury to your credit standing will outweigh any such advantage.

To separate a series of three or more words, phrases, or clauses:

The qualities to aim for in business correspondence are simplicity, conciseness, accuracy, and fact.

Mr. Dixon has the experience you require, the friendly approach that holds customers, and a resourcefulness and confidence that enable him to tackle his assignments without fumbling and hesitation.

Always make sure of the credit terms, of the delivery date, and of shipping instructions.

(In such series the trend, today, is to place the comma before the **and** or **or**; but so many writers omit it that its use is optional. Whichever style you use, be consistent and omit or retain the comma throughout.)

To separate two adjectives each of which individually modifies the noun:

He is a sound, clear-headed businessman.

The comma here takes the place of the conjunction **and.** The sentence might be written, for example, "He is a sound and clear-headed businessman."

The difference may be seen in two adjectives where the second is essentially part of the noun. "He is a brilliant market analyst." It would be an absurdity here to say, "He is a brilliant and market analyst."

To set off a long adverbial clause or phrase coming before the main clause:

When the Monday morning's mail was brought in by my secretary, I looked eagerly for that promised order from you.

Even here the trend is to omit the comma; and if you are inclined to modernism in punctuation, you have the option to do so.

To set off an introductory, verbal phrase (participial, gerund or infinitive):

Having investigated the matter, our accounting department reports that the bill is overdue three and a half months.

After studying your prospects, you may decide that only a fraction of them are worth going after.

To make sure that nothing goes astray, check with the original order before shipping.

The trend here, too, is to omit the comma. You have the option to do so, if you choose.

To set off an absolute phrase in a sentence:

Most people being honest, a suspicious attitude toward new customers is unwarranted.

To avoid confusion where, unless there were a comma, unrelated words would be read together.

In brief, accounts require periodic checking.

To separate the parts of geographical terms, addresses, etc.:

1245 Findlay Avenue, New York 53, N.Y.

To set off nouns in speech openings:

Mr. Chairman, honored guests, ladies and gentlemen:

To separate the year from any of its divisions:

December 25, 1954

(The tendency is to omit the comma between month and year—December 1954.)

To indicate omission of words that are understood:

Good paying customers earn consideration; poor payers, suspicion.

To set off contrasting statements:

What we ask for is fair play, not favors.

To set off non-restrictive phrases and clauses. (Whether an expression is restrictive or not can be simply tested. If its omission materially affects the meaning, it is restrictive; if the sentence could stand without it, it is non-restrictive.)

The directors, who were present, voted for the resolution.

The commas here indicate that the clause, "who were present," is non-restrictive. It is an incidental reference to their presence at the meeting. Without the commas it would restrict the observation to those of "the directors who were present" at the meeting.

To set off parenthetical expressions:

This order, as investigation disclosed, had not been properly entered.

To set off mild interjections:

Why, this sleeve measures an inch shorter than specified!

To set off appositional expressions:

The fact that it was made by Bausch and Lomb, the world-famous name in lenses, is your guarantee of camera-excellence.

To set off a sentence modifier:

Their credit position, nevertheless, is strong.

THE SEMICOLON

In its functions of pause and emphasis, and setting off of parts of sentences, the semicolon stands between the period and the comma.

USES OF THE SEMICOLON

To separate independent clauses not linked by a conjunction:

Man can have only a certain number of teeth, hair and ideas; there comes a time when he necessarily loses his teeth, hair, ideas.

To separate independent clauses linked by a conjunction where punctuation serves to give emphasis:

I know I can count on his business; but I sell him just as if he were a new account.

To separate clauses or phrases already containing commas:

Among those present were Walter Erskine, President of National Housing; Walter Pritchard, President of Tanner's Bank; Elwood McKettrick, President of Hudson Canneries. . . .

To set off a conjunctive adverb (therefore, nevertheless, moreover, etc.):

Mr. Price will be in Chicago in November; therefore, he will be unable to attend the conference.

To set off specifying words (namely, that is, for example, etc.) which introduce explanations or enumerations.

We are especially interested in having a demonstration of one of your lighting systems; namely, the overhead, louvre indirect system on page 16 of your catalogue.

INCORRECT USES OF THE SEMICOLON

In place of a comma to separate subordinate clauses or participial phrases in long sentences:

Mr. Campbell, our Western representative, now on his way back to the home office, where he is to render a full report; (,) has already informed us differently; (,) having met with none of the difficulties you enumerate. (**Note: Commas should be used in place of semicolons.**)

In place of a colon, following the salutation in a letter:

Dear Sir; (:) (**Note: Use the colon here.**)

In place of a comma, following the complimentary close in a letter:

> Sincerely yours; (,) (**Note: Use only the comma here.**)

THE COLON

The colon serves to prepare for some explicit elaboration. It calls for a longer pause than a period.

USES OF THE COLON

To introduce a series:

> There are three kinds of businessmen: the adventurer, the stand-patter, and the one who knows when to venture and when to stand pat.

To introduce a long or formal quotation:

> Mr. Compton wrote: "In these times it is difficult to estimate . . ."

To separate clauses where the second explains, amplifies, or contrasts with the first:

> A businessman needs principles, just as do other men of affairs: in the hurly-burly of trade, this may not be apparent, but when one inquires into most business deals one finds that principles have guided them throughout.

To stress a word, phrase, or clause that follows:

> American business can attribute its success to a single factor: competition.

To close a salutation and introduce the body of a letter:

> Dear Sir:

To separate or explain titles, followed by citations, bibliographical references:

> Mercury: A Magazine of Business

THE DASH

In typing, the dash is formed by two successive strokes of the hyphen key. In printing, it is the larger or m-dash as distinguished from the smaller n-dash used for hyphens. The function of the dash is to emphasize what it sets off. It has somewhat more force than the comma.

USES OF THE DASH

To mark an afterthought or a sudden sharp turn in thinking:

> Most businessmen are honest—at least along lines where custom, tradition, or trade associations have established standards or controls.

> Study your customer before you concoct your sales talk—"according to taste," as the recipes say.

To separate a parenthetical expression from the main communication:

> Mr. Howard's estimates—as market records show—correctly anticipated these changes.

To set off a word or words in apposition or amplification; especially when the words intervene. Commas or parentheses may also be used for this purpose: commas, when close to the main statement; parentheses, when remote. The dash is used for intermediate cases or when emphasis is desired. But individual feeling about the effect desired is the final arbiter:

> We want you to feel that this bonus is given to you not as a reward for sales, but in recognition of the qualities in your work—the resourcefulness and enterprise you have shown.

To set off words or words epitomizing a preceding series:

> Adam Smith, who made clear the sources of a nation's wealth; David Ricardo, who pointed to the creative role of free enterprise; Jeremy Bentham, who demonstrated the relationship between utility and happiness—these were the formulators of our economic principles.

To set off a word or words that will produce an effect of climax or anti-climax:

> He who laughs—lasts. (*Reader's Digest*)
> Poor sales letters have an introduction, a body, a climax—and an anti-climax.

To mark an unfinished sentence:

> "Real salesmen seldom become sales managers. They—"
> "Why not?"
> "They like selling too much."

THE PARENTHESIS

The parenthesis encloses supplementary or explanatory matter, more remote in its relevance than that set off by comma or dash. Avoid its overuse. Too many parentheses are distracting and tend to obscure the meaning.

One does not willingly become a debtor unless he is a certain type of neurotic (particularly the kind that resembles those called accident-prone, who are strangely unaware of whirling knives or oncoming vehicles).

THE BRACKET

Brackets enclose matter entirely independent of the sentence.

USES OF THE BRACKET

To correct or call attention to an error in a text. The word sic (Latin for "thus") is used in quotations to indicate that a word was misspelled in the original, not by the author using the quotation:

This great industry was founded in 1854 [this is the correct date; not 1853, as given in some accounts] and has since developed a number of accessory industries.
Salesmanship has it's [sic] laws, like any other field of endeavor.

To mark a comment by the writer:

The trouble with such business methods [I exclude certain types of installment selling] is that they put a premium on extravagance.

To mark an explanatory addition:

The distinguishing feature of Harry's [Henry Madison's] method is that he considers research the indispensable preliminary to action.

To enclose parentheses within parentheses:

No less a personage than James Brown (joining Elbert Hopkins, Vincent Craig [of International Freighters], Dalton Trowbridge, and others) has testified to the effectiveness of this procedure.

QUOTATION MARKS

Double quotation marks are customarily used; single quotation marks, generally, serve subsidiary purposes.

USES OF QUOTATION MARKS

To enclose a direct quotation:

Mr. Caulfield reported, "This year's sales are the best in our company's history."

To set off technical terms, colloquialisms, etc., to indicate that the writer is aware of, or wishes to call attention to, their special character:

There are many items to take up. "In re" the Hopkins account, I would say . . .
There is far too much of the "racket buster" in Brown's composition for me to have much confidence in his constructive capacity.

To enclose titles of sections of a longer work:

"The Credit Inquiry" is the key chapter of Mr. Anderson's valuable book, *Credit and Business*.

(Italicizing the title of the book, in such cases, is commoner practice, today, than enclosing it between quotation marks; but the latter is still optional.)

SPECIAL USES OF QUOTATION MARKS

When a quotation extends over several paragraphs, double marks are used before each paragraph and at the close of the final paragraph to indicate that the quotation is concluded:

"Cotton futures showed a rise. This development confirmed earlier forecasts.
"Wool futures dipped. This, too, confirmed our forecasts.
"Artificial fabrics, however, remained at the same level. This contradicted our forecasts of a rise. Our analysts feel that this indicated a delayed reaction—they continue in their conviction that a rise is due."

Quotations within quotations are set off by single marks:

"So our analyst reports. And he adds, 'Unless the rains come soon, the harvest will be small and prices will rise.' "

In punctuating matter enclosed in quotation marks, periods and commas are invariably put inside the quotation marks:

"It is impossible," Jones remarked, "to do business with a man who rejects the common rules of business."

All other punctuation marks go inside the quotation marks unless they are part of the quotation:

He asked, "Did you investigate the account?" Was his order, "I want you to investigate the account"?

Quotations that are restrictive require no punctuation.

Mr. Dobbs declared that he was "more concerned with a businessman's good credit than in any other reported goodness."

THE ELLIPSIS

The three spaced periods called the **ellipsis** indicate that something has been omitted as irrelevant, or has been interrupted or left unfinished; the ellipsis may also be used to express hesitation:

Business scarcely realized the development of the Welfare State . . . which now confronts us full-grown.
The witness answered, "If I could only remember . . ." but did not go on.
He paused. "If . . . if I should confess, what then?"

When the ellipsis is used at the end of the sentence, it appears to consist of four spaced periods. But this is the only occasion when, even in appearance, more than three periods may be used.

Avoid excessive use of the ellipsis. Its overuse is another of the signs of the "schoolgirl style."

THE HYPHEN

The hyphen indicates that two words are becoming associated. When the association is very common, the tendency is to run the hyphenated words together as one. For example, basketball was once written basket ball, then basket-ball; now it is run together.

USES OF THE HYPHEN

To join two or more words used as a single adjective preceding their noun:

most favored-nation clause
iron-clad principles

To join two or more words together as a single noun:

hero-worship

To join an adjective and a participle to form a compound adjective:

ready-made clothing

To join an adjective and a noun ending in d or ed:

bird-brained politician

To separate compound numbers, fractions used as adjectives, and compound fractions:

twenty-one years
twenty-first year
twenty-one twenty-fifths

To avoid confusion:

A fraud-hating businessman
It is necessary to re-form the committee.
Should there be any damage we will re-cover the chair.

To avoid clumsy spellings where, without the hyphen, too many identical consonants or vowels would occur together, or a lower case letter and a capital letter would come together:

hall-lamp, re-echo, un-American

To separate prefixes self and ex (meaning former) from the rest of a compound word:

self-reliance, ex-president

To join fanciful, coined, or duplicating words:

A come-up-and-see-me-sometime glance.
A know-it-all merchant.

To separate two or more compounds with a common base:

Bright-er-est
1- and 2-inch nails.

To divide a word at the end of a line. Such division should be by syllables. If you do not know how the syllables divide, consult a dictionary:

prof-it, per-fect.

One syllable words should never be divided. Do not try to divide **spared,** for example.

Avoid dividing a word after a single letter. Don't divide a-loud, e-ventual, etc.

WHAT NOT TO HYPHEN

Two or more words used as an adjective, when they follow the word that they modify:

These ideas were out of date (**not** out-of-date) years ago.

When words used together as an adjective are within quotation marks:

"Good neighbor" (**not** "good-neighbor") policy, except when the words were originally hyphenated, as:
"blue-pencil" habit.

When such words are capitalized:

South American (**not** South-American) trade.

When a prefix or suffix and a root are joined·

antibiotic, clockwise.

THE APOSTROPHE

This punctuation mark indicates omission of letters in a word.

USES OF THE APOSTROPHE

To indicate a word contraction:

it's (but only for it is)
'tis (for it is)
mornin' (colloquial for morning)
B'klyn (for Brooklyn)

To form the possessive case of a noun:

Singular: John's orders. Customer's choice.
Plural: Joneses' orders. Gentlemen's choice.
Group: Collins and Winthrop's order. The Board of Directors' choice.

To form the possessive singular without the **s** where another s would be harsh or awkward:

Holmes's credit. Holmes' standing.

To form the possessive plural except where the plural does not end in **s.**

boys' trousers, men's trousers

USES OF APOSTROPHE S ('s)

To form the possessive of a group of words containing a single idea, add the apostrophe **s** ('s) to the last word.

The fruit grower and canner's interests demand attention.
The fruit grower's and the canner's profit are differently affected by the weather.

To form coined plurals, and standard plurals of letters, numbers, and symbols referred to as words:

The x's equal the y's.
C.I.O.'s, A.F. of L.'s, and their equivalents.

INCORRECT USE OF APOSTROPHE S

To form possessive pronouns:

it's (**correct,** its)
her's (**correct,** hers)
their's (**correct,** theirs)
your's (**correct,** yours)

To form the possessive of a noun that stands for an inanimate object:

The location of the comma (**not** the comma's location), except in some idiomatic construction:
Duty's call, wit's end, etc.

CAPITAL LETTERS

Use an initial capital letter to mark:

Proper names: John D. Rockefeller
Proper adjectives: English, Texan.

Ethnic groups, religions: Negro, Protestants, Judaism

Deity: God, Buddha, He, His

Days and months: Monday, January

Companies, organizations, clubs: National Association of Manufacturers, Associated Press, General Motors Corporation, Rotary Club.

Geographical divisions: The Mississippi River, The South, Mt. Washington, The North Pole, Broadway.

Official bodies: The United States Senate.

Titles of distinction: The Dean of Canterbury, Chairman of the Board.

Personifications: The Throne appoints the Chancellor, The Chair recognizes Mr. Simmons.

To mark the first word of sentences, lines of verse, full quotations:

He certainly puts business before pleasure.

Early to bed, and early to rise
Makes a man healthy, wealthy and wise.

He told the customer, "If we make a promise, we keep it."

To mark the pronoun I and the interjection O:

But when I called he was out.
Let me see thy light once more, O Sun!

To mark a word signifying a family relationship, when used like a name:

Yes, Father said he would.

MISUSES OF CAPITALIZATION

That "schoolgirl style" we have referred to in overuses of exclamations, dashes and ellipses, is also characterized by overuse of capitals. Avoid it. But such overuse is sometimes allowable for emphasis in posters, display advertising, and sales letters. And a special use of capital letters is made in order forms (see section on Orders in the chapter on Miscellaneous Business Letters).

Capitals should not be used:

To mark general or class names:

His ambition was to be a bank president. (Not Bank President)

On retiring to enter this company he was a three star general (not Three Star General).

He was a democrat in principle but did not belong to the Democratic Party. (Not he was a Democrat . . .)

To mark a point of the compass except where it designates a geographical division:

Our salesmen go everywhere—north, south, east and west. (Not North, South, East and West)

The South has become an industrial region. (Here South is correct.)

To mark the season of the year:

spring, summer, autumn, winter. (Not Spring, Summer, Autumn, Winter)

ITALICS

In print italics are slanted letters in place of perpendicular letters. In handwriting or typing, italics are indicated by underlines. Their purpose is to direct attention to the italicized words. Overuse of italics for emphasis is another favorite indulgence of the "schoolgirl style." Avoid it.

USES OF ITALICS

To emphasize or contrast:

Consider what he *is*, not what he *was*.

To indicate a foreign language derivation:

Our representative is *en route*.

To indicate titles of plays, operas, books, symphonies, periodicals, etc.

Hamlet, Tosca, Gone With the Wind, The Eroica Symphony, The New Yorker, the New York *Times*.

To indicate names of ships or planes:

The *Normandie*, the *Spirit of St. Louis*.

To indicate a word, letter or number, as such:

The antonym of *part* is *whole*.
He knows a *p* from a *q*.
Many of us still believe *thirteen* is unlucky.

ABBREVIATIONS

Abbreviations should be distinguished from **contractions** such as **don't, isn't, Int'l,** which are not followed by periods.

Abbreviations should be capitalized only when the unabbreviated words are capitalized. Periods usually follow the words and help to identify them as abbreviations. Chemical abbreviations, however, are not followed by periods since in chemical compounds this would be confusing; e.g., Cu (copper), CuO (copper oxide). All chemical abbreviations are capitalized.

In coining an abbreviation **for your own convenience,** use the first three letters or the three most characteristic letters of the word, and add a **d** or a **g** to indicate participle. Thus, **lic., licd., licg.,** for **license, licensed, licensing;** and **whs., whsd., whsg.,** for **warehouse, warehoused, warehousing.**

Plurals of abbreviations are formed by adding **s.** But where the abbreviation is a single letter it is usually doubled, as in **pp.** for **pages, LL.D.** for **Doctor of Laws.**

In forming possessives of plurals the same procedure is followed as in the unabbreviated words; as **Dr.'s, Drs.'**

Multiple names are usually abbreviated by their initials; as **FBI** (Federal Bureau of Investigation), **NAM** (National Association of Manufacturers), **CIO** (Congress of Industrial Organizations).

The same abbreviations may be used for nouns (or verbs) and for words derived from them; as **Nor.** for **Norway, Norwegian; opt.** for **option, optional; del.** for **deliver, delivery.**

Abbreviations of adjectives that would otherwise be identical with those of nouns, as **r.f.** (radio frequency), use a hyphen as **r.-f. waves** (radio frequency waves).

As a general rule, when writing to others use standard abbreviations that are clear and unmistakable (every good dictionary includes accepted abbreviations). A safe rule to follow is: **When in doubt, spell it out.**

The forms in the following brief and select list of abbreviations are widely used by authoritative sources:

a.—acre
A.A.A.—American Automobile Association
A.B.—Bachelor of Arts; also, able-bodied seaman
abbr. (or abbrev.)—abbreviation
AC—alternating current
acct.—account
ad val.—**ad valorem** (on the value)
advt.—advertisement
agt.—agent
alt.—altitude
amt.—amount
assn.—association
asst.—assistant
atty.—attorney
av.—average
bal.—balance
bbl.—barrel
bd.—board
bf.—boldface
bu.—bushel
bul.—bulletin
bur.—bureau
c.—copyright
C.C.—Chamber of Commerce
C.O.D.—cash (or collect) on delivery
cont.—continued
cor.—corrected
corp.—corporation
C.P.A.—Certified Public Accountant
Cr.—credit, creditor
do.—ditto (the same)
doz.—dozen, dozens
e.g.—**exempli gratia** (for example)

167

et al.—**et alii** (and others)
ff.—and the following pages
f.o.b.—free on board
govt.—government
hr.—hour
ht.—height
ib. (or ibid.)—**ibidem** (in the same place)
i.e.—**id est** (that is)
incl.—including, inclusive
int.—interest
introd.—introduction
IOU—I owe you
jour.—journal
lb.—**libra** (pound)
Ltd.—limited
mdse.—merchandise
memo.—memorandum
mfg.—manufacturing
mgr.—manager

mi.—mile, miles
min.—minute, minutes
mph—miles per hour
natl.—national
n.d.—no date
Pat. Off.—Patent Office
pd.—paid
pro tem.—**pro tempore** (temporarily)
Q.E.D.—**quod erat demonstrandum** (which was to
  be demonstrated)
recd.—received
rect. (or rept.)—receipt
rpm—revolutions per minute
Ry.—Railway
secy.—secretary
wk.—week
wt.—weight
yd.—yard
yr.—year

SALUTATIONS TO BE USED WHEN ADDRESSING DIGNITARIES

GOVERNMENT OFFICIALS

The President
  My dear Mr. President:
  My dear President McKinley:
  Sir:

Cabinet Officers
  My dear Mr. Secretary:
  My dear Secretary Adams:
  My dear Mr. Lowell:
  Sir:

Judges
  My dear Judge Garth:
  My dear Sir:

Military Officials
  My dear General Atwater:
  My dear General:
  My dear Sir:

MEMBERS OF THE CLERGY

The Pope
  Your Holiness:
  Most Holy Father:

Cardinal
  Your Eminence:

Archbishop
  Most Reverend Archbishop:
  Most Reverend Sir:

Bishop (Roman Catholic)
  Your Excellency:

Bishop (Episcopalian)
  Right Reverend and Dear Sir:
  Dear Bishop Mather:

Bishop (Methodist)
  Dear Sir:
  Dear Bishop Bradford:

Priest (Roman Catholic)
  Reverend Father:
  Dear Father Malachy:

Clergyman
  Dear Sir:
  Reverend Sir:

Rabbi
  Reverend Sir:
  Dear Sir:
  Dear Rabbi Lewisohn:
  Dear Dr. Wise:

Mother Superior
  Reverend Mother:
  My dear Reverend Mother Noonan:

Nun
  Reverend Sister:
  Dear Sister Anne:

EDUCATORS

President of a College
  Dear Sir:
  Dear President Gallagher:

President of a Catholic College
  Very Reverend and dear Father:
  Dear Father Malachy:

President of a Theological Seminary
  Dear President Weston:
  Dear Dr. Weston:

Dean of a College

    Dear Dean Walters:

    Dear Sir:

    Dear Dr. Walters:

FOREIGN DIGNITARIES

Prime Minister

    My dear Mr. Prime Minister:

    My dear Mr. Teetering:

Duke or Duchess

    My Lord Duke:

    Your Grace:

    Madam:

Baron or Baroness

    My Lord:

    Madam:

Ambassador

    Excellency:

    My dear Mr. Ambassador:

WORDS OFTEN CONFUSED OR WRONGLY USED

Accept—To take something offered. **Except**—To exclude.

Adapt—To adjust or to fit. **Adopt**—To take, receive, or assume as one's own.

Affect—To influence. **Effect**—To accomplish.

Agree to . . . a proposal or plan. **Agree with** . . . a person.

Alright—Incorrect. Use **all right.**

Among—Used when speaking of more than two. **Between**—Used when speaking of two. (Among those present . . . Between New York and Chicago . . .)

Amount—Applies to mass or bulk. **Number**—To units. (A large amount of money; a large number of employees.)

Apt—Suited, pertinent, inclined, capable of learning. **Liable**—Responsible for consequences. **Likely**—Probable. They are often incorrectly used as synonyms.

As—Used to introduce a clause. **Like**—Most correctly used to introduce a phrase. General usage, however, is making the two interchangeable colloquially.

As regards, In regard to—Common misuse is in **regards** to. The word **about** is normally preferable to either of the above phrases. **Harrison wrote nothing about the Jenkins order** is clearer than **Harrison wrote nothing in regard to** or **as regards the Jenkins order.**

Awful—Its proper meaning is **awe-inspiring** or **appalling;** it is loosely used as a synonym for ugly, bad, shocking, ludicrous, very.

Because of—Introduces an adverbial phrase; **due to,** an adjective phrase.

    Our entire sales plan has had to be changed because of this delay.

    Our abandonment of the plan is due to this delay.

Beside, Besides—Beside means "at the side of"; besides, "in addition."

Contact—Becoming acceptable as a synonym for **get in touch with,** but its overuse has led to sloppy substitutions for many other terms. Better use specific terms such as **write to, talk to, meet, telephone, call upon, inform, ask about,** where these are meant.

Continual—Implies regular but interrupted succession; **continuous,** constant and uninterrupted succession.

    The continual rains of Florida are the boon of its citrus industry.

    The continuous roar of traffic in the business district may partly account for the tensions of New York business men.

Data—Technically **data** is the plural of **datum;** but datum is seldom used and data functions as a collective singular, as well as the plural. The plural verb is preferred.

Disinterested—Means impartial; **uninterested** means not interested.

Disregardless, Irregardless—Misused for **regardless.**

Doubt that—Implies some uncertainty; **doubt whether**—implies considerable uncertainty.

Emigrant—One who leaves his country; **immigrant**—one who enters another country to settle in it.

Equally as good—A confusion of **equally good** with **as good as.** Either of the two latter usages is preferable.

Etc.—Abbreviation for **et cetera,** Latin for **and so forth.** Use sparingly and avoid **and etc.,** which means "and and so forth."

Fewer—Less. Fewer applies to countable things; less to measurable. (The **fewer** the mistakes; the **less** the cost.)

Good—Is an adjective only. **Well** may be used as an adjective or an adverb. (**This product is good,** but not **this product sells good.**)

If—Introduces a condition. **Whether** introduces an indirect question, an expression of doubt, or an alternative.

If the strike is called, we cannot guarantee delivery.

He asked whether the strike had been called.

He wondered whether there would be a strike.

He guaranteed delivery whether there would be a strike or not.

Imply, Infer—Imply means to suggest or hint; infer means to conclude or derive from.

The chairman implied that a strike was imminent.

His audience inferred from his remarks that it would be wise to stock up on this item.

Individual, Party, Person—Party means a group of people, except in legal terminology where it means one involved in a transaction; person and individual both mean a single human being; but person is a somewhat more respectful term than individual.

In, Into—In implies location, situation, position; into implies direction or motion toward a location.

In the United States strict observance of these regulations has effectively barred the entry of East European products into the country.

Incredible, Incredulous—Incredible means unbelievable or too far-fetched for belief; incredulous means skeptical or disinclined to belief.

Latter, Last—Latter means the second mentioned of two things. When there are more than two, use **last, last-named,** or **last-mentioned.**

Leave, Let—Leave means to depart; let means to allow. They should not be used interchangeably.

Lie, Lay—Lie is an intransitive verb meaning to recline: lay is a transitive verb meaning to put or place. The trouble spots are these:

lie—(present) ⎤
lay—(past) ⎬ to recline
lain—(perfect) ⎦

lay—(present) ⎤
laid—(past) ⎬ to put
laid—(perfect) ⎦

Loan, Lend, Borrow—Both **loan** and **lend** may be used interchangeably although **lend** is preferred, but neither may substitute for borrow, which means to accept a loan. In general, the giver **lends,** the taker **borrows.**

I will borrow a hundred dollars from Jones (not **lend** or **loan**).

Nowhere, Nowheres—The former only is correct.

Off of—Of is superfluous. Off is sufficient by itself.

Keep off this property is **correct; keep off of** this property is **incorrect.**

Raise, Rise—Raise is a transitive verb and requires an object; rise is an intransitive verb.

The audience rises when the conductor raises his baton.

Reason is because—Use either **the reason is** or **because,** which means **for this reason.**

The reason I am late is because the subway stalled (**incorrect**).

I am late because the subway stalled, **or** The reason I am late is that the subway stalled.

Said—When used to mean **previously mentioned,** should be restricted to legal documents.

Someplace, Anyplace, Noplace, Everyplace—Incorrectly substituted for somewhere, anywhere, nowhere, everywhere.

Their, There, They're—Confused because of the same sound. **Their** is a possessive pronoun; **there,** an adverb meaning at that place or at that point; **they're** is a contraction for **they are.**

If they're ready to settle, we'll be there too, ready to consider any offer of theirs.

Unique—Means the only one of its kind. Should not be confused with unusual, rare, or outstanding.

WORDS AND EXPRESSIONS TO AVOID

SUPERFLUOUS, OVERFORMAL, FLABBY, TACTLESS, HACKNEYED LANGUAGE

According to our records—Often superfluous and can be omitted.

Acknowledge receipt of your letter—Overformal. Better, **We thank you for your letter.**

(Please) advise—Better **inform** or **tell** unless actually soliciting advice.

Agreeable to your letter—Old fashioned.

Along these lines—Better, **the gist of his remarks** or simply **like.**

Amount of, preceded by **in the, to the, for the—** Better say **check** or **remittance for $—.**

(Please) arrange to return—Sufficient to say, **please return.**

As per your letter—**As per** is a legal term, therefore out of place in an ordinary letter. Better, **according to** or **as mentioned in.**

As stated above—Better to repeat what you stated, or **as I have mentioned.**

As yet—For **yet.**

Assuring you of—Old fashioned.

As to—Awkward.

At all times, at this time—Usually superfluous.

At hand—Usually superfluous.

Attached you will find—Overformal. Better, **we are attaching** or **we are enclosing.**

At the present time—**Now** is preferable.

At this writing—Formal. Better **now.**

At your earliest convenience, at an early date, at the earliest possible moment—Overformal. Better say **soon.**

Awaiting your favor—Better, **please let us hear from you soon.**

Beg—Relic of old-fashioned courtesy, now abandoned in business correspondence.

Claim—Avoid in the sense of **to assert** or **assertion;** might antagonize.

Communication—Formal. Better, **message, letter, report, inquiry,** etc.

Complaint—Aggressive sound. Usually better to say **request for adjustment.**

In compliance with your request—Overformal.

Contents noted—Superfluous.

(To) date—Overformal. "To date we have not received"—better, **we have not yet received.**

Deal—Improperly used for **transaction.**

It is desired that we receive—Inactive, weak, and longwinded. Better, **we want to receive** or **we'd appreciate receiving.**

We have duly investigated—**Duly** is superfluous.

Each and every—**Each** or **every** is sufficient by itself.

Early date—May mean two or three days or two or three weeks. Better be specific.

Enclosed please find—Better **here is** or **I enclose.**

Esteemed—Old-fashioned.

Even date—(meaning today). Better be specific. Say **your letter of this morning** or **of December — 19—.**

Event—Avoid "in the event that." **If** is preferable.

Favor—In sense of letter—old-fashioned, better say **your letter of ——.** Only proper, nowadays, when referring to a specific act of kindness.

For the reason that—**Because** is preferable.

Forward—**Send** or **ship** are preferable.

For your information—Superfluous. Omit.

Hand you—**Send our check** or **enclose our check** preferable.

Have for acknowledgment—Simpler to say "thanks."

Herewith—Superfluous.

Hoping—Weak and usually superfluous. Avoid, especially as dangling participle before complimentary close of letter.

Inasmuch as—Just say, **because.**

(We are) in receipt of—Overformal. Better, **we have received** or **thank you for.**

In order to—Just say **to.**

In reference to—Overformal, avoid. Better, **about.**

In regard to—Just say **about.**

In reply would wish to—Overformal, avoid.

Instant—Abbreviated as Inst., meaning the current month. A legal term, out of place in ordinary correspondence. Better name the month—instead of "the 5th Inst." say **October 5.**

In the nature of—Long-winded. Just say **like.**

It is the hope of the undersigned—for **I hope.**

Kindly let us know—Kindly is old fashioned. **Please let us know** is preferable.

Liberty (May we take the liberty to . . .)—Usually no liberty involved. Preferable to be direct and say **may we.**

Line—Sometimes inaccurately used in sense of a business.

(To) lineup—Vague. Better say **try to interest, try to sell,** etc.

Lot—Often inaccurately used to indicate quantity. Watch it.

Miss—Avoid using alone. Always use with a name.

Must say—Avoid. Just say it.

Oblige—Antiquated.

Our Mr. . . . .—Pretentious. If name does not sufficiently identify him, describe him as **Mr. . . . ,** **our representative,** or **our Chicago manager,** etc.

Passive constructions—Avoid them. Recast when convenient into active construction. Instead of **The goods ordered by you have been shipped,** say **We have shipped the goods you ordered.**

Permit me to say—No permission needed; just say it.

Pertaining to—**About** is better.

Pleasure (We take pleasure in)—Overformal. Better, **We are sending** or **are glad to send.**

Posted—In sense of informed, is a poor usage. Better say **informed** or **well informed.**

Prior to—**Before** is better.

Pronoun—Should not be omitted because of risk of sounding curt. Avoid, "Goods received. Sending check today." Better say, "We have received the goods and are sending you our check today."

Proposition—Avoid using the term in the sense of task. "To ship this order during the Christmas rush will be a difficult proposition" is not as good as "To ship this order during the Christmas rush will be difficult."

Proximo—(Abbreviated as prox.) Meaning next month. Legal term, out of place in ordinary business correspondence. Say **next month.**

Pursuant to your order—Overformal. Better say **following your directions.**

Recent date—your letter of—Preferable, **your letter** or **your order of . . .** (give date).

Regret—When used the following way: **we regret very deeply,** or **most sincerely,** overformal. Better, **I'm sorry,** or **I regret.**

Replying, Regarding, Referring—Weak. Avoid hanging participles. The simple straight statement is usually more direct and forceful.

Return mail—Shopworn. Better, **this week.**

Same—Stilted. Instead of "We received the goods and found same satisfactory," "We received the goods and found them satisfactory."

State—Not as good as simple word **say** or some other expression. For example: Instead of **as stated above,** use **as we have said** or merely repeat the statement.

Thanking you in advance—A trite device; may antagonize as unwarranted.

Thank you again—Once is enough.

Trust—**Hope, believe, think,** etc. preferable.

Ultimo—(Abbreviation ult.) Meaning last month. A legal term, out of place in business correspondence. Better say, **last month.**

Under separate cover—Use sparingly. Better specify means of shipment, **we are sending you by parcel post.**

(The) Undersigned—Overformal. Preferable to say **I.**

Valued—Formal word. Avoid expressions like **your valued patronage.**

We—In place of I, is right only when emphasis is on action by the firm. Otherwise it is preferable to say **I.**

Wish to say—Say it.

Would say—Say it.

(The) Writer—Overformal. Don't hesitate to say **I.**

GLOSSARY OF TERMS COMMONLY USED IN BUSINESS AND FORMAL CORRESPONDENCE

Abstract of Title—Record summarizing deeds, mortgages, and other documents and transactions affecting title to a piece of real estate.

Accessory after the Fact—One who knowingly aids the criminal after a criminal act.

Accessory before the Fact—One who instigates or aids in a crime but takes no part in its commission.

Accommodation Paper—Negotiable paper bearing the endorsement of a person who thereby lends his credit to the maker of the paper.

Account—Right to transact business in a bank by depositing money or its equivalent therein; a salesman's customers; business transacted with a firm or an individual; right to conduct business with a firm by establishing credit; record of business transactions with a firm or an individual.

Accountant—One skilled in keeping the accounts of a firm and responsible for their accuracy. Certified Public Accountant (abbrev. CPA), corresponding to a Chartered Accountant in England, is one who has qualified for a certificate from the state and is consequently engaged to check on and certify the accuracy of a firm's books.

Account Sales—Record delivered by a broker or commission merchant to the owner of a consignment of goods, showing the amount and sale prices of goods sold and deductions for commissions and freight and other expenses.

Actuary—One whose profession is to calculate insurance risks and premiums.

Adjust (in insurance)—To determine the sum to be paid in settlement of a loss covered by a policy. **Adjustor, Adjuster**—one who makes the settlement in claims arising out of losses or complaints with the purpose of avoiding possible litigation.

Administrator, Administratrix—A person appointed by a court to settle an estate.

Advertising—Promotion of business through notices in the public prints, on posters, by radio, television, or other media. **Classified Advertising**—small advertisements listed alphabetically. **Display Advertising**—large advertisements usually using illustrations and type arrangements for effect. **Poster Advertising**—advertising on large cards posted in public places. **Outdoor Advertising**—very large advertising posted on roadside structures, on top of buildings, on sides of wall, etc. **Car Card Advertising**—small posters inserted in panels on cars, busses, railroad cars, etc. **Radio Advertising**—advertising over the radio with an "advertiser" paying the cost of programs as "sponsor." **Television Advertising**—advertising over television with an "advertiser" paying the cost of programs as "sponsor." **Mail Order Advertising**—advertising by mail or periodical advertisements, leading to purchases transacted by mail.

Affiant—A signer of an affidavit.

Affidavit—An attestation of the truth of a written statement.

Affiliate—A company in financial association with another.

Agent—Person or company acting for another person or company.

Agreement—Mutual consent to terms of trade or employment, usually in written form.

Allocation—Apportionment of goods in short supply so that all companies, when the government is the allocator, or all customers, when a company is the allocator, may secure a share assigned according to their regular consumption or their comparative immediate needs.

Allowance—A customary deduction from the gross weight of goods; in law, a sum in addition to regular taxable costs awarded by the court; a reduction in cost allowed the purchaser by the seller.

Amortization—Gradual liquidation of a mortgage or other debt by periodic payments in addition to interest.

Announcer—A person hired by a radio station or commercial sponsor to introduce radio programs and performers.

Annuity (in insurance)—Annual or periodic income to the insured for life or for a specified long term.

Appeal—Resort to a higher court for review of a lower court's decision in the hope of having it reversed, or the case retried.

Appraise—To set a value on goods, land, the estate of a deceased person; to estimate loss as by fire, etc.; **Appraisal**—act of appraising or the stated result after appraising; **Appraiser**—one designated by court or appointed by agreement to set a value on property.

Appreciate—To increase in value; **Appreciation**—a rise in value.

Arbitrage—Purchase of stock in one market for profitable resale in another.

Arbitration—Submission of a dispute to judgment by a third party agreed on by both parties to the dispute.

Arraignment—Formal summoning of accused into court where indictment is read to him and he is called upon to plead "guilty" or "not guilty."

Arrival Notice—Announcement by transportation company to consignee when shipment reaches destination.

Arson—Deliberate burning of a house (in some states, of any property); a statutory crime.

Assess—To set a value for taxation; to impose a fine; to impose a contribution as a "lodge assessment." **Assessment**—a valuation of property; a fine; an imposed contribution; **Assessor**—one appointed or elected to value property for taxation.

Asset Currency (in banking)—Currency secured exclusively by the general assets of the issuing bank as distinguished from that secured by special deposit of government bonds, commercial paper, etc.

Assets (Property)—In accounting, items on balance sheet of business showing book values of its resources as at a given date; **Fixed or Permanent Assets**—land, building, machinery, capital stock of another company which can be used repeatedly; **Current, Liquid or Floating Assets**—cash or materials which can be used only at one time; **Quick Assets**—cash or goods which can be immediately disposed of without loss.

Association—Organization of a large number of people to transact business; if not incorporated, members are liable for its debts as in a partnership.

Attachment—Court order authorizing seizure of property, usually pending outcome of trial.

Auction—Public sale of property by competitive bidding of prospective buyers.

Auctioneer—A person whose job it is to conduct auction sales.

Audit—A verification of accounts; to make an audit.

Auditor—A person authorized to examine accounts.

Backlog—Amount of orders remaining to be filled.

Balance (in bookkeeping)—To prepare an accounting of assets and liabilities; the money in a bank account left after current withdrawals.

Balance Sheet—Statement of financial condition showing current assets and liabilities.

Bank—Institution where money or other property is deposited. A **National Bank** is one organized under the National Bank Act; it functions as a commercial bank but may have trust and savings departments, depending on the laws of the state in which it operates. A **State Bank** is organized under state laws; it operates as a commercial bank, but may have trust and savings departments. A **Commercial Bank** does business primarily in short-term and seasonal loans to business organizations. A **Savings Bank** does business primarily in savings and their investment, but may also do commercial banking where state law permits. A **Trust Company** acts as fiduciary agent for trust funds of individuals or corporations; if part of commercial bank, trust funds are separate from bank funds. The **Federal Reserve Bank** is a banker's bank acting under the Federal Reserve Act as agent for the government in relations with other banks. The **Land Bank** lends money on real estate mortgages under terms of the Federal Farm Loan Act.

Bank Discount—Interest deducted in advance.

Banker—Officer of a bank. **Investment Banker** is one who supplies capital in securities, and finances transactions or advises on investments. **Private Banker** generally lends money to finance international projects, may also engage in commercial banking.

Bankruptcy—Condition of a company unable to meet its debts. In **Voluntary Bankruptcy**, the company petitions to be declared bankrupt; in

Involuntary Bankruptcy, a creditor or group of creditors is the petitioner.

Bargain—Agreement or terms of a sale; purchase of material at an advantage.

Barter—Direct exchange of commodities without use of money.

Bear—One with a pessimistic attitude toward business; one who anticipates downswings in the market, as opposed to Bull.

Beneficiary—One in whose benefit a gift, trust fund income, or insurance money, is drawn.

Bequeath—To will personal property (property other than realty).

Bid—A possible offer at which goods will be supplied or work performed.

Big Board—A term for the New York Stock Exchange.

Bill—Account of or invoice for goods sold or work done. Abbreviation for "bill of exchange," now chiefly designating piece of paper money.

Bill of Lading—Certificate drawn up and signed by transportation company, enumerating articles being shipped; acts as contract and receipt for shipment.

Binder—A sum of money or other valuable consideration binding parties to a contract.

Black Market—Trading that violates legal restrictions such as price ceilings, etc.

Blanket—Covering everything, rather than a specified item, such as blanket insurance, etc.

Block (in currency)—Legal prohibition or restriction of foreign credit, currency, securities or other property, usually during war; e.g., blocked currency.

Blue Chip—A stock regarded as an especially good investment.

Board of Directors—Group of persons directing affairs of a company, corporation, or association.

Board Room—Room in which Board of Directors meets; room in brokerage office containing board on which is posted records of transactions, prices, etc.

Board of Trade—Organization for advancement of business, usually of an industry or geographical area such as a town or state.

Bourse—The Paris Stock Exchange.

Bond—An interest-bearing certificate of indebtedness; a bond differs from stock in not representing ownership. In actuality, bonds are long-term interest-bearing notes representing loans; or goods being manufactured, stored, or transported under care of bonded agencies.

Bonded Debt—Bond issue representing indebtedness.

Bonus—Extra goods shipped without charge on an order; sum given to employee in addition to contracted wages or salary.

Bookkeeper—One who keeps "books" or accounts of a company; generally distinguished from an accountant in having less formal training and lower status.

Book Value—Value given to assets on the books of owner, may be above or below current market value.

Boycott—Organized effort to prevent purchases of goods produced by a certain firm or industry and usually arising out of labor trouble.

Brand Name—Name of manufactured article registered to prevent copying.

Breach of Contract—Refusal to carry out terms of a contract in whole or in part.

Brief—Lawyer's statement of his client's case, containing legal citations supporting it.

Broker—Agent; one who buys or sells for another on commission.

Bucket Shop—A dishonest brokerage house where the customer's money is gambled with, against the customer's interest.

Budget—Plan for the expenditure of income.

Building and Loan Association—Association of investors whose savings are used to finance home construction and make loans on improved real estate.

Bull—One with optimistic attitude toward business; one who anticipates upswings in the market; opposite of Bear.

Bullion—Bars of gold and silver intended for coinage.

Business—Commercial transaction; organization conducting commercial transactions.

Business cycle—Recurrent succession of business fluctuations loosely divided into prosperity, crisis, liquidation, depression, recovery.

Call—Purchased rights to demand a certain amount of goods at a fixed price or within a fixed time; demand for payment of money as on a stockholder, member of a mutual insurance company, etc., to pay installment of subscription to capital, or a contribution to meet losses.

Call Loan—One which may be terminated by either party at any time.

Call Money—Money that must be returned when demanded.

Cancel—To annul an order for goods or services.

Capacity—Calculated space of any form of container from warehouse or ship to carton.

Capital—A stock of accumulated wealth; amount of property and funds as distinguished from income.

Capitalism—An economic system in which capital plays a leading part in production and distribution.

Capitalist—One who uses capital for investment.

Capital Stock—Shares of a corporation considered as an aggregate.

Capital Surplus—Profits, such as from sale of stock above par value, other than earned surplus.

Carrier—A company transporting passengers or freight, e.g., railroad, airlines, bus or trucking company, etc.

Cartel—International combination allocating markets and supplies, and fixing prices in order to eliminate competitive buying and selling.

Catalogue—A list, usually with illustrations and textual description, of items for sale at announced prices.

Ceiling—Maximum wage, rent, etc., fixed by the government.

Certified Check—Bearing the signature or stamp of the cashier of the bank on which it is drawn. Its significance is that the sum has been withdrawn from the account of the drawer and the bank assumes responsibility for payment.

Chain Store—Branch of a large system of stores belonging to a single ownership.

Chamber of Commerce—A board of trade; an association to promote the commerce of a community, state or nation.

Charter—Certificate from the state approving the organization of a company and authorizing it to do business in the approved form.

Check—A standard form of written order to a bank to make a designated payment out of a depositor's balance.

Circulation—In a periodical, the number of purchasers by subscription or individual sales; in a store, movement of customers in and out.

Clearing House—Organization maintained by a banking group to exchange checks and adjust accounts among its members.

Closed Corporation—One in which all stock is privately held in a few hands; it usually may not be disposed of by holders without the consent of the other holders.

C.O.D.—Abbreviation for "cash on delivery." In C.O.D. transactions, goods must be paid for at the time of delivery.

Code—An arrangement of words, letters or other symbols to achieve secrecy or brevity in communication; a set of rules governing the conduct of a business.

Codicil—Addition to a will, modifying some provision in it.

Collateral—Property used as security for a loan.

Collective Bargaining—Negotiations between employers and a committee of their workers and/or representatives of the union.

Co-Maker—One who shares obligations of another by endorsing a contract.

Commercial Paper—Promissory notes of a large, reputable firm; dealt in by note brokers and sold to banks which discount them and, in that way, realize interest on them.

Commission—Percentage or allowance made to broker or agent for transacting business for another, e.g., salesman's commission.

Company—Association of persons for carrying on commercial or industrial enterprise; may be partnership, corporation or other joint enterprise.

Complaint (in law)—Statement of the cause of an action; the person initiating the complaint is called the complainant. In commerce, customer's charge of faulty goods, delivery or other service.

Comptroller—Auditor with the rank of executive.

Consign—To send or address goods by bill of lading, etc., to an agent in another place to be stored, sold or otherwise cared for.

Consignee—One to whom goods are shipped.

Consignment—Transaction in which purchase is not final; unsold goods may be returned to consignor.

Consumer—Ultimate purchaser or user of merchandise.

Contingent Order (in advertising)—Space in small circulation media to be paid for by returns from the advertisement.

Contract—Witnessed agreement, usually in writing, the terms of which are legally enforceable.

Contractor—One who specializes in a certain type of work; e.g., building contractor. **Sub-contractor**—one who performs part of a piece of work; e.g., plumbing sub-contractor.

Convenience Merchandise—Goods kept in a store for the convenience of certain customers.

Cooperative—A business enterprise or association with the object of producing, purchasing, selling, or occupying quarters at common savings to members by eliminating middle-man fees and profits.

Copy—Text of advertising; duplicate of an original letter or of an article of commerce. Ordinarily, carbon copy duplication of typing.

Copyright—Exclusive publication rights, now extended to cover plays, movie scenarios and movie films and radio and television scripts; other pieces of creative work are copyrighted **after** publication. Application must be made to Register of Copyrights, Library of Congress, Washington 25, D.C.

Corner—To secure such control of stock or commodities as to be able to dictate quotation prices.

Corporation—A business association operating on a state franchise and with liability limited to the amount of the investment.

Co-Sign—To assume joint responsibility in indebtedness by adding one's signature to the note of another.

Cottage Industry—One where operations are performed by workers at home.

Countermand—To reverse a personal order.

Courts—Where cases involving offenses against the law or claims protected by the law are tried. Courts where large claim cases are tried include Superior, Circuit, certain District, Chancery or County courts. Courts where small claim cases are tried are Justice courts, presided over by a Justice of the Peace, and include Magistrate's court and certain District courts.

Covenant—Promise of some future action, made in contracts and other legal papers.

Coverage—The amount and type of protection against risks agreed on in an insurance policy.

Credit—Financial standing influencing sales to a concern on deferred payment; permission to defer payment for a certain period.

Creditor—One who extends credit; lender.

Credit Line—Amount of credit extended; e.g., "X's credit line is $2,000." Also, reproduction of signature, symbol or other acknowledgment in print to signify the originator or owner of writing, photographs or illustrations.

Credit Rating—Summary of credit line as published in Dun & Bradstreet or other credit house ratings and reports.

Cum Div—With dividend declared or pending.

Curb Market—The usual reference is to the American Stock Exchange (formerly New York Curb Exchange), formerly conducted out-of-doors but now housed in a building of its own; it is the second largest stock market in the United States.

Custom—Generally accepted practice, company practice; customer's account.

Customer—Person or concern purchasing goods.

Cut—In printing, zinc etching, or copper or zinc halftone, usually reproducing a picture or hand-lettering.

Cutback—Reduction in production schedule; reduction in salary or other compensation.

Damage—Loss in merchandise, machinery, service, productive capacity or trade standing. Compensation for such damage may be claimed depending on the circumstances, in a court of law.

Dead Spot—Store location at point of little traffic.

Dead Stock—Unsaleable merchandise.

Debenture—Synonym for debt; documentary evidence of debt.

Debit and Credit Memoranda—Issued by companies to effect necessary adjustments in the course of business transactions.

Decontrol—Removal of government restrictions on prices, rents, etc.

Deduction—Sum or money subtracted from amount to be paid for goods or services.

Deed—Contract by which real estate is conveyed by one party to another; **Warranty Deed** contains a guarantee to clear title ownership; **Quick Claim Deed** relinquishes rights of former owner without guaranteeing clear title to purchaser; **Joint Tenancy Deed** transfers property to two or more owners with the provision that the survivor will own the entire property; **Trust Deed** is given as security for a debt and is a form of mortgage; **Tax Deed** is received by purchaser at a tax sale.

Defalcation—Misappropriation of money placed in trust; the sum misappropriated.

Default—To fail in fulfilling a contract or other financial obligation.

Deficit—Amount by which expenses exceed income, liabilities exceed assets, production falls below expectation.

Deflation—Decline in prices, volume of production, etc., usually accompanied by unemployment.

Delaware Corporation—A corporation chartered in Delaware to take advantage of low incorporation fees and tax rates.

Demand—Desire to purchase commodity together with capacity to pay for it.

Demand Bill or Draft—A bill payable at sight, or on demand.

Demand Item—Article in constant demand, which must be carried in stock constantly.

Demand Loan—Loan payable on demand.

Demand Note—Note payable on demand.

Demurrage—Charge by transportation company for detention of carriers beyond allotted time.

Deposit—Money or equivalent entrusted for safekeeping with another, as in a bank; money given as partial payment in a transaction or as a binder in a contract.

Deposition—Testimony given by witness unable to appear in court.

Depreciation—Decline in value, usually as a result of loss through wear, neglect, exposure, etc. Machinery is usually calculated to suffer an annual depreciation of 10% in value through wear.

Depression—Deep and prolonged decline of industrial and general business activity.

Deteriorate—To spoil or lose quality with time, e.g., food and certain manufactured articles such as photographic film.

Detriment—Damage by intangible cause, such as injury to a firm's reputation through rumors.

Devise—To will property in real estate.

Director—Person entrusted with determining policies and decisions of a firm.

Disbursements—Payments to meet bills.

Discount—Allowance for cash or quick payment; **Trade Discounts** are discounts from wholesale prices allowed to customers and scaled according to amount of purchases and other considerations.

Distributor—Person or company through whom goods reach the consuming public; **Wholesale**

Distributors supply **Retail Distributors** who serve the public directly.

Dividend—Money paid to shareholders or depositors as share of profits.

Dock Receipt—Signed by steamship company for freight delivered to dock.

Draft—Papers by which one party, usually the seller, orders another party, usually the buyer, to deliver to a third party, usually a bank, a sum to be credited to the account of the first party. Used to assure payment and to secure settlement of unpaid accounts, since rejection of a draft when presented by the bank is recorded and affects credit standing.

Drawee—Bank on which check or draft is drawn.

Drawer—Person who draws money from his bank account by check.

Dry Goods—Commodities made from fabrics.

Due Bill—In brokerage business, a type of IOU by broker, promising to deliver certain stocks not available at time of sale; also used for promised future delivery of dividends, etc.

Dummy—Sample of proposed book, magazine, or booklet to show size, format, and sample pages.

Dummy Corporation—One organized solely for intermediate purposes, and not for open business activity.

Duplicate—Copy or identical likeness, e.g., duplicate of bill.

Duty—Payment imposed by the government on goods imported, exported, or consumed, such as customs duties, excises, etc.

Earned Income—Income derived from wages, salary, or fees in return for labor, advice or management services.

Earned Surplus—Balance of profits and income remaining after deducting losses, dividends, and transfers to capital stock, etc.

Earnest Money—Deposit or binder; a sum of money paid to seal a bargain and to be deducted from purchase payment.

Economy—Organization of the production, distribution, and consumption of goods in a community.

Efficiency Engineer—A person whose profession it is to plan or change production methods to secure greater economy and efficiency.

Embezzle—To fraudulently appropriate to one's own use property entrusted to him.

Endorse (also Indorse)—To sign one's name as a payee or to indicate co-responsibility for payment on a check, bill, note, or other document.

Enterprise—In association with the word "free" or "private" has come to replace "capitalism" to differentiate the non-socialist from the socialist type of economy.

Entrepreneur—One who takes commercial risks; enterpriser.

Entry—Item in a business record.

Equity—In real estate, difference between value of property and owner's debt on it. In margin buying difference between market value of a stock and customer's indebtedness for its purchase.

Escrow—Papers or money in keeping of responsible third party such as a bank, held until certain conditions are fulfilled.

Estate—Property in lands or tenements, sometimes inaccurately used for property other than lands or tenements; total property left by a deceased person.

Estimate—Statement of amount of goods to be produced or stored or of sum for which certain work will be done.

Ex-Bonus
Ex-Coupon
Ex-Dividend
Ex-Interest
Ex-Privileges
Ex-Rights
} Earnings or privileges not included in the purchase of particular shares.

Exchange—Transfer of goods; place where business interests of a certain sort meet for transaction, e.g., stock exchange, cotton exchange, etc.

Executor (Executrix)—One designated to carry out terms of a will.

Execution—Carrying out of terms of a will or a court order.

Expedite—To accelerate production or distribution of goods or rendering of service.

Expediter—One whose job it is to expedite or facilitate business and other transactions.

Export-Import Bank of Washington—Organized by the government in 1934 to facilitate foreign trade.

Express—Shipment by fast or unobstructed transportation; via Railway Express Agency.

Facsimile—Exact copy not necessarily of same size; photostat can serve as satisfactory facsimile.

Factor—Commercial agent who sells or buys goods for others on commission; commission agent.

Factory—Building where manufacture of goods is carried on.

Fail—To become insolvent.

Fee—Compensation for professional or special services; fixed charge for services of a public officer, e.g., sheriff's fee.

Feeder—Branch line in railroad, bus, or air transport that connects with trunkline.

Fee Simple—Unrestricted title to property.

Felony—Crime whose penalty is death or prison sentence.

Fiduciary—In trust; a fiduciary is a trustee.

Finance—Management of money matters.

Financial Rating—Financial information carried in directory such as *Moody's Manual*.

Firm—Correct meaning is partnership; in common usage, any business organization.

Fiscal—Relating to finance, e.g., U.S. fiscal year, period in which annual taxes are collected.

Fixtures—Fixed equipment in business or professional premises.

Foreclosure—Transfer of property to mortgagee when mortgagor defaults on interest payment.

Franchise—Special commercial rights granted by a city to operator of a public conveyance, e.g., a bus line; special rights granted by a manufacturer to a dealer.

Freight Bill—Prepared by transportation company and rendered to receiver or sender, depending on who is paying the freight charges.

Freight Claim—Also called "Loss and Damage Claim" or "Overcharge Claim," claim on transportation company for loss, damage or overcharge.

Fund—Cash or specified assets set aside for a specific purpose.

Funded Debt—Fund set up for payment of long-term indebtedness.

Funded Reserve—A reserve for which a fund has been invested to earn income.

Futures—In commodity exchange, contracts for subsequent delivery, as of a crop not yet harvested.

Garnishee—To take over property or money to satisfy a debt or a claim. A claimant may "garnishee" a defendant's wages.

Gold Standard—Rating of currency in terms of supposed value in gold.

Good will—Intangible asset resting on a special earning power gained through advertising, reputation, good business methods, favorable location, business standing, etc.

Gray Market—Trading by undercover methods, in between black market and regular market methods.

Gross—As a number, 12 dozen or 144; as an adjective, indicating a complete sum before deductions have been made, e.g., gross income before deduction of taxes, expenses, etc.

Handbill—Printed announcement handed out to passers-by.

Handicrafts—Goods produced by hand, e.g., certain pottery, woven goods, embroidery, basket work, etc.

Hedging—Stock trading in which sales or purchases are made to offset or "hedge" against possible loss in other transactions. "Puts and calls" are a form of hedging.

Heir—Person entitled by law or terms of a will to an inheritance.

High Pressure—To make sales of goods not actually needed or desired.

Holding Company—One organized to buy and hold stock of another company.

Holographic Will—One entirely in the handwriting of the testator, not valid in some states.

Huckster—One who prepares radio or television advertising, usually with methods of exaggerated showmanship.

Hypothecation—Pledging of collateral. Governments may "hypothecate" tax revenues as security for a loan. Property may be "hypothecated" for payment of a debt. Its earnings may be so used and the property remain with the debtor; but if payment is defaulted, the creditor may demand sale of the property to secure payment of the debt.

Identification—Driver's license, social security card, or other document required as identification in check payments at stores, hotels, or other public places.

Implement—To find means to carry out an agreement.

Impulse Item—Something marketed to appeal to spontaneous decision of customer, usually novelties and luxuries as opposed to staples or necessities.

Income Group—Classification of people according to earnings.

Incorporate—To secure a charter of incorporation from a state, and to organize operations under its provisions.

Indemnify—To make secure against loss or damage; to make good a loss or damage.

Indenture—Sealed agreement of which each party concerned holds a signed copy.

Index—Stock market term referring to listed price quotations of securities traded on the market and analyzed for trends.

Indictment—Formal grand jury charge against a person accused of a major crime.

Industry—Collectively, manufacturing as contrasted to agriculture; any branch of production, e.g., shoe industry, paper industry, etc.

Inflation—Rise in prices where income advance fails to keep up with prices.

Injunction—Court order restraining certain action.

Insert—Something added in a document; an enclosure in a mailing.

Insolvency—Inability to meet current financial obligations.

Installment—Periodic payment on a time-payment purchase. The British equivalent is "hire-purchase."

Institutional Advertising—Directed not at immediate sales but at increasing prestige leading to consideration of a company as an established institution.

Instrument—Person or document useful in accomplishing a stated purpose.

Interest—Payment by borrower for use of borrowed money measured in percentages and units of time; **simple** interest is payment on principal alone; **compound** interest is payment of accrued interest added to capital; **penal** interest is payment of special interest by defaulting debtor.

Interstate Commerce—Commerce across state boundaries.

Intestate—Descriptive of a property holder who dies without leaving a will. Division of property will then be made according to state inheritance laws.

Intrastate Commerce—Commerce within a state.

Inventory—Record of merchandise on hand and in stock rooms; **perpetual** inventory is one maintained by recording every sale and receipt of goods on an inventory card. Usually inventories are made at periodic intervals.

Investment—Money or other property risked with expectation of profit.

Investment Trust—Company whose business is investment in securities and bond issue, and which markets its own securities on the basis of these investments.

Invoice—A bill itemizing goods shipped and their prices.

IOU—Document bearing the letters "IOU" and a notation of a sum of money. If signed, an IOU has legal status as a debit account.

Island Counter—Table displaying or carrying goods for sale in such a position in a store that customers may walk around it.

Joint Stock Company—Large partnership with some of the features of a corporation.

Journal—Bookkeeping record in which transactions are first entered.

Judgment—Court decision; in a civil trial for damages, the sum awarded to the plaintiff.

Jury—Of two kinds. The **grand** jury consists of 12 to 23 persons who serve as an investigating body and dismiss or indict a suspect, depending on the evidence at hearings. Functions only in cases involving major crimes. **Petit** jury, an ordinary jury, usually consisting of 12 persons who hear civil suits and cases of minor law-breaking.

Kickback—Unauthorized payment out of wages, prices, or fees as extortion or bribery.

Know-How—Technical skill gained through training and experience.

Kraft—Strong brown paper used in packing for shipping.

Landlord—Owner of real estate; usually reference is to owner of specified building.

Layout—Sketch of a proposed advertisement, booklet, etc., in store merchandising, arrangement of merchandise.

Lease—A contract for the temporary conveyance of property, usually in consideration of rent.

Ledger—Account book. In larger sense, accounting in general.

Legacy—Inheritance through a will.

Legal Standard—Measure of value in gold or silver established by a government for the rating of its currency.

Legal Tender—Money that may lawfully be used in settlement of debts.

Lessee—Tenant under a lease.

Lessor—One who grants a lease.

Letters Patent—Document transferring title to public lands or rights to inventions (see Patent).

Liability—Indebtedness; **current** liabilities are short term debts such as taxes, accounts payable, etc., to be met within the year; **fixed** liabilities are long term debts such as mortgages, bonds, etc.; **deferred** liabilities are advance payments such as rent or interest before they come due.

Libel—Written statement held to be damaging to person or business about which it is made. To be distinguished from **slander**, which is a damaging statement made orally.

License—Legal permission to sell certain goods, e.g., a liquor license; or to practice a profession; or to sell goods on the street, e.g., a peddler's license, etc.

Lien—Legal right to property in payment of debt; usually has priority over other claims, e.g., tax lien, mechanics lien, etc.

Limit Order—Order to buy or sell stock at or above or below a specified price.

Line—Type of merchandise offered for sale, e.g., line of pearl buttons.

Liquid—Convertible into cash, e.g., liquid assets.

Liquidate—To convert assets into cash, generally in reference to business in financial difficulty and in need of ready cash.

List Price—Selling price as listed in catalogue.

Loan—Money lent on interest.

Lockout—Shutting out of employees during a labor dispute. Now illegal.

Logotype—Trademark or symbol used by a firm in its advertising.

Long and Short—To be **long** is to hold stock in expectation of a rise; to be **short** is to sell stocks one does not own, in a falling market, in expectation of buying them in at a still lower quotation and profiting from the difference.

Lots—In real estate, specified arrangement of ground; in the stock market, number of shares traded in. **Round** lots are those in round numbers, such as 100 shares; **odd** lots are transactions in lots under 100.

Maintenance of Membership—Clause in labor contract making it obligatory upon workers to keep in good standing in the union in order to retain jobs.

Malfeasance—Wrongful action: To be distinguished from **nonfeasance**, failure to perform an action agreed upon; and **misfeasance**, performance of an agreed action in such a way as to violate the rights of others.

Malice Aforethought—Intentional or planned injury.

Manifest—Invoice of a ship's cargo, for evidence at customs house.

Manufacture—Conversion of raw materials into a finished product, e.g., converting iron ore into steel plate.

Margin—Money deposited with a broker as security on stock purchases; thus margin may be forfeited if stock quotations take an adverse turn.

Markdown—Lowering of prices, usually to make sales for slow-moving goods.

Market—In general, the range for buying and selling; in particular, the range for buying and selling in a particular field, e.g., the stock market, the cotton market, etc.

Market Order—Order to sell at the market price of the day on which the order is issued.

Mark-Up—Amount added, in selling price, to wholesale price to cover overhead and profit.

Marshall Plan—Plan to extend economic aid abroad, initiated by George C. Marshall as United States Secretary of State in 1947.

Mass Market—The general public considered as potential consumers.

Mass Production—Large scale, mechanized production designed to lower production costs to permit purchase by the majority of potential consumers.

Maximum Hours—Limit of time workers may be employed without overtime payment.

Mediation—Resort to third party in disputes between employer and worker; not as conclusive as arbitration.

Melon—Extra dividend on stock, distributing surplus earnings or profits.

Merger—Consolidation of two or more companies into one.

Metes and Bounds—Dimensions and boundaries of a parcel of real estate.

Mill—A machine for grinding, pressing, stamping, or almost every repetitive process; a building or group of buildings containing manufacturing machinery.

Minimum Wage—Lowest limit of wages that may be paid to workers.

Minor—Person under legal age to assume certain responsibilities. The age varies—it is different for marriage, for business transaction, or for liability to criminal charges.

Model Change-Over—Reorganization of manufacturing process for the manufacture of a new model (sometimes called **mark**) of an article.

Monopoly—Exclusive control of an industry or some form of trade.

Morris Plan Company—Makes small personal loans for repayment in installments.

Mortgage—Transfer of rights in property as security for a loan or for other considerations. **Real estate** mortgages are on land and improvements upon it; **chattel** mortgages cover other forms of property; **crop** mortgage is a chattel mortgage on crops; a **first** mortgage is one which has priority in any claims on the property over subsequent mortgages (**second** and **third** mortgages, etc.).

Mortgage Certificates—Certificates for small shares of large first mortgages or first mortgage bonds. Issued by mortgage customers to investors.

National Advertising—Advertising in periodicals or over radio and television, nationwide in scope.

Negotiable—Salable or transferable as payment for debts.

Net—Sum, after deductions have been made, e.g., net income after expenses, taxes, etc. have been taken out.

Nonfeasance—see Malfeasance.

Notary Public—A person authorized by state law to witness and certify to the authenticity of signatures affixed to documents or statements in his presence.

Number—Item of manufacture; usually refers to item in a catalogue.

O.K.—With signature, constitutes endorsement or approval of something presented in writing. According to popular belief, from Old Kinderhook, birthplace of Martin van Buren, and used by his supporters in his campaign for the presidency.

Omnibus Clause—Section in a contract covering several items not specifically covered elsewhere in the document.

One Day Order—Order for stock transaction on a certain day, and cancelled if not executed on that day.

Open Order—Order for a stock transaction to be executed at any time and to hold good until notice of withdrawal is received. Also called GTC (Good till cancelled) order.

Option—First choice or right to obtain goods or services without competition for a specified period, e.g., ten days' option.

Order—Customer's itemized description of goods desired for purchase.

Overhead—Fixed expenses, such as rent, salaries, maintenance costs, etc.

Overstock—Goods in excess of current demand.

Over-the-Counter Trading—Trading by private dealers in securities not listed on the stock exchange.

Package—Combined merchandise and/or services, offered as a unit, in a "package deal," e.g., radio or television program in which script, actors, announcer, etc., are all provided as a unit in a "package program."

Pamphlet—Paper-covered booklet used as advertising or to convey information about a business.

Panic—Sudden widespread fright over financial situation causing artificial depression through sales of securities and other property.

Paper—Documents of any sort, negotiable notes, bills, etc.

Par—Normal or face value of securities.

Parcel—Package of goods; piece of property; to apportion merchandise in small lots to provide some supply to all accounts.

Parity—Rate of exchange at which different currencies acquire equal purchasing power.

Partnership—Defined in Uniform Partnership Act: "An association of two or more persons to carry on as co-owners of a business for profit"; except in "limited partnership" in which liability of certain partners is restricted to the amount of capital contributed, partners are individually liable for debts contracted by the business.

Passbook—A book borne by customer, containing records of credit purchases; also bankbook.

Passing a Dividend—Failure to declare an expected dividend.

Patent—Right granted by the government for a term of seventeen years, for the exclusive production of an invented article or for an improvement on an article, not renewable.

Patent Attorney—One specializing in the preparation of patent applications and in the search to de-termine that the invention is new and does not infringe on previous patents.

Patent Office—Government bureau that registers patent applications and issues "letters patent," granting patent rights.

Patron—Customer.

Patronage—Business given by a customer.

Pattern (in industry)—A model made for duplication as in metal casting, dress manufacture, etc.

Pattern-Maker—One who makes patterns needed in industry.

Pay—To make an acceptable return, usually in money, for property delivered, or services rendered; remuneration such as wages or salaries.

Payee—Person to whom money has been, or is to be, paid.

Paymaster—One under whose management wage or salary payments are made.

Payroll—Paymaster's list of those entitled to wages or salary.

Peculation—Embezzlement.

Peg—To hold market prices at a set value by manipulating purchases or sales.

Pension—Payment made through grant, insurance, or other arrangement to person retired from employment, business, or public office.

"Percents"—Investments such as bonds or other securities, described by their interest rate, e.g., 3%.

Perpetual Trust—Trust estate with no prescribed duration.

Personal Property or Personal Estate—Property other than real estate.

Personnel—Employed staff.

Petition—Written application to a court instituting an action or requesting action upon a matter before it.

Petition in Bankruptcy—Written application by a debtor or his creditors that he be declared bankrupt.

Petty Cash—Cash fund used to make small payments.

Photo Engraving—Process of reproducing pictures through photography, where printing surface is in relief in contrast to lithography or gravure.

Photostat—Photographic process for reproducing documents, drawings, etc.; a document or drawing so reproduced.

Pica—12-point type, usually used on typewriters and in other print where readability is desired.

Picket—Person, during a strike, standing or walking back and forth before entrance of business to discourage non-striking employees or customers from entering.

Piece Goods—Fabrics sold by pieces or fixed lengths.

Pilot Plant—A business operated to determine rates to be charged in its industry.

Pipeline—Piping over long distances used in the transportation of oil or gas.

Piracy—Infringement on copyrighted or patent property rights.

Pit—Section of Chicago Board of Trade where a specific commodity is traded; e.g., wheat pit.

Pivotal—A stock whose quotations influence the course of the market.

Planned Economy—Economical organization, usually of a state, in which production is arranged to prevent or reduce fluctuation and waste.

Plant—The building, machinery, etc., taken together that are used in a unit of industrial production.

Plantation—Large scale farming operation, carried on by hired labor; e.g., rubber plantation.

Plastics (in industry)—Synthetic materials mainly produced by molding process.

Pledge—Piece of property given as security for a loan.

Point—Unit used in quoting prices on stocks. In the United States, one point usually stands for $1 a share.

Point System—Method of wage payment by time units of work performed. Also called the "Bedaux System," from its originator.

Policy—Contract of insurance; guiding principles of a concern, usually determined or governed by a Board of Directors.

Pool—Merger of property or financial interests of a group, usually with the expectation of manipulating the market in its favor.

Portal-to-Portal Pay—Payment for time spent, as in mines, in passing to and from the entrance of the actual place of work.

Position—On produce exchanges, undertaking to make delivery in a given month; e.g., October position.

Possession—Such control of property as to give exclusive legal enjoyment of it.

Posthumous—Taking effect after death.

Power of Attorney—Legal authority to act for another, not as a lawyer, but to carry out transactions.

Practice—Professional service; e.g., legal practice; customary procedure of a firm.

Pre-Fab—A prefabricated article, usually a house or small industrial building, to facilitate speedy erection.

Preference Shop—One where, by agreement between union and management, preference is given to union members in employment, promotion, and tenure, but management may employ non-union workers if union cannot supply qualified personnel.

Preferred Stock—Issue which receives preference over common stock in dividends or distribution of assets.

Premium (in insurance)—Money or other consideration paid by the insured according to terms of contract. (In economics)—Greater value of one currency over another; additional payment for loan of money. (On the stock market)—Amount above par that securities are being quoted at; sum paid for an option.

Prepaid—Paid in advance.

Price—Value at which goods are exchanged or services rendered.

Pricing—Setting a price on goods.

Primary Markets—Markets in farm produce such as foods or fibers.

Principal—Actual party to transaction as distinguished from agent; money or other property on which interest is earned.

Priority—Precedence as in transportation, goods production, delivery of order, etc.

Privilege—Option on the sale or purchase of securities on specified terms.

Probate—Proof established by legal procedures; e.g., probate of a will.

Process—A method of manufacture or of rendering services.

Production—Creation of goods having value to purchasers; e.g., agricultural production, industrial production.

Profit—What remains after production and sales costs have been deducted.

Profit and Loss—Accounting, after a given period, to determine condition of a business.

Promissory Note—Note undertaking payment of a debt at a specified time or occasion.

Promoter—One who initiates organization of a company, floating of securities, or other business undertaking.

Property—Things owned; real property is property in real estate, while personal property or personal estate refers to all other possessions of value.

Proprietor—Owner; one with legal right to possession.

Proxy—To act for another; one whose voting rights are entrusted to another, the usual reference being to voting of stock holders.

Public Domain—The field of property rights belonging to the public at large, such as manufacturing processes or literary properties not, or no longer, covered by patents and copyrights.

Public Utility—Company servicing the general public, such as a railroad, supplier of electricity, etc.

Put and Call—To "put" is to deliver, according to agreement, specified stock at a specified price to a buyer who receives a payment for this service. The privilege of "putting" may be sold to a third party. To "call" is to receive on demand specified stock at a specified price from a seller who is paid for this service. The privilege of "calling" may be sold to a third party.

Pyramid—To engage in transactions in banking or stock market, using gains as "margin" for further purchases or sales, in order to take continuous advantage of a market trend.

Qualified—Fit to do required work.

Quantity—Used relatively, usually in references to goods in bulk, e.g., "These castings can be supplied in any reasonable quantity."

Quantity Theory of Money—Economic theory that changes in quantity of money in circulation affect price levels and currency values.

Query—To recheck a shipment, a shipper or an account; may refer to goods, invoices, personnel, etc.; e.g., "Please query Hobson, rubber tape shipment overdue at warehouse."

Quit Claim—Document in legal form relinquishing some property right.

Quotations—Statements, oral or written, of market prices of stocks, bonds or commodities.

Quotation Board—Board in brokerage office on which market quotations are displayed.

Rebate—Repayment of a percentage of sum received in payment for goods or services. Rebate may be allowed for damage, delay, or savings in shipping costs, etc.

Receipt—Signed paper in evidence that goods or money has been received.

Receipts—Earnings of a business for a given period; e.g., "today's receipts."

Receiver—Person, firm, or bank appointed by courts to conduct a business declared bankrupt.

Recession—Decline in industrial activity, not so drastic as a depression.

Redemption—Payment of outstanding loans; e.g., redemption of a bond issue.

Referee—Appointed by court to hear evidence and render decision in business disputes.

Refund—Return of entire amount paid for goods or services, usually because of their unsatisfactory nature.

Reimburse—Repay money expended by another. An agent will be reimbursed for costs incurred during his operation.

Reorganization—Reestablishment of insolvent business with the consent of creditors and under court supervision, with the aim of avoiding receivership costs and forced sale losses.

Requisition—Order for supplies, materials, etc.

Rescued—Withdrawal of order or instructions.

Restrictive—Limiting. A restrictive covenant is a clause in a document setting certain conditions, as in real estate contracts restricting residence to certain races.

Retail Trade—Trade with consumers.

Retirement—Withdrawal from circulation, e.g., retirement of a currency.

Revenue—Source of income, usually referring to governmental income from taxation.

Revenue Bond—Short-term issue in anticipation of revenue payments.

Rigged Market—Subject to manipulation so that it does not reflect real values.

Rollback—Price reduction to previous levels, usually by government action.

Royalty—Share of profits paid by manufacturer to inventor (or owner of an invention), author, etc. or to his heirs.

Runaway—Removal of business to a region of low labor costs as an employer measure in labor trouble.

Sabotage—Obstruction, malicious waste of materials, or spoilage of product by workers during labor trouble.

Sales Engineering—Computing and adjusting installation and production costs from plans, as a means of promoting sales of equipment and machinery to a specific industry or factory.

Salvage—Goods rescued from shipwreck or other disaster.

Sample—A representative piece of an article offered for sale; e.g., swatch of cloth.

Scab—Opprobrious term, used in labor relations for person employed in place of strikers or refusing to strike with his fellow workers.

Schedule—Systematic listing of time for production or other performance in manufacturing, transportation, distribution, etc.

Search—To verify status of a property; e.g., mortgage title search, patent search, etc.

Seat—Membership in the Stock Exchange entitling one to share in its assets and the privilege of trading there.

Security—(Chiefly used in the plural.) Stock certificates, bonds, or other documentary evidence of indebtedness giving the possessor the right to claim property secured by the document; **listed** security is one which, by meeting certain requirements, is listed for trading on the Stock Exchange.

Self-Mailer—Advertising message that can be sent by mail without enclosure in an envelope. A sticker or stamp is affixed to hold pages or folded edges together.

Shakeout—Minor decline in industrial activity in course of adjustment after inflation.

Shape-up—Hiring of dockworkers by selection of applicants at piers, usually arbitrarily, at the discretion of labor supervisor.

Shortage—Something missing from inventory or from cash, due to theft, loss, or error.

Silver Standard—Rating of currency in terms of a specified value in silver.

Sinking Fund—Fund continually added to and invested toward the payment of bonds or other maturing debts.

Sitdown Strike—One where striking employees stay in or at their places of work to prevent operation of machinery by others.

Slander—Oral statement held to be damaging to person or business about whom it is made. To be distinguished from **libel,** which is a damaging written statement.

Sleeper—Film, book, novel, or other property or article of trade that gains unexpected commercial success, doing better business than other items for which greater sales were anticipated.

Slowdown—Slowing down of work operations, without actual walkout, as a worker tactic in labor dispute.

Smog—Saturation of air with smoke or other industrial exhausts leading to fog conditions.

Social Security—System and fund set up, under the Social Security Act, to insure security in old age. The fund is made up of compulsory contributions by employers and employees.

Solicit—To seek business accounts.

Solvency—Capacity to meet financial obligations.

Specie—Metal (hard) money as distinguished from paper currency.

Specimen—Sample of minerals, ores, plants, or other things that are complete units of their kind.

Speculation—Buying or selling with chance of high profits and risk of considerable loss.

Spot Announcement (in radio advertising)—A commercial not part of a sponsored program.

Spot Delivery—In stock market, immediate delivery of stock.

Staple—An established product; e.g., oil is a staple of Texas.

Statement—List of unpaid items in a business account; a **financial** statement is a listing of assets and liabilities.

Statute of Limitations—Law setting time limit for legal action.

Stipulation—Condition specified in agreement or contract, usually something undertaken by buyer to bolster his credit.

Stock—Share of ownership in an incorporated business; supply of merchandise for sale; **common** stock is ordinary stock as distinguished from **preferred** stock, which takes precedence over it in distribution of assets or dividends; **guaranteed** stock is one whose dividends are guaranteed by another company.

Stockpile—Reserve supply of essential material.

Strike—Refusal by employees to work unless demands, generally for pay increases, vacations, and other benefits are met. Usually accompanied by picketing of the premises of the business affected.

Strike-Breaking—Coercive action with the intention of defeating strike action.

Sublease—To lease all or part of premises one has leased.

Sublet—To rent all or part of premises one has rented.

Subpoena—Court order served on witnesses summoning them to give testimony.

Subsidiary—A company, control of whose stock is held by another company.

Subsidy—Agreed sum paid, over and above market charges, to assure supply or service that would otherwise be unavailable because of lack of profit.

Substandard—Below standard quality.

Supermarket—Departmentalized branch in chain store system, where some departments may be rented as concessions, and doing a gross annual business of a specified figure, usually $100,000.

Supply—Amount of goods for sale at a given price.

Surplus—Oversupply; amount by which assets exceed liabilities and capital; amount of goods on hand above current demand.

Swindle—To defraud; dishonest business transaction.

Swindler—One who defrauds.

Swindle Sheet—Expense account, when padding or the possibility of padding is implied.

Syndicate—Group organized for special financing, such as purchase and resale of certain securities or underwriting of a stock issue, purchasing it at a discount.

Take-Home Pay—What is left of earnings after withholding tax and other deductions have been made.

Tariff—Schedule of duties imposed on importers and exporters.

Tax—To exact payment, usually payment exacted by government to provide revenue for its operations.

Tax Sale—Sale of a property to recover unpaid taxes.

Technological—Referring to technical processes or changes in industry; e.g., technological unemployment.

Tenant—Occupant of premises, generally one who pays rent for the occupancy.

Tenders—Sealed bids or offers for securities.

Terms—Terms of payment; prearranged conditions for payment of a debt; e.g., cash in 30 days, $5 down and $1 a week, etc.

Testator—One who makes a will.

Ticker—Machine in which messages are stamped on paper tape, used in reporting market quotations.

Tie-in Sale—Where additional product must be purchased to effect purchase of a certain article.

Title—All factors combined which accord right to exclusive possession of property.

Tool Engineering—New branch of engineering concerned with perfecting new machinery processes, equipment and use of raw material in preparation for production of a new product or a new model.

Tracer—Investigation designed to trace article undelivered by post office or transportation company; one who makes such an investigation.

Trade Acceptance—Bill of exchange governing purchase price, drawn by seller upon buyer whose endorsement constitutes "acceptance."

Trade Agreement—Agreement between employer and union, fixing wages, hours, working conditions.

Trade Edition or Trade Book—Edition designed for general public as distinguished from educational and professional use.

Trademark—Coined name, monogram, logotype, signature, picture, distinctively designed words or name, symbol, emblem or device, which may be registered in the Government Patent Office for exclusive use by the applicant. Registration term is 20 years and may be renewed.

Trade Name—Name or other symbol under which a firm does business and protected by common law against attempt to deceive customers by use of a similar name by a competing firm.

Trade Paper—Endorsed notes (two or more names) given in payment for merchandise; a periodical published in the interest of a certain branch of business.

Transcript—Letter-perfect copy of a document, which does not seek to reproduce exact appearance of original.

Travelers Checks—Issued by banks, travel agencies, American Express, and Western Union for the convenience of travelers.

Treasury Bills—Short-term government offerings, bearing no interest, but sold at a discount to buyers.

Treasury Certificates—Interest-bearing certificates of indebtedness issued in place of short-term bonds.

Trust—Holding of property by a responsible person or bank (trustee) for the good of another person (beneficiary).

Turnover—Number of times, within a specified period such as a year, in which a given commodity is sold out.

Upgrade—To advance an employee, a work process or a product in rank, earnings, price or quality.

Venue—Place where case is tried. **A change of venue** may be granted with the object of securing a fairer trial.

Volume—Amount of business done.

Voucher—A receipt or other proof of money paid, vouches for the accuracy of the terms of a transaction.

Wages—Payment for labor.

Waive—To voluntarily forego a right.

Warrant—Order for the payment of money or delivery of goods or documents; in banking, primarily written order for the payment of money.

Wash Sale—Fictitious trading to give an appearance of activity to inactive stocks.

Wharfage—Fee for use of piers.

Wholesale—Sale of goods to dealers for resale to retail merchants.

Will—Testament of a property-holder directing the distribution of his property after his death.

Window Dressing—Manipulations in financial statement to give it a more favorable appearance than is due.

Withholding Tax—Income tax payment deducted at source, as from wages, dividends, etc.

Without Prejudice—A contract term signifying that the agreement will not injure any prior or subsequent rights.

Zoning—Laws governing real estate, setting off special areas for special types of occupation; e.g., residence, business, hospitals, etc.